THE PENTAGON PAPERS

ABRIDGED EDITION

THE PENTAGON PAPERS

ABRIDGED EDITION

EDITED BY

George C. Herring

McGraw-Hill, Inc.
New York St. Louis San Francisco Auckland Bogotá
Caracas Lisbon London Madrid Mexico City Milan
Montreal New Delhi San Juan Singapore
Sydney Tokyo Toronto

This book was set in Times Roman by Arcata Graphics/Kingsport.
The editors were Niels Aaboe and Sheila H. Gillams;
the production supervisor was Louise Karam.
The cover was designed by Rafael Hernandez;
cover photo: UPI.
R. R. Donnelley & Sons Company was printer and binder.

This book is printed on recycled, acid-free paper containing a minimum of 50% recycled de-inked fiber.

THE PENTAGON PAPERS
Abridged Edition

2 3 4 5 6 7 8 9 0   DOH   9 0 9 8 7 6 5 4

ISBN 0-07-028380-X

Library of Congress Cataloging-in-Publication Data

Pentagon Papers.   Selections
The Pentagon Papers / George C. Herring, editor.—Abridged ed.
        p.   cm.
    Includes bibliographical references.
    ISBN 0-07-028380-X
    1. United States—Foreign relations—Vietnam.   2. Vietnam—Foreign
relations—United States.   3. Vietnam—Politics and
government—1945–1975.   4. Vietnamese Conflict, 1961–1975.
I. Herring, George C., (date).   II. Title.
E183.8.V5P425   1993
327.730597—dc20
                                                      92-32172

ABOUT THE EDITOR

GEORGE C. HERRING is Alumni Professor of History at the University of Kentucky. He received his M.A. and Ph.D. degrees in history from the University of Virginia. He is the author of numerous scholarly articles and books including, most importantly, *America's Longest War: The United States and Vietnam.* He served as editor of the journal *Diplomatic History* from 1982 to 1986 and as President of the Society for Historians of American Foreign Relations in 1989. In 1991, he was a Fulbright Scholar at the University of Otago, New Zealand.

CONTENTS

PREFACE

From the time I began teaching courses on the Vietnam war, in January 1973, I regularly assigned the *New York Times* book *The Pentagon Papers* as basic reading. The volume contained the most important documents then available on the war. It gave an inside view of policy-making rare for any historical event, particularly one so recent and still so controversial. It explained as nothing else did at the time how and why the United States had become involved in Vietnam and why, ultimately, it failed to accomplish what it had set out to do. Thus, although the documents ended in 1967, six years before the end of the American phase of the war, they dealt with the most fundamental questions raised by that war.

As a consequence, when Chris Rogers of McGraw-Hill proposed many years later that I put together a new edition of these long-out-of-print documents, I responded enthusiastically. In earlier times, I had found the papers an indispensable teaching tool, and I missed being able to use them during the years they were out of print. I was delighted to have the opportunity to make them available again in usable form.

This edition is significantly abridged. I have omitted the commentary of the *New York Times* authors, all of which was done under the pressure of urgent deadlines and much of which is now out of date. I have included only those documents I regard as the most important, and I have tried to eliminate those that duplicate material contained in others. I have tried to keep my own editing as unobtrusive as possible and to let the documents themselves tell the story. At the beginning of each of the seven chapters, I have written a brief introduction that provides background for the chapter and helps put the documents in context by summarizing the main events of the period they cover. For each document, I have written a brief headnote that highlights the significance of the document. In the text of the documents, I have included in brackets the first names and positions of people not otherwise completely identified. At the end of the book, I have provided a glossary of the acronyms and abbreviations that appear in profusion in these pages—and without which modern governments appear unable to function—and a bibliography of works relating to the *Pentagon Papers.*

I am grateful to Times Books for their permission to reprint the documents as originally published in *The Pentagon Papers as Published by The New York Times.*

I am grateful to a number of people for assistance with this project. My editors at McGraw-Hill have been unfailingly supportive and helpful. My friend and editor, first at Knopf and then at McGraw-Hill, Chris Rogers, suggested this volume and persuaded me to do it. David Follmer, my first editor at Knopf and then later my editor at McGraw-Hill, helped to push the volume through to completion. And Niels Aaboe, with whom I worked on the second edition of *America's Longest War,* assisted in the completion of this project. Howard Jones, University of Alabama, and Michael Schaller, University of Arizona offered helpful critiques in their review of the manuscript. Much of my work was done in Dunedin, New Zealand, and I am grateful to Laurie Cox and the New Zealand–United States Educational Foundation and to Otago University for the Fulbright award that got me away from obligations that frustrated, if they did not completely stymie, scholarly endeavors. And I especially thank my good friends Rob and Kathie Rabel and my colleagues in the department of history at Otago for making me feel at home many thousands of miles from Kentucky.

Dottie Leathers's name appears in all my books, and it deserves a very special place in this one. I suspect, in fact, that she did more work than I, putting the documents on disk a long time ago and repeatedly reminding me that I was neglecting this—and other—projects. Even more important was the assistance and support she provided between 1988 and 1991 when I served as history department chair at the University of Kentucky. I could not have made it without her, and for this—and everything else—I am grateful.

George C. Herring

INTRODUCTION

The documents printed in this volume comprise a small portion of the much larger body of historical materials known as the Pentagon Papers. This collection remains today, more than twenty years after its release, the single most important documentary source on U.S. policy-making during the Vietnam War. Its leak to and subsequent publication by *The New York Times* in 1971 was one of the great journalistic "scoops" of recent history, and the court case that followed posed, as few others have, the fundamental issue of government secrecy against the people's right to know.

The Pentagon Papers originated out of the disillusionment of Secretary of Defense Robert S. McNamara with the war that had once borne his name. In the Kennedy and early Johnson years, Vietnam was sometimes referred to as "McNamara's War," and the hard-driving former businessman, slogging through Vietnam, pointing at crisis spots on a map, and reeling off statistics, was a symbol of the can-do spirit that had driven the United States into Vietnam and seemed to ensure its eventual success. We now know that as early as December 1965, less than six months after the first major increments of U.S. combat forces had been dispatched to Vietnam, McNamara had concluded that the war could not be won militarily. He remained in government for nearly two years, pursuing various schemes in a desperate and for him excruciating effort to reconcile his disillusionment with the war and his loyalty to President Lyndon Baines Johnson. In late 1967, after recommending to Johnson radical changes in Vietnam policy, he was removed from the Defense Department and appointed president of the World Bank.

In the spring of 1967, apparently as part of his process of disillusionment, McNamara ordered compilation of what would become known as the Pentagon Papers. The reason is not entirely clear. He later claimed that he sought to compile the essential documents so that scholars could determine where the United States had gone wrong and the alternatives it might have pursued. He may also have been seeking immediate answers to some of the questions that had perplexed him since 1965, and he may even have hoped to use the results of the study to alter the policy he had concluded was bankrupt. McNamara's silence on his motives has kept scholars guessing for more than two decades.

Although his instructions called for an "encyclopedic" review of U.S. policy in Vietnam, he could not have foreseen the proportions the study would eventually assume. The original timetable called for completion in three to six months by a staff of six people. Assigned to a task force headed by Morton Halperin and under the immediate supervision of Leslie Gelb in the Pentagon's International Security Affairs division, the study in fact required the efforts of thirty-six people, along with numerous part-time consultants and collaborators. It was not completed until early 1969, nearly a year after McNamara left office. The finished product comprised 47 volumes, more than 7000 pages, and an estimated 2½ million words. It weighed 60 pounds! Comprehensive in coverage and based on extensive research in official records, it provided detailed analysis of U.S. involvement in Vietnam from the end of World War II to 1967, with particular emphasis on the Kennedy-Johnson years. It included voluminous supporting documents.

The finished product divulged from the files of government itself a considerable amount of government duplicity. Regarding the Tonkin Gulf affair of August 1964, for example, the Pentagon documents revealed that the Johnson administration had for months sought increased power to escalate the conflict in Vietnam and had seized upon the alleged incidents to secure those powers from Congress. Nor had the administration revealed at the time of these allegedly unprovoked attacks its own clandestine warfare against North Vietnam: commando raids that may have provoked the attacks if indeed they took place.

Other documents traced increased American involvement in Vietnam and showed repeated deception about it. The papers revealed the extent to which the Truman administration had aided French efforts to suppress the Vietminh insurgency, something only vaguely known before. They touched on the nationalist aspirations of Ho Chi Minh's Vietminh as well as American fears about the economic consequences of the "loss" of Southeast Asia. They made clear the manner in which the United States had subverted the Geneva Accords that ended the First Indochina War in 1954. They showed how the Kennedy administration had turned a still-limited commitment into a vital interest. They exposed the Johnson administration's repeated dissembling about its plans and actions in Vietnam.

Originally designed as an in-house study and routinely classified "top secret," the papers in time would attain a notoriety McNamara had never intended. Upon leaving the Pentagon in 1969, Halperin and Gelb placed a set of the documents in the RAND Corporation, a private think tank with close ties to the Department of Defense. There they came under the scrutiny of Daniel Ellsberg, an economist and former marine officer who had served in Vietnam, had once firmly supported the war, and had compiled a section of the papers.

Like McNamara, Ellsberg had long since determined that the war was unwinnable. He had also concluded that it was immoral, and the more disturbed he became about it the more troubled he became about his own role. By this time a RAND consultant, Ellsberg secured access to the Pentagon documents for a study of the lessons of Vietnam. They revealed what he had come to suspect, that the war had been waged by lies and deception. He eventually concluded that by making the papers available to the public, he might expiate his own wrongdoing and spread to others his own outrage, thereby increasing popular pressures on the new Nixon administration to end the war. Thus in dark of night, with the help of his children and at his own personal expense, he secretly xeroxed the top-secret study.

Making the documents available proved more difficult. He first planned to release them in conjunction with the Vietnam antiwar moratorium of October 15, 1969, hoping to trigger a protest that would force President Richard Nixon's hand. But Nixon's silent-majority speech and Vietnamization plan cut the ground from beneath the moratorium and Ellsberg. He then turned to antiwar senator J. William Fulbright (D-Ark.), reasoning that hearings on the papers by Fulbright's dovish Senate Foreign Relations Committee would stimulate opposition to the war. But Fulbright's staffers were wary of trafficking in and releasing classified documents they suspected were stolen. The senator would go no further than ask Secretary of Defense Melvin Laird to turn them over to him. When Laird predictably refused, Fulbright let the matter die. Ellsberg subsequently determined to pursue more drastic measures. In February 1971, he turned the volumes over to *New York Times* correspondent Neil Sheehan, a young journalist who had spent considerable time in Vietnam and had undergone a similar conversion from "hawk" to "dove."

For that most eminent of American journalistic institutions, the Ellsberg windfall presented a most difficult and painful dilemma. The sober, respectable paper had to decide whether to print still-classified documents that dealt with an ongoing war. Executives, editors, reporters, and lawyers spent long hours arguing over the meaning of patriotism and journalistic ethics. They weighed the risks of publication and nonpublication for *The New York Times,* the journalistic profession, and the nation. While the debate raged, four reporters, three copy editors, and an arsenal of support personnel were holed up under the tightest security in the New York Hilton hotel working on what was called "Project X."

Advocates for publication eventually carried the day, and on Sunday, June 13, 1971, *The New York Times* published the first installment of a projected series based on the Pentagon Papers. From Ellsberg's standpoint, the timing could not have been better. The United States had been involved in full-scale war in Vietnam for six years, and despite President Nixon's promises of peace and his commitment to a phased withdrawal of U.S. forces, there was little indication by the summer of 1971 that the conflict was nearing an end. Polls showed a dramatic rise in public frustration and disillusionment. Domestic protest, which had quieted in Nixon's first year in office, was again on the increase. A massive demonstration in Washington earlier in the spring had provoked one of the worst riots in the capital's history.

Well aware of the risks it was taking in publishing documents still classified, *The New York Times* cautiously downplayed its initial story. What Sheehan aptly called a "thermonuclear vial" would soon explode, however, provoking a classic confrontation between government and the press, adding to popular disillusionment with the war, and spurring Nixon to take steps that through a near-incredible train of events led directly to the Watergate scandal and his eventual resignation. Publication of the Pentagon Papers came as a profound shock to the Nixon administration. As some of Nixon's advisers were quick to point out, the papers exposed the sins of his Democratic predecessors and could be conveniently used to discredit them, especially John F. Kennedy, despised by many Republicans. It is also possible that if nothing had been done, attention would not have been drawn to the papers.

But Nixon and his national security adviser, Henry Kissinger, both saw grave consequences if they did not stop publication. Nixon later claimed that the leak caused panic throughout the government. The supersecret National Security Agency feared that its codes would be compromised; the CIA, that the names of informants would be divulged. Kissinger's secret initiative to the People's Republic of China—the key to the administration's "Grand Design" for a new world order—was then nearing a successful conclusion, and the men worried that at this critical point the Chinese government might conclude that the United States was too unreliable to be a diplomatic partner. Nixon also felt that a vital principle was at stake. It was the role of government, not *The New York Times,* to determine what documents should be made public and when. Applying to domestic matters the doctrine of credibility that so profoundly influenced his foreign policy, he also insisted that if the administration did not do something, the situation would encourage further leaks, possibly of more current secrets, and completely undermine security in government.

Nixon thus tried to prevent publication of the papers. He first attempted through private threats to dissuade *The New York Times* from further publication. When that failed, the administration took the unprecedented step of obtaining from the federal courts a temporary restraining order preventing the newspaper from publishing additional material from the Pentagon study.

The court case that followed was of extraordinary significance. *The New York Times,* of course, argued First Amendment rights and harked back to legal precedents holding that prior restraint on publication was the most sinister and dangerous threat to freedom of expression. The government argued that materials already published had prejudiced the interests of the United States and that publication of additional material would do irreparable injury to the national security. The case could not be made that publication would damage the war effort, since most of the documents were over three years old, did not contain military information, and in some instances had already been made public. Government attorneys rested their case on the larger fear that permitting the newspaper to publish would encourage other leaks that would damage the government's ability to function. Attorneys also cited damage already done to U.S. diplomatic relations with allies such as Australia and Canada through leakage of the papers.

The case was eventually settled in favor of *The New York Times.* After issuing a temporary restraining order barring publication, presiding judge Murray Gurfein, a recent Nixon appointee, decided in favor of the newspaper. When the government secured yet another restraining order from the court of appeals, *The New York Times* asked for review by the U.S. Supreme Court. After an unprecedented Saturday morning session, six of the nine justices held that the government had failed to meet the tests for prior restraint. Four justices were so persuaded by the inadequacy of the government's case that they would have ruled for the newspaper without any oral argument. Justices Hugo Black and William O. Douglas opposed such restraints in all cases. Justice William Brennan opposed them in all cases except the extremely unlikely circumstance in which the country was at war and the government proved that publication would do real and lasting damage to the war effort. Justice Thurgood Marshall held that no statute of Congress allowed the sort of relief sought by the government.

Justices Potter Stewart and Byron White determined the outcome. Their opinion, which established the legal precedent for the case, held that in the absence of explicit authorization from Congress they could not agree to prior restraint on publication unless the disclosures would "surely result in direct, immediate, and irreparable damage to our nation or its people." The government had not met that test in this case. Thus on June 30, 1971, the Court denied the government's request for a permanent injunction against publication.

This much publicized clash between government and press gave the Pentagon Papers far more attention than they would have received otherwise, and the Supreme Court decision opened the floodgates. *The New York Times* resumed publication and gave the papers prominent play over the next few weeks. The *Washington Post*, which had also secured a set of the papers, published its own series. Excerpts began appearing in newspapers across the nation, and the leak became a raging torrent. By the end of 1971, moreover, compilations of the Pentagon Papers had been published in book form in three different editions. *The New York Times* published a 677-page version, *The Pentagon Papers*, which included extensive documents and the summaries of the original studies of the documents done by its own reporters in 1971. Mike Gravel of Alaska, another Senate dove, arranged with Beacon Press to print a much fuller four-volume edition. The government then released its own twelve-volume version, which contained most of the original study.

The Pentagon Papers had a profound impact on the United States in a critical period. Publication of the papers strengthened public and congressional opposition to continued American involvement in Vietnam. Few people read them, to be sure. Still, the relevations in them—or, perhaps more accurately, the reports of the revelations—challenged the myth of America as a reluctant participant in the war, added to an already large credibility gap between public and government, and gave legitimacy to some of the key arguments of the antiwar opposition.

Publication of the papers also stiffened the spines of journalists. It signaled the passing of an era when newspapers could be expected to play by the rules in handling matters that the government deemed confidential. For better or worse, it marked the end of media collaboration as an integral part of the national security state. It ushered in a new era of press militancy in which journalists would see their primary function as exposing government sins rather than simply reporting what government said and did. Indeed, it is possible that without *The Pentagon Papers* exposure of Watergate would not have occurred.

Publication of the papers had other, ultimately quite ironic effects, especially for the Nixon administration. Persuaded that Ellsberg was part of a vast conspiracy to subvert the government and determined in any event to make an example of him, the Nixon administration had the Justice Department indict him and his collaborator, Anthony Russo, for theft and espionage.

After a long delay, the trial finally got under way in Los Angeles in the spring of 1972, and it attracted almost as much attention as the event that had precipitated it. It posed again the fundamental issue of government secrecy versus the public's right to know. On the part of both sides, it took the form of a vendetta. Nixon was determined to destroy Ellsberg. On the other hand, the defendants hoped to convert the trial into a public forum on government secrecy and the morality and legality of the war.

The case hinged on the basic question of whether release of the Pentagon Papers had adversely affected the security of the United States. The prosecution held that information in the papers could have been used to the detriment of the national security. The defense, on the other hand, attempted to show that neither the volumes as a whole nor any part of them met the tests of espionage as defined by the law. Using the work of a small army of researchers, many of them student volunteers who had joined Ellsberg's crusade against the government and the war, the defense produced excerpts from books, newspapers, and unclassified documents to show that information in the papers was already available to the public.

Just as the lawyers were presenting their final arguments, the proceedings in Los Angeles became entwined with the simultaneous Wa-

tergate revelations of abuses of power in the Nixon administration. In
fact, they had been connected from the beginning. As the story subsequently unfolded, the administration had not stopped at instituting legal
action against Ellsberg. Determined not merely to prosecute but also to
destroy him, the White House had authorized a secret "plumbers"
group to discredit Ellsberg and other dissidents.

The actions of the plumbers had profoundly ironic consequences. In
search of information to embarrass Ellsberg, they had burglarized the
office of his psychiatrist. In addition, records of wiretaps possibly relevant to the Ellsberg case had mysteriously disappeared from FBI files,
and the White House had attempted to influence the judge by offering
him a top-level government position. Ruling that these "bizarre" events
had "incurably infected the prosecution" of the case, the judge on May
11, 1973, dismissed the charges against Ellsberg and Russo. The trial
thus ended without even addressing the vital issues raised by the case.

Even more ironic—and more important—Nixon's efforts to defend
the nation's security against Ellsberg and others like him eventually
contributed to the downfall of his presidency. It was, after all, the leak
of the Pentagon Papers that led to creation of the plumbers group and to
a multifaceted effort to undermine and suppress the antiwar opposition.
The bungling, often illegal actions of the plumbers, in turn, led to the
Watergate investigations, which, in turn, forced Nixon to resign the
presidency.

In an even more ironic twist, in reaction to the Pentagon Papers and
to defend his embattled Vietnam policy, Nixon took actions that provoked congressional restrictions on presidential power and, through the
Watergate revelations, further undermined presidential authority. Thus
he and his successor, Gerald Ford, could do nothing when the North
Vietnamese challenged the 1973 peace agreement, and there was no option but to acquiesce in the fall of South Vietnam in 1975. Consequently, through a curious, even remarkable train of events, the study
that McNamara may have ordered in 1967 to provide a way out of Vietnam finally, eight years later, contributed to that result—although certainly not in the way intended.

In terms of the law, the First Amendment, and the system of security
classification that led to the case, the longer-term consequences of the
Pentagon Papers appear less significant. In many ways, the victory of
the press was a hollow one. A majority of the Supreme Court left open
not only the possibility of prior restraints in other cases but also of
criminal sanctions upon the press. The fact that the government had

tried to stop publication was troubling, and the fact that it had tried to
censor the press for the first time could be considered a defeat of sorts.
And although the government had a very weak case, the courts did restrain *The New York Times* from publication for a period of weeks. That
in itself could be seen as a threat to the First Amendment.

In the area of foremost interest to historians, the Pentagon Papers
case had no impact whatever on the system of secrecy that keeps documents under wraps long after their connection to national security has
disappeared. In the case of Vietnam, as a result of leakage of the papers, historians knew far more sooner than they would have known otherwise, and declassification of other documents was facilitated. Within
a short time, however, the system of security classification was tightened rather than loosened, and the obstacles to historians increased
rather than diminished.

The *New York Times* book *The Pentagon Papers* was the smallest
of the three editions and the one best known to the public. Published
in July 1971, it became an instant best-seller, and it eventually sold
more than 1 million copies. It was widely used in college classrooms
in the 1970s, and for many years it was basic reading for anyone interested in the origins and outcome of American involvement in
Vietnam.

The *New York Times* edition contained only a fragment of the original papers. Less than 700 pages in length, it was divided into ten chapters covering the period from 1945 to 1968 (eight of them dealing with
the years 1961 to 1968). The original Pentagon study consisted of a series of long analyses written by Department of Defense officials, each
backed up by extensive supporting documents and each dealing with a
particular chronological period or a specific topic such as pacification,
the air war, or the advisory effort in support of the South Vietnamese.
In the newspaper's edition, each chapter was based on the original papers and written by one of the four *New York Times* authors. All but
one of the chapters included extensive documents from the original
study, and most of them included at least short excerpts from the analyses. The writers worked closely within the parameters set by the authors of the Pentagon study itself. Their chapters were summaries of the
chapters in the original. Additional material was brought in only when
it was deemed necessary to provide context for the general reader.

The most important component of the *New York Times* edition was,
of course, the documents, and they are what has been reprinted in this
version. The documents presented by the *New York Times* edition com-

prise only a small portion of the documentation in the Pentagon Papers as a whole and represent only a tiny part of the vast documentation on American policy-making in Vietnam that is currently available to scholars. Nevertheless, they retain great value now, twenty years after their original release. They provide the background for and the context of the major Vietnam decisions in the two decades from the end of World War II to the commitment of U.S. combat forces in 1965. They explain the decisions in the words of the policymakers themselves. They elaborate in full and in the bureaucratic language of the day the larger assumptions upon which the policymakers acted and the "operational codes" under which they worked. They reveal how the government system operated at the height of the Cold War national security state, and the cloak of secrecy in which it was shrouded. "To read the Pentagon Papers in their vast detail," Neil Sheehan wrote in the introduction to the *New York Times* edition, "is to step through the looking glass into a new and different world," a world with a "set of values, a dynamic, a language and a perspective quite distinct from the public world of the ordinary citizen and of the other two branches of the Republic—Congress and the judiciary" (p. xii). The Pentagon Papers remain today an indispensable source for understanding why the United States intervened in Vietnam and why, ultimately, it failed to achieve its objectives.

THE
PENTAGON
PAPERS

ABRIDGED EDITION

Origins of Involvement, 1946–1960

From 1950 to 1960, the Truman and Eisenhower administrations laid the foundation for large-scale U.S. involvement in Vietnam. In 1946, war had broken out between Ho Chi Minh's Communist-led Vietminh and a France determined to reestablish control over its colonies in Indochina. From the outset, that war posed a serious dilemma for the United States. The Truman administration was reluctant to support French colonialism at a time when nationalism was in the ascendant throughout the world. On the other hand, eager to secure French backing for its Cold War policies in Europe, the United States found it increasingly difficult to resist French appeals for help in Vietnam. And the Communist ties of Ho and his Vietminh made it impossible in a Cold War setting for the United States to support the Vietminh revolution. Thus, from 1946 to 1950, the United States claimed to be neutral but in fact pursued a neutrality heavily skewed in France's favor.

After February 1950, the United States abandoned any pretense of neutrality. The intensification of the Cold War in Europe, the victory in China of Mao Tse-tung's Communists, and the outbreak of hot war in Korea in June 1950 led the Truman administration to extend to East Asia the containment policy already applied in Europe. Persuaded that the loss of Vietnam to communism might, through a dominolike effect, cause the loss of all Southeast Asia, the administration, as part of this change of policy, began to supply direct economic and military aid to France for the war in Vietnam. The Eisenhower administration continued and even expanded the policy initiated by its predecessor, and by 1954 the United States was paying close to 80 percent of the cost of France's war in Indochina.

France's defeat in 1954 led to an American commitment to create in the southern part of Vietnam an independent, non-Communist government as a bulwark against further Communist expansion in Southeast Asia. Even with enormous American aid, France was unable to suppress the Vietminh forces, and its disastrous defeat in May 1954 at the remote fortress of Dienbienphu doomed its military effort in Indochina. The United States at first took a hostile approach toward the ensuing peace conference at Geneva. Ultimately, however, when the conferees agreed on a temporary partition of Vietnam, the Eisenhower administration saw an opportunity, free of the taint of French colonialism, to strengthen the U.S. position in what was considered a critical part of the world. The United States paid lip service to the Geneva Accords, signed on July 21, 1954, but in fact supported the efforts of Ngo Dinh Diem, a non-Communist nationalist, to build an independent government in South Vietnam. In October 1954, Eisenhower made a carefully qualified commitment to Diem that resulted in a major economic and military aid program and defiance of the provisions of the Geneva Accords calling for elections in 1956.

The American experiment in nation-building was imperiled by 1960. Diem at first achieved striking successes, with U.S. help routing internal forces arrayed against him and launching a sweeping and highly effective campaign of repression against those Vietminh who had stayed in South Vietnam after the 1954 armistice. As the decade wore on, however, the deficiencies of his leadership became obvious. He relied almost entirely on his family, especially his sinister brother Ngo Dinh Nhu. He proved incapable of rallying the people of South Vietnam to his side or of developing effective economic or political programs. At the same time, his heavy-handed repression stimulated opposition to his rule and spurred the Vietminh to organize a revolt against him. North Vietnam soon supported the efforts of the newly organized National Liberation

Front (NLF), and by 1960 a full-scale insurgency had been launched against the Diem government. As Ambassador Elbridge Durbrow warned in the last document included in this chapter, by the end of the decade this insurgency threatened the very existence of the U.S.-backed government of South Vietnam.

Ho Chi Minh's 1946 Appeal for Help

Between 1945 and 1949, Vietminh leader Ho Chi Minh issued
several appeals to the United States for recognition of Vietnamese independence and support in his war against France.
This February 27, 1946, cable from U.S. diplomat Kenneth
Landon in Hanoi reports one such appeal. The United States
ignored Ho's overtures, in part for fear of alienating its more
important European ally, France, and in part out of suspicion
of Ho's past Communist ties.

Ho Chi Minh handed me 2 letters addressed to President of USA,
China, Russia, and Britain identical copies of which were stated to have
been forwarded to other governments named. In 2 letters . . . Ho Chi
Minh request USA as one of United Nations to support idea of Annamese independence according to Philippines example, to examine the
case of the Annamese, and to take steps necessary to maintenance of
world peace which is being endangered by French efforts to reconquer
Indochina. He asserts that Annamese will fight until United Nations interfered in support of Annamese independence. The petition addressed
to major United Nations contains:

    A   Review of French relations with Japanese where French In-
dochina allegedly aided Japs:
    B   Statement of establishment on 2 September 1945 of PENW
Democratic Republic of Viet Minh:
    C   Summary of French conquest of Cochin China began 23 Sept
1945 and still incomplete:
    D   Outline of accomplishments of Annamese Government in
Tonkin including popular elections, abolition of undesirable taxes, expansion of education and resumption as far as possible of normal economic activities:
    E   Request to 4 powers: (1) to intervene and stop the war in In-
dochina in order to mediate fair settlement and (2) to bring the Indochi-
nese issue before the United Nations organization.

    The petition ends with the statement that Annamese ask for full in-
dependence in fact and that in interim while awaiting UNO decision the
Annamese will continue to fight the reestablishment of French imperialism. Letters and petition will be transmitted to Department soonest.

NSC 1952 Policy Study on Southeast Asia

This National Security Council (NSC) document of early 1952, "United States Objectives and Courses of Action with Respect to Southeast Asia," articulated the rationale behind U.S. support for the French in Vietnam and clearly revealed the dilemmas that faced the United States in working with France. It also indicated the willingness of the United States to intervene militarily in the war, if, as in Korea, the Chinese got involved. The perceptions stated here of the importance of Southeast Asia to U.S. security and of Vietnam to Southeast Asia continued to influence U.S. policy after France's defeat and in fact undergirded the U.S. commitment in Vietnam until at least the mid-1960s.

OBJECTIVE

1   To prevent the countries of Southeast Asia from passing into the communist orbit, and to assist them to develop will and ability to resist communism from within and without and to contribute to the strengthening of the free world.

GENERAL CONSIDERATIONS

2   Communist domination, by whatever means, of all Southeast Asia would seriously endanger in the short term, and critically endanger in the longer term, United States security interests.

    a   The loss of any of the countries of Southeast Asia to communist aggression would have critical psychological, political and economic consequences. In the absence of effective and timely counteraction, the loss of any single country would probably lead to relatively swift submission to or an alignment with communism by the remaining countries of this group. Furthermore, an alignment with communism of the rest of Southeast Asia and India, and in the longer term, of the Middle East (with the probable exceptions of at least Pakistan and Turkey) would in all probability progressively follow: Such widespread alignment would endanger the stability and security of Europe.

    b   Communist control of all of Southeast Asia would render the U.S. position in the Pacific offshore island chain precarious and would seriously jeopardize fundamental U.S. security interests in the Far East.

    c   Southeast Asia, especially Malaya and Indonesia, is the principal world source of natural rubber and tin, and a producer of petroleum and other strategically important commodities. The rice exports of Burma and Thailand are critically important to Malaya, Ceylon and Hong Kong and are of considerable significance to Japan and India, all important areas of free Asia.

d The loss of Southeast Asia, especially of Malaya and Indonesia, could result in such economic and political pressures in Japan as to make it extremely difficult to prevent Japan's eventual accommodation to communism.

3 It is therefore imperative that an overt attack on Southeast Asia by the Chinese Communists be vigorously opposed. In order to pursue the military courses of action envisaged in this paper to a favorable conclusion within a reasonable period, it will be necessary to divert military strength from other areas thus reducing our military capability in those areas, with the recognized increased risks involved therein, or to increase our military forces in being, or both.

4 The danger of an overt military attack against Southeast Asia is inherent in the existence of a hostile and aggressive Communist China, but such an attack is less probable than continued communist efforts to achieve domination through subversion. The primary threat to Southeast Asia accordingly arises from the possibility that the situation in Indochina may deteriorate as a result of the weakening of the resolve of, or as a result of the inability of the governments of France and of the Associated States to continue to oppose the Viet Minh rebellion, the military strength of which is being steadily increased by virtue of aid furnished by the Chinese Communist regime and its allies.

5 The successful defense of Tonkin is critical to the retention in non-Communist hands of mainland Southeast Asia. However, should Burma come under communist domination, a communist military advance through Thailand might make Indochina, including Tonkin, militarily indefensible. The execution of the following U.S. courses of action with respect to individual countries of the area may vary depending upon the route of communist advance into Southeast Asia.

6 Actions designed to achieve our objectives in Southeast Asia require sensitive selection and application, on the one hand to assure the optimum efficiency through coordination of measures for the general area, and on the other, to accommodate to the greatest practicable extent to the individual sensibilities of the several governments, social classes and minorities of the area.

COURSES OF ACTION

Southeast Asia

7 With respect to Southeast Asia, the United States should:
 a Strengthen propaganda and cultural activities, as appropriate, in relation to the area to foster increased alignment of the people with the free world.
 b Continue, as appropriate, programs of economic and technical assistance designed to strengthen the indigenous non-communist governments of the area.
 c Encourage the countries of Southeast Asia to restore and expand their commerce with each other and with the rest of the free world, and stimulate the flow of the raw material resources of the area to the free world.
 d Seek agreement with other nations, including at least France, the UK, Australia and New Zealand, for a joint warning to Communist China regarding the grave consequences of Chinese aggression against Southeast Asia, the issuance of such a warning to be contingent upon the prior agreement of France and the UK to participate in the courses of action set forth in paragraphs 10 c, 12, 14 f (1) and (2) and 15 c (1) and (2), and such others as are determined as a result of prior trilateral consultation, in the event such a warning is ignored.
 e Seek UK and French agreement in principle that a naval blockade of Communist China should be included in the minimum courses of action set forth in paragraph 10c below.
 f Continue to encourage and support closer cooperation among the countries of Southeast Asia, and between those countries and the United States, Great Britain, France, the Philippines, Australia, New Zealand, South Asia and Japan.
 g Strengthen, as appropriate, covert operations designed to assist in the achievement of U.S. objectives in Southeast Asia.
 h Continue activities and operations designed to encourage the overseas Chinese communities in Southeast Asia to organize and activate anti-communist groups and activities within their own communities, to resist the effects of parallel pro-communist groups and activities and, generally, to increase their orientation toward the free world.
 i Take measures to promote the coordinated defense of the area, and encourage and support the spirit of resistance among the peoples of Southeast Asia to Chinese Communist aggression and to the encroachments of local communists.

Indochina

8 With respect to Indochina the United States should:

    a Continue to promote international support for the three Associated States.

    b Continue to assure the French that the U.S. regards the French effort in Indochina as one of great strategic importance in the general international interest rather than in the purely French interest, and as essential to the security of the free world, not only in the Far East but in the Middle East and Europe as well.

    c Continue to assure the French that we are cognizant of the sacrifices entailed for France in carrying out her effort in Indochina and that, without overlooking the principle that France has the primary responsibility in Indochina, we will recommend to the Congress appropriate military, economic and financial aid to France and the Associated States.

    d Continue to cultivate friendly and increasingly cooperative relations with the Governments of France and the Associated States at all levels with a view to maintaining and, if possible, increasing the degree of influence the U.S. can bring to bear on the policies and actions of the French and Indochinese authorities to the end of directing the course of events toward the objectives we seek. Our influence with the French and Associated States should be designed to further those constructive political, economic and social measures which will tend to increase the stability of the Associated States and thus make it possible for the French to reduce the degree of their participation in the military, economic and political affairs of the Associated States.

    e Specifically we should use our influence with France and the Associated States to promote positive political, military, economic and social policies, among which the following are considered essential elements:

        (1) Continued recognition and carrying out by France of its primary responsibility for the defense of Indochina.

        (2) Further steps by France and the Associated States toward the evolutionary development of the Associated States.

        (3) Such reorganization of French administration and representation in Indochina as will be conducive to an increased feeling of responsibility on the part of the Associated States.

        (4) Intensive efforts to develop the armies of the Associated

States, including independent logistical and administrative services.

(5) The development of more effective and stable Governments in the Associated States.

(6) Land reform, agrarian and industrial credit, sound rice marketing systems, labor development, foreign trade and capital formation.

(7) An aggressive military, political, and psychological program to defeat or seriously reduce the Viet Minh forces.

(8) U.S.-French cooperation in publicizing progressive developments in the foregoing policies in Indochina.

9 In the absence of large scale Chinese Communist intervention in Indochina, the United States should:

a Provide increased aid on a high priority basis for the French Union forces without relieving French authorities of their basic military responsibility for the defense of the Associated States in order to:

(1) Assist in developing indigenous armed forces which will eventually be capable of maintaining internal security without assistance from French units.

(2) Assist the French Union forces to maintain progress in the restoration of internal security against the Viet Minh.

(3) Assist the forces of France and the Associated States to defend Indochina against Chinese Communist aggression.

b In view of the immediate urgency of the situation, involving possible large-scale Chinese Communist intervention, and in order that the United States may be prepared to take whatever action may be appropriate in such circumstances, make the plans necessary to carry out the courses of action indicated in paragraph 10 below.

c In the event that information and circumstances point to the conclusion that France is no longer prepared to carry the burden in Indochina, or if France presses for an increased sharing of the responsibility for Indochina, whether in the UN or directly with the U.S. Government, oppose a French withdrawal and consult with the French and British concerning further measures to be taken to safeguard the area from communist domination.

10 In the event that it is determined, in consultation with France, that Chinese Communist forces (including volunteers) have overtly intervened in the conflict in Indochina, or are covertly participating to such an extent as to jeopardize retention of the Tonkin Delta area by French Union forces, the United States should take the following measures to assist these forces in preventing the loss of Indochina, to repel the aggression and to restore peace and security in Indochina:

a   Support a request by France or the Associated States for immediate action by the United Nations which would include a UN resolution declaring that Communist China has committed an aggression, recommending that member states take whatever action may be necessary, without geographic limitation, to assist France and the Associated States in meeting the aggression.

b   Whether or not UN action is immediately forthcoming, seek the maximum possible international support for, and participation in, the minimum courses of military action agreed upon by the parties to the joint warning. These minimum courses of action are set forth in subparagraph c immediately below.

c   Carry out the following minimum courses of military action, either under the auspices of the UN or in conjunction with France and the United Kingdom and any other friendly governments:

   (1) A resolute defense of Indochina itself to which the United States would provide such air and naval assistance as might be practicable.

   (2) Interdiction of Chinese Communist communication lines including those in China.

   (3) The United States would expect to provide the major forces for task (2) above; but would expect the UK and France to provide at least token forces therefor and to render such other assistance as is normal between allies, and France to carry the burden of providing, in conjunction with the Associated States, the ground forces for the defense of Indochina.

11 In addition to the courses of action set forth in paragraph 10 above, the United States should take the following military actions as appropriate to the situation:

a   If agreement is reached pursuant to paragraph 7-e, establishment in conjunction with the UK and France of a naval blockade of Communist China.

b   Intensification of covert operations to aid anti-communist guerrilla forces operating against Communist China and to interfere with and disrupt Chinese Communist lines of communication and military supply areas.

c   Utilization, as desirable and feasible, of anti-communist Chinese forces, including Chinese Nationalist forces in military operations in Southeast Asia, Korea, or China proper.

  d Assistance to the British to cover an evacuation from Hong Kong, if required.

  e Evacuation of French Union civil and military personnel from the Tonkin delta, if required.

12 If, subsequent to aggression against Indochina and execution of the minimum necessary courses of action listed in paragraph 10-c above, the United States determines jointly with the UK and France that expanded military action against Communist China is rendered necessary by the situation, the United States should take air and naval action in conjunction with at least France and the U.K. against all suitable military targets in China, avoiding insofar as practicable those targets in areas near the boundaries of the USSR in order not to increase the risk of direct Soviet involvement.

13 In the event the concurrence of the United Kingdom and France to expanded military action against Communist China is not obtained, the United States should consider taking unilateral action.

French Seek U.S. Air Intervention at Dienbienphu

This cable from the U.S. ambassador to France, Douglas Dillon, to Secretary of State John Foster Dulles, April 5, 1954, reports an urgent French request for U.S. air intervention to help save the beleaguered outpost at Dienbienphu.

URGENT. I was called at 11 o'clock Sunday night and asked to come immediately to Matignon where a restricted Cabinet meeting was in progress. On arrival [French foreign minister Georges] Bidault received me in [Prime Minister Joseph] Laniel's office and was joined in a few minutes by Laniel. They said that immediate armed intervention of U.S. carrier aircraft at Dien Bien Phu is now necessary to save the situation.

    [French general Henri] Navarre reports situation there now in state of precarious equilibrium and that both sides are doing best to reinforce—Viet Minh are bringing up last available reinforcements which will way outnumber any reinforcing French can do by parachute drops. Renewal of assault by reinforced Viet Minh probable by middle or end of week. Without help by then fate of Dien Bien Phu will probably be sealed.

[French general Paul] Ely brought back report from Washington that [Admiral Arthur] Radford [chairman, U.S. Joint Chiefs of Staff] gave him his personal (repeat personal) assurances that if situation at Dien Bien Phu required U.S. naval air support he would do his best to obtain such help from U.S. Government. Because of this information from Radford as reported by Ely, French Government now asking for U.S. carrier aircraft support at Dien Bien Phu. Navarre feels that a relatively minor U.S. effort could turn the tide but naturally hopes for as much help as possible. French report Chinese intervention in Indochina already fully established as follows:

First. Fourteen technical advisors at [Vietnamese general Vo Nguyen] Giap's headquarters plus numerous others at division level. All under command of Chinese Communist General Ly Chen-hou who is stationed at Giap headquarters.

Second. Special telephone lines installed maintained and operated by Chinese personnel.

Third. Forty 37 mm. anti-aircraft guns radar-controlled at Dien Bien Phu. These guns operated by Chinese and evidently are from Korea. These AA guns are now shooting through clouds to bring down French aircraft.

Fourth. One thousand supply trucks of which 500 have arrived since 1 March, all driven by Chinese army personnel.

Fifth. Substantial material help in guns, shells, etc., as is well known.

Bidault said that French Chief of Air Staff wished U.S. be informed that U.S. air intervention at Dien Bien Phu could lead to Chinese Communist air attack on delta airfields. Nevertheless, government was making request for aid.

Bidault closed by saying that for good or evil the fate of Southeast Asia now rested on Dien Bien Phu. He said that Geneva would be won or lost depending on outcome at Dien Bien Phu. This was reason for French request for this very serious action on our part.

He then emphasized necessity for speed in view of renewed attack which is expected before end of week. He thanked U.S. for prompt action on airlift for French paratroops. He then said that he had received Dulles' proposal for Southeast Asian coalition, and that he would answer as soon as possible later in week as restricted Cabinet session not competent to make this decision.

New Subject. I passed on [U.S. general Lauris] Norstad's concern that news of airlift (DEPTEL 3470, April 3) might leak as planes assembled. [French minister of defense René] Pleven was called into the room. He expressed extreme concern as any leak would lead to earlier Viet Minh attack. He said at all costs operation must be camouflaged as training exercise until troops have arrived. He is preparing them as rapidly as possible and they will be ready to leave in a week. Bidault and Laniel pressed him to hurry up departure date of troops and he said he would do his utmost.

U.S. Rejects French Plea

This cable from Dulles to Dillon, April 5, 1954, made clear that the United States would not intervene without congressional approval, which in turn depended upon British participation. Despite vigorous efforts, Dulles could not secure commitments of such support from Britain, and the administration refused to intervene to save Dienbienphu.

As I personally explained to Ely in presence of Radford, it is not (rpt not) possible for U.S. to commit belligerent acts in Indochina without full political understanding with France and other countries. In addition, Congressional action would be required. After conference at highest level, I must confirm this position. U.S. is doing everything possible as indicated my 5175 to prepare public, Congressional and Constitutional basis for united action in Indochina. However, such action is impossible except on coalition basis with active British Commonwealth participation. Meanwhile U.S. prepared, as has been demonstrated, to do everything short of belligerency.

FYI. U.S. cannot and will not be put in position of alone salvaging British Commonwealth interests in Malaya, Australia and New Zealand. This matter now under discussion with UK at highest level.

French Response

This cable from Dillon to Dulles, April 5, 1954, reported French reaction to the U.S. refusal to intervene at Dienbienphu.

I delivered message DEPTEL 3482 to Bidault Monday evening. He asked me to tell Secretary that he personally could well understand position US Government and would pass on your answer to Laniel.

He asked me to say once more that unfortunately the time for formulating coalitions has passed as the fate of Indochina will be decided in the next ten days at Dien-Bien-Phu. As I left he said that even though French must fight alone they would continue fighting and he prayed God they would be successful.

Instructions to U.S. Delegation to Geneva Conference

This cablegram from Dulles to Undersecretary of State Walter Bedell Smith, May 12, 1954, reveals the wariness with which the United States approached the Geneva Conference, its concern about the possible outcome of the negotiations, and its determination to retain complete freedom of action.

The following basic instructions, which have been approved by the President, and which are in confirmation of those already given you orally, will guide you, as head of the United States Delegation, in your participation in the Indochina phase of the Geneva Conference.

1 The presence of a United States representative during the discussion at the Geneva Conference of "the problem of restoring peace in Indochina" rests on the Berlin Agreement of February 18, 1954. Under that agreement the U.S., UK, France, and USSR agreed that the four of them plus other interested states should be invited to a conference at

Geneva on April 26 "for the purpose of reaching a peaceful settlement of the Korean question" and agreed further, that "the problem of restoring peace in Indochina" would also be discussed at Geneva by the four powers represented at Berlin, and Communist China and other interested states.

2   You will not deal with the delegates of the Chinese Communist regime, or any other regime not now diplomatically recognized by the United States, on any terms which imply political recognition or which concede to that regime any status other than that of a regime with which it is necessary to deal on a de facto basis in order to end aggression or the threat of aggression, and to obtain peace.

3   The position of the United States in the Indochina phase of the Geneva Conference is that of an interested nation which, however, is neither a belligerent nor a principal in the negotiation.

4   The United States is participating in the Indochina phase of the Conference in order thereby to assist in arriving at decisions which will help the nations of that area peacefully to enjoy territorial integrity and political independence under stable and free governments with the opportunity to expand their economies, to realize their legitimate national aspirations, and to develop security through individual and collective defense against aggression, from within or without. This implies that these people should not be amalgamated into the Communist bloc of imperialistic dictatorship.

5   The United States is not prepared to give its express or implied approval to any cease-fire, armistice, or other settlement which would have the effect of subverting the existing lawful governments of the three aforementioned states or of permanently impairing their territorial integrity or of placing in jeopardy the forces of the French Union in Indochina, or which otherwise contravened the principles stated in (4) above.

6   You should, insofar as is compatible with these instructions, cooperate with the Delegation of France and with the Delegations of other friendly participants in this phase of the Conference.

7   If in your judgment continued participation in the Indochina phase of the Conference appears likely to involve the United States in a result inconsistent with its policy, as stated above, you should immediately so inform your Government, recommending either withdrawal or the limitation of the U.S. role to that of an observer. If the situation develops such that, in your opinion, either of such actions is essential under the circumstances and time is lacking for consultation with Washington, you may act in your discretion.

8   You are authorized to inform other delegations at Geneva of these instructions.

Joint Chiefs of Staff 1954 War Plans for Indochina

On several occasions during the spring of 1954, the United States appears to have come close to military intervention in Indochina. Had this occurred, as the following Joint Chiefs of Staff memorandum to Secretary of Defense Charles E. Wilson, May 26, 1954, indicates, the military had contingency plans calling for air and naval action against China and for the use of atomic weapons.

1   Reference is made to the memorandum by the Acting Secretary of Defense, dated 18 May 1954, subject as above, wherein the Joint Chiefs of Staff were requested to prepare certain studies, and agreed outline answers to certain questions relating thereto, for discussion with the Acting Secretary of Defense on or before 24 May, and for subsequent submission to the National Security Council (NSC).

2   **a**   The Studies requested by the Acting Secretary of Defense were developed within the parameters prescribed in the memorandum by the Executive Secretary, NSC, dated 18 May 1954, subject as above. This memorandum is interpreted as assuming no concurrent involvement in Korea. This assumption may be quite unrealistic and lead to malemployment of available forces. The Joint Chiefs of Staff desire to point out their belief that, from the point of view of the United States, with reference to the Far East as a whole, *Indochina is devoid of decisive military objectives and the allocation of more than token U.S. armed forces in Indochina would be a serious diversion of limited U.S. capabilities.* The principal sources of Viet Minh military supply lie outside Indochina. The destruction or neutralization of these sources in China proper would materially reduce the French military problems in Indochina.

   b   In connection with the above, it may be readily anticipated that, upon Chinese Communist intervention in Indochina, the French would promptly request the immediate deployment of U.S. ground and air forces, additional naval forces, and a considerable increase in MDAF armament and equipment. The Joint Chiefs of Staff have stated their belief that committing to the Indochina conflict naval forces in excess of a Fast Carrier Task Force and supporting forces as necessary in accordance with the developments in the situation, of basing substantial air forces in Indochina, will involve maldeployment of forces and reduce readiness to meet probable Chinese Communist reaction elsewhere in the Far East. Simultaneously, it is necessary to keep in mind the considerable Allied military potential available in the Korea-Japan-Okinawa area.

c   In light of the above, it is clear that denial of these forces to Indochina could result in a schism between the United States and France unless they were employed elsewhere. However, it should be noted that the Joint Chiefs of Staff have plans, both approved and under consideration, which provide for the employment of these forces in combat operations outside Indochina. Nevertheless, it is desired to repeat that this particular report is responsive to the question of U.S. intervention in Indochina only.

ASSUMING THE CHINESE COMMUNISTS INTERVENE

3   Strategic Concept and Plan of Operation

Seek to create conditions through the destruction of effective Communist forces and their means for support in the Indochina action and by reducing Chinese Communist capability for further aggression under which Associated States forces could assume responsibility for the defense of Indochina. In the light of this concept the major courses of action would be as follows:

a   Employing atomic weapons, whenever advantageous, as well as other weapons, *conduct offensive air* operations against *selected military targets in Indochina and against those military targets in China, Hainan,* and other Communist-held offshore islands which are being used by the Communists *in direct support of their operations,* or which threaten the security of U.S. and allied forces in the area.

b   Simultaneously, French Union Forces, augmented by U.S. naval, and air forces, would exploit by coordinated ground, naval and air action such successes as may be gained as a result of the aforementioned air operations in order to destroy enemy forces in Indochina.

c   Conduct coordinated ground, naval, and air action to destroy enemy forces in Indochina.

d   In the light of circumstances prevailing at the time, and subject to an evaluation of the results of operations conducted under subparagraphs *a* and *b* above, be prepared to take further action against Communist China to reduce its war-making capability, such as:

(1) Destruction of additional selected military targets. In connection with these additional targets, such action requires an enlarged but highly selective atomic offensive in addition to attacks employing other weapons systems.

(2) Blockade of the China coast. This might be instituted progressively from the outset.

(3) Seizure or neutralization of Hainan Island.

(4) Operations against the Chinese mainland by Chinese Nationalist forces. . . .

ASSUMING CHINESE COMMUNISTS DO NOT INTERVENE

9 Strategic Concept and Plan of Action

Seek to create conditions by destroying effective Communist forces in Indochina, under which the Associated States forces could assume responsibility for the defense of Indochina. In the light of this concept, the major courses of action which would be undertaken are as follows:

a *Conduct air operations* in support of allied forces in *Indochina*. The employment of atomic weapons is contemplated in the event that such course appears militarily advantageous.

b Simultaneously, French Union Forces augmented by such armed forces of the Philippines and Thailand as may be committed would, in coordination with U.S. naval and Air Force forces, conduct coordinated ground, naval and air action to destroy enemy forces in Indochina. . . .

Geneva Accords, July 1954

This "final declaration" of the Geneva Conference, signed by France and the Vietminh on July 21, 1954, comprises the so-called Geneva Accords of 1954 that ended the First Indochina War and laid the basis for the Second Indochina War. The Accords called for a cease-fire and placed strict limits on the introduction of foreign troops. They also called for national elections in 1956 to reunite a Vietnam presumed to be divided only temporarily. In the years after 1954, they would be honored by both sides more in the breach than in the observance.

THE "FINAL DECLARATION"

FINAL DECLARATION, dated the 21st July, 1954, of the Geneva Conference on the problem of restoring peace in Indo-China, in which the representatives of Cambodia, the Democratic Republic of Viet-Nam, France, Laos, the People's Republic of China, the State of Viet-Nam, the Union of Soviet Socialist Republics, the United Kingdom, and the United States of America took part.

   1   The Conference takes note of the agreements ending hostilities in Cambodia, Laos and Viet-Nam and organizing international control and the supervision of the execution of the provisions of these agreements.

   2   The Conference expresses satisfaction at the ending of hostilities in Cambodia, Laos and Viet-Nam; the Conference expresses its conviction that the execution of the provisions set out in the present declaration and in the agreements on the cessation of hostilities will permit Cambodia, Laos, and Viet-Nam henceforth to play their part, in full independence and sovereignty, in the peaceful community of nations.

   3   The Conference takes note of the declarations made by the Governments of Cambodia and of Laos of their intention to adopt measures permitting all citizens to take their place in the national community, in particular by participating in the next general elections, which, in conformity with the constitution of each of these countries, shall take place in the course of the year 1955, by secret ballot and in conditions of respect for fundamental freedoms.

   4   The Conference takes note of the clauses in the agreement on the cessation of hostilities in Viet-Nam prohibiting the introduction into Viet-Nam of foreign troops and military personnel as well as of all kinds of arms and munitions. The Conference also takes note of the declarations made by the Governments of Cambodia and Laos of their resolution not to request foreign aid, whether in war material, in personnel or in instructors except for the purpose of the effective defense of their territory and, in the case of Laos, to the extent defined by the agreements on the cessation of hostilities in Laos.

   5   The Conference takes note of the clauses in the agreement on

the cessation of hostilities in Viet-Nam to the effect that no military base under the control of a foreign State may be established in the regrouping zones of the two parties, the latter having the obligation to see that the zones allotted to them shall not constitute part of any military alliance and shall not be utilized for the resumption of hostilities or in the service of an aggressive policy. The Conference also takes note of the declarations of the Governments of Cambodia and Laos to the effect that they will not join in any agreement with other States if this agreement includes the obligation to participate in a military alliance not in conformity with the principles of the Charter of the United Nations or, in the case of Laos, with the principles of the agreement on the cessation of hostilities in Laos or, so long as their security is not threatened, the obligation not to establish bases on Cambodia or Laotian territory for the military forces of foreign powers.

6 The Conference recognizes that the essential purpose of the agreement relating to Viet-Nam is to settle military questions with a view to ending hostilities and that the military demarcation line is provisional and should not in any way be interpreted as constituting a political or territorial boundary. The Conference expresses its conviction that the execution of the provisions set out in the present declaration and in the agreement on the cessation of hostilities creates the necessary basis for the achievement in the near future of a political settlement in Viet-Nam.

7 The Conference declares that, so far as Viet-Nam is concerned, the settlement of political problems, effected on the basis of respect for the principles of independence, unity and territorial integrity, shall permit the Viet-Namese people to enjoy the fundamental freedoms, guaranteed by democratic institutions established as a result of free general elections by secret ballot. In order to ensure that sufficient progress in the restoration of peace has been made, and that all the necessary conditions obtain for free expression of the national will, general elections shall be held in July 1956, under the supervision of an international commission composed of representatives of the Member States of the International Supervisory Commission, referred to in the agreement on the cessation of hostilities. Consultations will be held on this subject between the competent representative authorities of the two zones from 20 July 1955 onwards.

8 The provisions of the agreements on the cessation of hostilities intended to ensure the protection of individuals and of property must be most strictly applied and must, in particular, allow everyone in Viet-Nam to decide freely in which zone he wishes to live.

9 The competent representative authorities of the Northern and

Southern zones of Viet-Nam, as well as the authorities of Laos and Cambodia, must not permit any individual or collective reprisals against persons who have collaborated in any way with one of the parties during the war, or against members of such persons' families.

10 The Conference takes note of the declaration of the Government of the French Republic to the effect that it is ready to withdraw its troops from the territory of Cambodia, Laos, and Viet-Nam, at the requests of the Governments concerned and within periods which shall be fixed by agreement between the parties except in the cases where by agreement between the two parties, a certain number of French troops shall remain at specified points and for a specified time.

11 The Conference takes note of the declaration of the French Government to the effect that for the settlement of all the problems connected with the re-establishment and consolidation of peace in Cambodia, Laos and Viet-Nam, the French Government will proceed from the principle of respect for the independence and sovereignty, unity, and territorial integrity of Cambodia, Laos and Viet-Nam.

12 In their relations with Cambodia, Laos and Viet-Nam, each member of the Geneva Conference undertakes to respect the sovereignty, the independence, the unity and the territorial integrity of the above-mentioned states, and to refrain from any interference in their internal affairs.

13 The members of the Conference agree to consult one another on any question which may be referred to them by the International Supervisory Commission, in order to study such measures as may prove necessary to ensure that the agreements on the cessation of hostilities in Cambodia, Laos and Viet-Nam are respected.

U.S. Response to Geneva Accords

This July 1954 statement by Undersecretary of State Smith reveals the persisting aloofness of the United States toward the Geneva proceedings and its unwillingness to commit itself to support of the Accords. In fact, after July 1954, the United

States would violate both the letter and the spirit of the agreements reached at Geneva.

As I stated on July 18, my Government is not prepared to join in a declaration by the Conference such as is submitted. However, the United States makes this unilateral declaration of its position in these matters:

"The Government of the United States being resolved to devote its efforts to the strengthening of peace in accordance with the principles and purposes of the United Nations takes note of the agreements concluded at Geneva on July 20 and 21, 1954 between (a) The Franco-Laotian Command and the Command of the Peoples Army of Viet-Nam; (b) the Royal Khmer Army Command and the Command of the Peoples Army of Viet-Nam; (c) Franco-Vietnamese Command and the Command of the Peoples Army of Viet-Nam and of paragraphs 1 to 12 inclusive of the declaration presented to the Geneva Conference on July 21, 1954 and declares with regard to the aforesaid agreements and paragraphs that (i) it will refrain from the threat or the use of force to disturb them, in accordance with Article 2 (4) of the Charter of the United Nations dealing with the obligation of members to refrain in their international relations from the threat or use of force; and (ii) it would view any renewal of the aggression in violation of the aforesaid agreements with grave concern and as seriously threatening international peace and security.

"In connection with the statement in the declaration concerning free elections in Viet-Nam my Government wishes to make clear its position which it has expressed in a declaration made in Washington on June 29, 1954, as follows:

" 'In the case of nations now divided against their will, we shall continue to seek to achieve unity through free elections supervised by the United Nations to insure that they are conducted fairly.'

"With respect to the statement made by the representative of the State of Viet-Nam, the United States reiterates its traditional position that peoples are entitled to determine their own future and that it will not join in an arrangement which would hinder this. Nothing in its declaration just made is intended to or does indicate any departure from this traditional position.

"We share the hope that the agreements will permit Cambodia, Laos and Viet-Nam to play their part, in full independence and sovereignty, in the peaceful community of nations, and will enable the peoples of that area to determine their own future."

Edward Lansdale Report on CIA Operations in Vietnam, 1954–1955

This classic account of the CIA mission to Vietnam headed by the legendary Edward Lansdale chronicles the overt and covert activities launched by the United States in the aftermath of the Geneva Conference to weaken the Vietminh government in North Vietnam and strengthen the Diem government in the South.

I. FOREWORD

This is the condensed account of one year in the operations of a "cold war" combat team, written by the team itself in the field, little by little in moments taken as the members could. The team is known as the Saigon Military Mission. The field is Vietnam. There are other teams in the field, American, French, British, Chinese, Vietnamese, Vietminh, and others. Each has its own story to tell. This is ours.

The Saigon Military Mission entered Vietnam on 1 June 1954 when its Chief arrived. However, this is the story of a team, and it wasn't until August 1954 that sufficient members arrived to constitute a team. So, this is mainly an account of the team's first year, from August 1954 to August 1955.

It was often a frustrating and perplexing year, up close. The Geneva Agreements signed on 21 July 1954 imposed restrictive rules upon all official Americans, including the Saigon Military Mission. An active and intelligent enemy made full use of legal rights to screen his activities in establishing his stay-behind organizations south of the 17th Parallel and in obtaining quick security north of that Parallel. The nation's economy and communications system were crippled by eight years of open war. The government, including its Army and other security forces, was in a painful transition from colonial to self rule, making it a year of hot-tempered incidents. Internal problems arose quickly to points where armed conflict was sought as the only solution. The enemy was frequently forgotten in the heavy atmosphere of suspicion, hatred and jealousy.

The Saigon Military Mission received some blows from allies and the enemy in this atmosphere, as we worked to help stabilize the government and to beat the Geneva time-table of Communist takeover in the north. However, we did beat the time-table. The government did become stabilized. The Free Vietnamese are now becoming unified and learning how to cope with the Communist enemy. We are thankful that we had a chance to help in this work in a critical area of the world, to be positive and constructive in a year of doubt.

II. MISSION

The Saigon Military Mission (SMM) was born in a Washington policy meeting in early 1954, when Dien Bien Phu was still holding out against the encircling Vietminh. The SMM was to enter into Vietnam quietly and assist the Vietnamese, rather than the French, in unconventional warfare. The French were to be kept as friendly allies in the process, as far as possible.

The broad mission for the team was to undertake paramilitary operations against the enemy and to wage political-psychological warfare. Later, after Geneva, the mission was modified to prepare the means for undertaking paramilitary operations in Communist areas rather than to wage unconventional warfare. . . .

III. HIGHLIGHTS OF THE YEAR

a. Early Days

The Saigon Military Mission (SMM) started on 1 June 1954 when its Chief, Colonel Edward G. Lansdale, USAF, arrived in Saigon with a small box of files and clothes and a borrowed typewriter, courtesy of an SA-16 flight set up for him by the 13th Air Force at Clark AFB. Lt-General John O'Daniel and Embassy Chargé Rob McClintock had arranged for his appointment as Assistant Air Attaché, since it was improper for U.S. officers at MAAG at that time to have advisory conferences with Vietnamese officers. Ambassador [Donald] Heath had concurred already. There was no desk space for an office, no vehicle, no safe for files. He roomed with General O'Daniel, later moved to a small house rented by MAAG. Secret communications with Washington were provided through the Saigon station of CIA.

There was deepening gloom in Vietnam. Dien Bien Phu had fallen. The French were capitulating to the Vietminh at Geneva. The first night in Saigon, Vietminh saboteurs blew up large ammunition dumps at the airport, rocking Saigon throughout the night. General O'Daniel and Chargé McClintock agreed that it was time to start taking

positive action. O'Daniel paved the way for a quick first-hand survey of the situation throughout the country. McClintock paved the way for contacts with Vietnamese political leaders. Our Chief's reputation from the Philippines had preceded him. Hundreds of Vietnamese acquaintanceships were made quickly.

Working in close cooperation with George Hellyer, USIS Chief, a new psychological warfare campaign was devised for the Vietnamese Army and for the government in Hanoi. Shortly after, a refresher course in combat psywar was constructed and Vietnamese Army personnel were rushed through it. A similar course was initiated for the Ministry of Information. Rumor campaigns were added to the tactics and tried out in Hanoi. It was almost too late.

The first rumor campaign was to be a carefully planted story of a Chinese Communist regiment in Tonkin taking reprisals against a Vietminh village whose girls the Chinese had raped, recalling Chinese Nationalist troop behavior in 1945 and confirming Vietnamese fears of Chinese occupation under Vietminh rule; the story was to be planted by soldiers of the Vietnamese Armed Psywar Company in Hanoi dressed in civilian clothes. The troops received their instructions silently, dressed in civilian clothes, went on the mission, and failed to return. They had deserted to the Vietminh. Weeks later, Tonkinese told an excited story of the misbehavior of the Chinese Divisions in Vietminh territory. Investigated, it turned out to be the old rumor campaign, with Vietnamese embellishments.

There was political chaos. Prince Buu Loc no longer headed the government. Government ministries all but closed. The more volatile leaders of political groups were proposing a revolution, which included armed attacks on the French. Col. Jean Carbonel of the French Army proposed establishing a regime with Vietnamese (Nungs and others) known to him close to the Chinese border and asked for our backing. Our reply was that this was a policy decision to be made between the FEC top command and U.S. authorities.

Oscar Arellano, Junior Chamber International vice-president for Southeast Asia, stopped by for a visit with our Chief; an idea in this visit later grew into "Operation Brotherhood."

On 1 July, Major Lucien Conein arrived, as the second member of the team. He is a paramilitary specialist, well-known to the French for his help with French-operated maquis in Tonkin against the Japanese in 1945, the one American guerrilla fighter who had not been a member of the [Archimedes] Patti [OSS] Mission. He was assigned to MAAG for cover purposes. Arranged by Lt-Col William Rosson, a meeting was held with Col Carbonel, Col Nguyen Van Vy, and the two SMM officers; Vy had seen his first combat in 1945 under Conein. Carbonel proposed establishing a maquis, to be kept as a secret between the four officers. SMM refused, learned later that Carbonel had kept the FEC Deuxieme Bureau informed. Shortly afterwards, at a Defense conference with General O'Daniel, our Chief had a chance to suggest Vy for a command in the North, making him a general. Secretary of State for Defense Le Ngoc Chan did so, Vy was grateful and remained so.

Ngo Dinh Diem arrived on 7 July, and within hours was in despair as the French forces withdrew from the Catholic provinces of Phat Diem and Nam Dinh in Tonkin. Catholic militia streamed north to Hanoi and Haiphong, their hearts filled with anger at French abandonment. The two SMM officers stopped a planned grenade attack by militia girls against French troops guarding a warehouse; the girls stated they had not eaten for three days; arrangements were made for Chinese merchants in Haiphong to feed them. Other militia attacks were stopped, including one against a withdrawing French artillery unit; the militia wanted the guns to stand and fight the Vietminh. The Tonkinese had hopes of American friendship and listened to the advice given them. Governor [name illegible] died, reportedly by poison. Tonkin's government changed as despair grew. On 21 July, the Geneva Agreement was signed. Tonkin was given to the Communists. Anti-Communists turned to SMM for help in establishing a resistance movement and several tentative initial arrangements were made.

Diem himself had reached a nadir of frustration, as his country disintegrated after the conference of foreigners. With the approval of Ambassador Heath and General O'Daniel, our Chief drew up a plan of overall governmental action and presented it to Diem, with Hellyer as interpreter. It called for fast constructive action and dynamic leadership. Although the plan was not adopted, it laid the foundation for a friendship which has lasted.

Oscar Areliano [sic.] visited Saigon again. Major Charles T. R. Bohanan, a former team-mate in Philippine days, was in town. At an SMM conference with these two, "Operation Brotherhood" was born: volunteer medical teams of Free Asians to aid the Free Vietnamese who have few doctors of their own. Washington responded warmly to the idea. President Diem was visited; he issued an appeal to the Free World for help. The Junior Chamber International adopted the idea. SMM would monitor the operation quietly in the background.

President Diem had organized a Committee of Cabinet Ministers to handle the problem of refugees from the Communist North. The Committee system was a failure. No real plans had been made by the French or the Americans. After conferences with USOM (FOA) officials and with General O'Daniel, our Chief suggested to Ambassador Heath that he call a U.S. meeting to plan a single Vietnamese agency, under a Commissioner of Refugees to be appointed by President Diem, to run the Vietnamese refugee program and to provide a channel through which help could be given by the U.S., France, and other free nations. The meeting was called and the plan adopted, with MAAG under General O'Daniel in the coordinating role. Diem adopted the plan. The French pitched in enthusiastically to help. CAT asked SMM for help in obtaining a French contract for the refugee airlift, and got it. In return, CAT provided SMM with the means for secret air travel between the North and Saigon. . . .

b. August 1954

An agreement had been reached that the personnel ceiling of U.S. military personnel with MAAG would be frozen at the number present in Vietnam on the date of the cease-fire, under the terms of the Geneva Agreement. In South Vietnam this deadline was to be 11 August. It meant that SMM might have only two members present, unless action were taken. General O'Daniel agreed to the addition of ten SMM men under MAAG cover, plus any others in the Defense pipeline who arrived before the deadline. A call for help went out. Ten officers in Korea, Japan, and Okinawa were selected and rushed to Vietnam.

SMM had one small MAAG house. Negotiations were started for other housing, but the new members of the team arrived before housing was ready and were crammed three and four to a hotel room for the first days. Meetings were held to assess the new members' abilities. None had had political-psychological warfare experience. Most were experienced in paramilitary and clandestine intelligence operations. Plans were made quickly, for time was running out in the north; already the Vietminh had started taking over secret control of Hanoi and other areas of Tonkin still held by French forces.

Major Conein was given responsibility for developing a paramilitary organization in the north, to be in position when the Vietminh took over. . . . [His] . . . team was moved north immediately as part of the MAAG staff working on the refugee problem. The team had headquarters in Hanoi, with a branch in Haiphong. Among cover duties, this team supervised the refugee flow for the Hanoi airlift, organized by the French. One day, as a CAT C-46 finished loading, they saw a small child standing on the ground below the loading door. They shouted for the pilot to wait, picked the child up and shoved him onto the aircraft, which they promptly taxied out for its takeoff in the constant air shuffle. A Vietnamese man and woman ran up to the team, asking what they had done with their small boy, whom they'd brought to say goodbye to relatives. The chagrined team explained, finally talked the parents into going south to Free Vietnam, put them in the next aircraft to catch up with their son in Saigon. . . .

A second paramilitary team was formed to explore possibilities of organizing resistance against the Vietminh from bases in the south. This team consisted of Army Lt-Col Raymond Wittmayer, Army Major Fred Allen, and Army Lt Edward Williams. The latter was our only experienced counter-espionage officer and undertook double duties, including working with revolutionary political groups. Major Allen eventually was able to mount a Vietnamese paramilitary effort in Tonkin from the south, barely beating the Vietminh shutdown in Haiphong as his teams went in, trained and equipped for their assigned missions.

Navy Lt Edward Bain and Marine Captain Richard Smith were assigned as the support group for SMM. Actually, support for an effort such as SMM is a major operation in itself, running the gamut from the usual administrative and personnel functions to the intricate business of clandestine air, maritime and land supply of paramilitary materiel. In effect, they became our official smugglers as well as paymasters, housing officers, transportation officers, warehousemen, file clerks, and mess officers. The work load was such that other team members frequently pitched in and helped.

c.   September 1954

Highly-placed officials from Washington visited Saigon and, in private conversations, indicated that current estimates led to the conclusion that Vietnam probably would have to be written off as a loss. We admitted that prospects were gloomy, but were positive that there was still a fighting chance.

On 8 September, SMM officers visited Secretary of State for Defense Chan and walked into a tense situation in his office. Chan had just arrested Lt-Col Lan (G-6 of the Vietnamese Army) and Capt Giai (G-5 of the Army). Armed guards filled the room. We were told what had happened and assured that everything was all right by all three principals. Later, we discovered that Chan was alone and that the guards were Lt-Col Lan's commandos. Lan was charged with political terrorism (by his "action" squads) and Giai with anti-Diem propaganda (using G-5 leaflet, rumor, and broadcast facilities).

The arrest of Lan and Giai, who simply refused to consider themselves arrested, and of Lt Minh, officer in charge of the Army radio station which was guarded by Army troops, brought into the open a plot by the Army Chief of Staff, General Hinh, to overthrow the government. Hinh had hinted at such a plot to his American friends, using a silver cigarette box given him by Egypt's Naguib to carry the hint. SMM became thoroughly involved in the tense controversy which followed, due to our Chief's closeness to both President Diem and General Hinh. He had met the latter in the Philippines in 1952, was a friend of both Hinh's wife and favorite mistress. (The mistress was a pupil in a small English class conducted for mistresses of important personages, at their request.) . . .

While various U.S. officials including General O'Daniel and Foreign Service Officer Frank [name illegible] participated in U.S. attempts to heal the split between the President and his Army, Ambassador Heath asked us to make a major effort to end the controversy. This effort strained relations with Diem and never was successful, but did dampen Army enthusiasm for the plot. At one moment, when there was likelihood of an attack by armored vehicles on the Presidential Palace, SMM told Hinh bluntly that U.S. support would stop in such an event. At the same time a group from the Presidential Guards asked for tactical advice on how to stop armored vehicles with the only weapons available to the Guards: carbines, rifles and hand grenades. The advice, on tank traps and destruction with improvised weapons, must have sounded grim. The following morning, when the attack was to take place, we visited the Palace; not a guard was left on the grounds; President Diem was alone upstairs calmly getting his work done.

As a result of the Hinh trouble, Diem started looking around for troops upon whom he could count. Some Tonkinese militia, refugees from the north, were assembled in Saigon close to the Palace. But they were insufficient for what he needed. Diem made an agreement with General Trinh Minh The, leader of some 3,000 Cao Dai dissidents in the vicinity of Tayninh, to give General The some needed financial support; The was to give armed support to the government if necessary and to provide a safe haven for the government if it had to flee. The's guerrillas, known as the Lien Minh, were strongly nationalist and were still fighting the Vietminh and the French. At Ambassador Heath's request, the U.S. secretly furnished Diem with funds for The through the SMM. Shortly afterwards, an invitation came from The to visit him. Ambassador Heath approved the visit. . . .

The Northern SMM team under Conein had organized a paramilitary group, (which we will disguise by the Vietnamese name of Binh) through the Northern Dai Viets, a political party with loyalties to [Emperor] Bao Dai. The group was to be trained and supported by the U.S. as patriotic Vietnamese, to come eventually under government control when the government was ready for such activities. Thirteen Binhs were quietly exfiltrated through the port of Haiphong, under the direction of Lt Andrews, and taken on the first stage of the journey to their training area by a U.S. Navy ship. This was the first of a series of helpful actions by Task Force 98, commanded by Admiral Sabin.

Another paramilitary group for Tonkin operations was being developed in Saigon through General Nguyen Van Vy. In September this group started shaping up fast, and the project was given to Major Allen. (We will give this group the Vietnamese name of Hao). . . .

Towards the end of the month, it was learned that the largest printing establishment in the north intended to remain in Hanoi and do business with the Vietminh. An attempt was made by SMM to destroy the modern presses, but Vietminh security agents already had moved into the plant and frustrated the attempt. This operation was under a Vietnamese patriot whom we shall call Trieu; his case officer was Capt Arundel. Earlier in the month they had engineered a black psywar strike in Hanoi: leaflets signed by the Vietminh instructing Tonkinese on how to behave for the Vietminh takeover of the Hanoi region in early October, including items about property, money reform, and a three-day holiday of workers upon takeover. The day following the distribution of these leaflets, refugee registration tripled. Two days later Vietminh currency was worth half the value prior to the leaflets. The Vietminh took to the radio to denounce the leaflets; the leaflets were so authentic in appearance that even most of the rank and file Vietminh were sure that the radio denunciations were a French trick.

The Hanoi psywar strike had other consequences. Binh had enlisted a high police official of Hanoi as part of his team, to effect the release from jail of any team members if arrested. The official at the last moment decided to assist in the leaflet distribution personally. Police officers spotted him, chased his vehicle through the empty Hanoi streets of early morning, finally opened fire on him and caught him. He was the only member of the group caught. He was held in prison as a Vietminh agent.

d.   October 1954

Hanoi was evacuated on 9 October. The northern SMM team left with the last French troops, disturbed by what they had seen of the grim efficiency of the Vietminh in their takeover, the contrast between the silent march of the victorious Vietminh troops in their tennis shoes and the clanking armor of the well-equipped French whose Western tactics and equipment had failed against the Communist military-political-economic campaign.

The northern team had spent the last days of Hanoi in contaminating the oil supply of the bus company for a gradual wreckage of the engines in the buses, in taking the first actions for delayed sabotage of the railroad (which required teamwork with a CIA special technical team in Japan who performed their part brilliantly), and in writing detailed notes of potential targets for future paramilitary operations. (U.S. adherence to the Geneva Agreement prevented SMM from carrying out the active sabotage it desired to do against the power plant, water facilities, harbor, and bridge.) The team had a bad moment when contaminating the oil. They had to work quickly at night, in an enclosed storage room. Fumes from the contaminant came close to knocking them out. Dizzy and weak-kneed, they masked their faces with handkerchiefs and completed the job.

Meanwhile, Polish and Russian ships had arrived in the south to transport southern Vietminh to Tonkin under the Geneva Agreement. This offered the opportunity for another black psywar strike. A leaflet was developed by Binh with the help of Capt Arundel, attributed to the Vietminh Resistance Committee. Among other items, it reassured the Vietminh they would be kept safe below decks from imperialist air and submarine attacks, and requested that warm clothing be brought; the warm clothing item would be coupled with a verbal rumor campaign that Vietminh were being sent into China as railroad laborers.

SMM had been busily developing G-5 of the Vietnamese Army for such psywar efforts. Under Arundel's direction, the First Armed Propaganda Company printed the leaflets and distributed them, by soldiers in civilian clothes who penetrated into southern Vietminh zones on foot. (Distribution in Camau was made while columnist Joseph Alsop was on his visit there which led to his sensational, gloomy articles later; our soldier "Vietminh" failed in an attempt to get the leaflet into

Alsop's hands in Camau; Alsop was never told this story.) Intelligence
reports and other later reports revealed that village and delegation committees complained about "deportation" to the north, after distribution
of the leaflet. . . .

Contention between Diem and Hinh had become murderous. . . .
Finally, we learned that Hinh was close to action; he had selected 26
October as the morning for an attack on the Presidential Palace. Hinh
was counting heavily on Lt-Col Lan's special forces and on Captain
Giai who was running Hinh's secret headquarters at Hinh's home. We
invited these two officers to visit the Philippines, on the pretext that we
were making an official trip, could take them along and open the way
for them to see some inner workings of the fight against Filipino Communists which they probably would never see otherwise. Hinh reluc-
tantly turned down his own invitation; he had had a memorable time of
it on his last visit to Manila in 1952. Lt-Col Lan was a French agent
and the temptation to see behind-the-scenes was too much. He and Giai
accompanied SMM officers on the MAAG C-47 which General
O'Daniel made available for the operation. 26 October was spent in the
Philippines. The attack on the palace didn't come off.

e. November 1954

General Lawton Collins arrived as Ambassador on 8 November. . . .

Collins, in his first press conference, made it plain that the U.S.
was supporting President Diem. The new Ambassador applied pressure
on General Hinh and on 29 November Hinh left for Paris. His other key
conspirators followed.

Part of the SMM team became involved in staff work to back up
the energetic campaign to save Vietnam which Collins pushed forward.
Some SMM members were scattered around the Pacific, accompanying
Vietnamese for secret training, obtaining and shipping supplies to be
smuggled into north Vietnam and hidden there. In the Philippines, more
support was being constructed to help SMM, in expediting the flow of
supplies, and in creating Freedom Company, a non-profit Philippines
corporation, backed by President Magsaysay, which would supply Filipinos experienced in fighting the Communist Huks to help in Vietnam
(or elsewhere). . . .

On 23 November, twenty-one selected Vietnamese agents and two
cooks of our Hao paramilitary group were put aboard a Navy ship in
the Saigon River, in daylight. They appeared as coolies, joined the
coolie and refugee throng moving on and off the ship, and disappeared

one by one. It was brilliantly planned and executed, agents being
picked up from unobtrusive assembly points throughout the metropolis.
Lt Andrews made the plans and carried out the movement under the supervision of Major Allen. The ship took the Hao agents, in compart-
mented groups, to an overseas point, the first stage in a movement to a
secret training area.

f.   December 1954

. . . discussions between the U.S., Vietnamese and French had
reached a point where it appeared that a military training mission using
U.S. officers was in the immediate offing. General O'Daniel had a
U.S.-French planning group working on the problem, under Col.
Rosson. One paper they were developing was a plan for pacification of
Vietminh and dissident areas; this paper was passed to SMM for its assistance with the drafting. SMM wrote much of the paper, changing the
concept from the old rigid police controls of all areas to some of our
concepts of winning over the population and instituting a classification
of areas by the amount of trouble in each, the amount of control required, and fixing responsibilities between civil and military authorities. With a few changes this was issued by President Diem on 31 December as the National Security Action (Pacification) Directive. . . .

There was still much disquiet in Vietnam, particularly among anti-
Communist political groups who were not included in the government.
SMM officers were contacted by a number of such groups who felt that
they "would have to commit suicide in 1956" (the 1956 plebiscite
promised in the 1954 Geneva agreement), when the Vietminh would
surely take over against so weak a government. One group of farmers
and militia in the south was talked out of migrating to Madagascar by
SMM and staying on their farms. A number of these groups asked
SMM for help in training personnel for eventual guerrilla warfare if the
Vietminh won. Persons such as the then Minister of Defense and Trinh
Minh The were among those loyal to the government who also requested such help. It was decided that a more basic guerrilla training
program might be undertaken for such groups than was available at the
secret training site to which we had sent the Binh and Hao groups.
Plans were made with Major Bohanan and Mr. John C. Wachtel in the
Philippines for a solution of this problem; the United States backed the
development, through them, of a small Freedom Company training
camp in a hidden valley on the Clark AFB reservation.

Till and Peg Durdin of the N.Y. Times, Hank Lieberman of the

N.Y. Times, Homer Bigart of the N.Y. Herald-Tribune, John Mecklin of Life-Time and John Roderick of Associated Press, have been warm friends of SMM and worked hard to penetrate the fabric of French propaganda and give the U.S. an objective account of events in Vietnam. The group met with us at times to analyze objectives and motives of propaganda known to them, meeting at their own request as U.S. citizens. These mature and responsible news correspondents performed a valuable service for their country. . . .

g. January 1955

The Vietminh long ago had adopted the Chinese Communist thought that the people are the water and the army is the fish. Vietminh relations with the mass of the population during the fighting had been exemplary, with a few exceptions; in contrast, the Vietnamese National Army had been like too many Asian armies, adept at cowing a population into feeding them, providing them with girls. SMM had been working on this problem from the beginning. Since the National Army was the only unit of government with a strong organization through the country and with good communications, it was the key to stabilizing the situation quickly on a nation-wide basis. If Army and people could be brought together into a team, the first strong weapon against Communism could be forged.

The Vietminh were aware of this. We later learned that months before the signing of the Geneva Agreement they had been planning for action in the post-Geneva period; the National Army was to be the primary target for subversion efforts, it was given top priority by the Central Committee for operations against its enemy, and about 100 superior cadres were retrained for the operations and placed in the [words illegible] organization for the work which commenced even before the agreement was signed. We didn't know it at the time, but this was SMM's major opponent in a secret struggle for the National Army. . . .

General O'Daniel was anticipating the culmination of long negotiations to permit U.S. training of the Vietnamese Armed Forces, against some resistance on the part of French groups. In January, negotiations were proceeding so well that General O'Daniel informally organized a combined U.S.-French training mission which eventually became known as the Training Relations and Instruction Mission (TRIM) under his command, but under the overall command of the top French commander, General Paul Ely.

The French had asked for top command of half the divisions in the TRIM staff. Their first priority was for command of the division supervising National Security Action by the Vietnamese, which could be developed into a continuation of strong French control of key elements of both Army and population. In conferences with Ambassador Collins and General O'Daniel, it was decided to transfer Colonel Lansdale from the Ambassador's staff to TRIM, to head the National Security division. Colonel Lansdale requested authority to coordinate all U.S. civil and military efforts in this National Security work. On 11 January, Ambassador Collins announced the change to the country team, and gave him authority to coordinate this work among all U.S. agencies in Vietnam. . . .

President Diem had continued requesting SMM help with the guard battalion for the Presidential Palace. We made arrangements with President Magsaysay in the Philippines and borrowed his senior aide and military advisor, Col. Napoleon Valeriano, who had a fine combat record against the Communist Huks and also had reorganized the Presidential Guard Battalion for Magsaysay. Valeriano, with three junior officers, arrived in January and went to work on Diem's guard battalion. Later, selected Vietnamese officers were trained with the Presidential Guards in Manila. An efficient unit gradually emerged. Diem was warmly grateful for this help by Filipinos who also continuously taught our concept of loyalty and freedom.

The patriot we've named Trieu Dinh had been working on an almanac for popular sale, particularly in the northern cities and towns we could still reach. Noted Vietnamese astrologers were hired to write predictions about coming disasters to certain Vietminh leaders and undertakings, and to predict unity in the south. The work was carried out under the direction of Lt Phillips, based on our concept of the use of astrology for psywar in Southeast Asia. Copies of the almanac were shipped by air to Haiphong and then smuggled into Vietminh territory.

Dinh also had produced a Thomas Paine type series of essays on Vietnamese patriotism against the Communist Vietminh, under the guidance of Capt. Arundel. These essays were circulated among influential groups in Vietnam, earned front-page editorials in the leading daily newspapers in Saigon. Circulation increased with the publication of these essays. The publisher is known to SMM as the Dragon Lady and is a fine Vietnamese girl who has been the mistress of an anti-American French civilian. Despite anti-American remarks by her boy friend, we had helped her keep her paper from being closed by the government . . . and she found it profitable to heed our advice on the editorial content of her paper.

Arms and equipment for the Binh paramilitary team were being cached in the north in areas still free from the Vietminh. Personnel movements were covered by the flow of refugees. Haiphong was reminiscent of our own pioneer days as it was swamped with people whom it couldn't shelter. Living space and food were at a premium, nervous tension grew. It was a wild time for our northern team.

First supplies for the Hao paramilitary group started to arrive in Saigon. These shipments and the earlier ones for the Binh group were part of an efficient and effective air smuggling effort by the 581st [word illegible] Wing, U.S. Air Force, to support SMM, with help by CIA and Air Force personnel in both Okinawa and the Philippines. SMM officers frequently did coolie labor in manhandling tons of cargo, at times working throughout the night. . . . All officers pitched in to help, as part of our "blood, sweat and tears." . . .

By 31 January, all operational equipment of the Binh paramilitary group had been trans-shipped to Haiphong from Saigon, mostly with the help of CAT, and the northern SMM team had it cached in operational sites. Security measures were tightened at the Haiphong airport and plans for bringing in the Hao equipment were changed from the air route to sea. Task Force 98, now 98.7 under command of Captain Frank, again was asked to give a helping hand and did so. . . .

. . . Major Conein had briefed the members of the Binh paramilitary team and started them infiltrating into the north as individuals. The infiltration was carried out in careful stages over a 30 day period, a successful operation. The Binhs became normal citizens, carrying out every day civil pursuits, on the surface.

We had smuggled into Vietnam about eight and a half tons of supplies for the Hao paramilitary group. They included fourteen agent radios, 300 carbines, 90,000 rounds of carbine ammunition, 50 pistols, 10,000 rounds of pistol ammunition, and 300 pounds of explosives. Two and a half tons were delivered to the Hao agents in Tonkin, while the remainder was cached along the Red River by SMM, with the help of the Navy. . . .

j.   April 1955

. . . the Hao paramilitary team had finished its training at the secret training site and had been flown by the Air Force to a holding site in the Philippines, where Major Allen and his officers briefed the paramilitary team. In mid-April, they were taken by the Navy to Haiphong, where they were gradually slipped ashore. Meanwhile, arms and other equipment including explosives were being flown into Saigon via our smuggling route, being readied for shipment north by the Navy task force handling refugees. The White team office gradually became an imposing munitions depot. Nightly shootings and bombings in restless Saigon caused us to give them dispersed storage behind thick walls as far as this one big house would permit. SMM personnel guarded the house night and day, for it also contained our major files other than the working file at our Command Post. All files were fixed for instant destruction, automatic weapons and hand grenades distributed to all personnel. It was a strange scene for new personnel just arriving. . . .

Haiphong was taken over by the Vietminh on 16 May. Our Binh and northern Hao teams were in place, completely equipped. It had taken a tremendous amount of hard work to beat the Geneva deadline, to locate, select, exfiltrate, train, infiltrate, equip the men of these two teams and have them in place, ready for actions required against the enemy. It would be a hard task to do openly, but this had to be kept secret from the Vietminh, the International [Control] Commission [appointed by the Geneva Conference to supervise the cease-fire] with its suspicious French and Poles and Indians, and even friendly Vietnamese. Movements of personnel and supplies had had to be over thousands of miles. . . .

Ambassador Durbrow's Concern about Diem Government, 1960

This cablegram from Elbridge Durbrow, U.S. ambassador in Saigon, to Secretary of State Christian A. Herter, September 16, 1960, provides a candid assessment of the failure of the Diem government to take advantage of U.S. backing and build a strong base of support in South Vietnam. It indicates the extent to which, by late 1960, the very existence of the government was in jeopardy.

As indicated our [cables] 495 and 538 Diem regime confronted by two separate but related dangers. Danger from demonstrations or coup attempt in Saigon could occur earlier; likely to be predominantly non-

Communistic in origin but Communists can be expected to endeavor infiltrate and exploit any such attempt. Even more serious danger is gradual Viet Cong extension of control over countryside which, if current Communist progress continues, would mean loss free Viet-nam to Communists. These two dangers are related because Communist successes in rural areas embolden them to extend their activities to Saigon and because non-Communist temptation to engage in demonstrations or coup is partly motivated by sincere desire prevent Communist take-over in Viet-nam.

Essentially [word illegible] sets of measures required to meet these two dangers. For Saigon danger essentially political and psychological measures required. For countryside danger security measures as well as political, psychological and economic measures needed. However both sets measures should be carried out simultaneously and to some extent individual steps will be aimed at both dangers.

Security recommendations have been made in our 539 and other messages, including formation internal security council, centralized intelligence, etc. This message therefore deals with our political and economic recommendations. I realize some measures I am recommending are drastic and would be most [word illegible] for an ambassador to make under normal circumstances. But conditions here are by no means normal. Diem government is in quite serious danger. Therefore, in my opinion prompt and even drastic action is called for. I am well aware that Diem has in past demonstrated astute judgment and has survived other serious crises. Possibly his judgment will prove superior to ours this time, but I believe nevertheless we have no alternative but to give him our best judgment of what we believe is required to preserve his government. While Diem obviously resented my frank talks earlier this year and will probably resent even more suggestions outlined below, he has apparently acted on some of our earlier suggestions and might act on at least some of the following:

1   I would propose have frank and friendly talk with Diem and explain our serious concern about present situation and his political position. I would tell him that, while matters I am raising deal primarily with internal affairs, I would like to talk to him frankly and try to be as helpful as I can be giving him the considered judgment of myself and some of his friends in Washington on appropriate measures to assist him in present serious situation. (Believe it best not indicate talking under instructions.) I would particularly stress desirability of actions to broaden and increase his [word illegible]

support prior to 1961 presidential elections required by constitution before end April. I would propose following actions to President:

2   Psychological shock effect is required to take initiative from Communist propagandists as well as non-Communist oppositionists and convince population government taking effective measures to deal with present situation, otherwise we fear matters could get out of hand. To achieve that effect following suggested:

(A)   Because of Vice President Tho's knowledge of south where Communist guerrilla infiltration is increasing so rapidly would suggest that he be shifted from ministry national economy to ministry interior. (Diem has already made this suggestion but Vice President most reluctant take job.)

(B)   It is important to remove any feeling within armed forces that favoritism and political considerations motivate promotions and assignments. Also vital in order deal effectively with Viet Cong threat that channels of command be followed both down and up. To assist in bringing about these changes in armed forces, I would suggest appointment of full-time minister national defense. (Thuan has indicated Diem has been thinking of giving Thuan defense job.)

(C)   Rumors about Mr. and Mrs. [Ngo Dinh] Nhu [Diem's brother and sister-in-law] are creating growing dissension within country and seriously damage political position of Diem government. Whether rumors true or false, politically important fact is that more and more people believe them to be true. Therefore, becoming increasingly clear that in interest Diem government some action should be taken. In analogous situation in other countries including U.S. important, useful government personalities have had to be sacrificed for political reasons. I would suggest therefore that President might appoint Nhu to ambassadorship abroad.

(D)   Similarly Tran Kim Tuyen, Nhu's henchman and head of secret intelligence service, should be sent abroad in diplomatic capacity because of his growing identification in public mind with alleged secret police methods of repression and control.

(E)   One or two cabinet ministers from opposition should be appointed to demonstrate Diem's desire to establish government of national union in fight against VC.

3   Make public announcement of disbandment of Can Lao party [run by Nhu] or at least its surfacing, with names and positions of all members made known publicly. Purpose this step would be to

eliminate atmosphere of fear and suspicion and reduce public belief in favoritism and corruption, all of which party's semi-covert status has given rise to.

4 Permit National Assembly wider legislative initiative and area of genuine debate and bestow on it authority to conduct, with appropriate publicity, public investigations of any department of government with right to question any official except President himself. This step would have three-fold purpose: (A) find some mechanism for dispelling through public investigation constantly generated rumors about government and its personalities; (B) provide people with avenue recourse against arbitrary actions by some government officials; (C) assuage some of intellectual opposition to government.

5 Require all government officials to declare publicly their property and financial holdings and give National Assembly authority to make public investigation of these declarations in effort dispel rumors of corruption.

6 [Words illegible] of [word illegible] control over content of the Vietnamese publication [word illegible] magazines, radio, so that the [words illegible] to closing the gap between government and [words illegible] ideas from one to the other. To insure that the press would reflect, as well as lead, public opinion without becoming a means of upsetting the entire GVN [word illegible], it should be held responsible to a self-imposed code of ethics or "canon" of press-conduct.

7 [Words illegible] to propaganda campaign about new 3-year development plan in effort convince people that government genuinely aims at [word illegible] their welfare. (This suggestion [word illegible] of course upon assessment of soundness of development plan, which has just reached us.)

8 Adopt following measures for immediate enhancement of peasant support of government: (A) establish mechanism for increasing price peasant will receive for paddy crop beginning to come on market in December, either by direct subsidization or establishment of state purchasing mechanism; (B) institute modest payment for all corvee labor; (C) subsidize agroville families along same lines as land resettlement families until former on feet economically; (D) increase compensation paid to youth corps. If Diem asks how these measures are to be financed I shall suggest through increased taxes or increased deficit financing, and shall note that under certain circumstances reasonable deficit financing becomes a politically necessary measure for governments. I should add that using revenues for these fundamental and worthy

purposes would be more effective than spending larger and larger sums on security forces, which, while they are essential and some additional funds for existing security forces may be required, are not complete answer to current problems.

9 Propose suggest to Diem that appropriate steps outlined above be announced dramatically in his annual state of union message to National Assembly in early October. Since Diem usually [word illegible] message in person this would have maximum effect, and I would recommend that it be broadcast live to country.

10 At [words illegible] on occasion fifth anniversary establishment Republic of Vietnam on October 26, it may become highly desirable for President Eisenhower to address a letter of continued support to Diem. Diem has undoubtedly noticed that Eisenhower letter recently delivered to [Prince Norodon] Sihanouk [of Cambodia]. Not only for this reason, but also because it may become very important for us to give Diem continued reassurance of our support. Presidential letter which could be published here may prove to be very valuable.

Request any additional suggestions department may have and its approval for approach to Diem along lines paras 1 to 9.

We believe U.S. should at this time support Diem as best available Vietnamese leader, but should recognize that overriding U.S. objective is strongly anti-Communist Vietnamese government which can command loyal and enthusiastic support of widest possible segments of Vietnamese people, and is able to carry on effective fight against Communist guerrillas. If Diem's position in country continues deteriorate as result failure adopt proper political, psychological, economic and security measures, it may become necessary for U.S. government to begin consideration alternative courses of action and leaders in order achieve our objective.

John F. Kennedy and the Escalation of the War, 1961–1963

During its brief, 1000 days in office, the administration of John Fitzgerald Kennedy significantly escalated the U.S. commitment in Vietnam.

In his first year, Kennedy drastically increased U.S. aid to South Vietnam. The administration took office at a time when the Diem government was increasingly threatened by non-Communist and Communist foes alike, and Kennedy's debacle at the Bay of Pigs in Cuba, his agreement to negotiate a settlement in Laos, and the construction of the Berlin Wall in August 1961 increased the pressures on him to take a hard line in Vietnam. Thus, although he rejected proposals to send American combat troops to Vietnam, in the spring of 1961 and again late in the year, he took steps to increase the amount of U.S. military and economic aid and the number of U.S. military advisers. American advisers also began to take an increasingly active role in combat.

These measures brought no more than temporary results. The massive infusion of aid at first reversed the unfavorable military trend, and South Vietnamese forces for a brief period gained the upper hand. In time, however, the National Liberation Front learned to deal with helicopters and other modern weapons provided by the United States, and the South Vietnamese, their advantage removed, again began to suffer defeat. At Ap Bac in January 1963, NLF forces inflicted an especially disastrous defeat on numerically superior Army of the Republic of (South) Vietnam (ARVN) units.

In the summer of 1963, the United States faced new and more serious problems. While the South Vietnamese position steadily deteriorated in the countryside, an urban revolt among South Vietnam's Buddhists threatened to bring down the government. Diem's blatant discrimination against the Buddhists provoked protests, and when the government responded with outright repression, South Vietnam erupted in a frenzy of violence. On a Saigon street corner, a Buddhist monk immolated himself to dramatize the wrongs, and the picture appeared on television screens and in newspapers across the world.

Alarmed by Diem's response to the protest, the Kennedy administration eventually decided to dump him. Uncertain exactly what the Buddhists wanted and unclear in its own mind whether South Vietnam could survive with or without Diem, the administration equivocated for weeks before deciding to eliminate him. Finally, it gave the green light to a group of disaffected army officers. On November 1, a successful coup was mounted, and despite promises of safe haven Diem and Nhu were brutally murdered by the coup plotters in the back of an American armored personnel carrier. Kennedy himself was assassinated just three weeks later in Dallas, leaving the haunting question, What would he have done in Vietnam had he lived? The answer can never be known, of course. What is clear is that he drastically increased the commitment, both tangibly and rhetorically. With the coup, moreover, the United States assumed responsibility for the South Vietnamese government to a degree it had not had before. Kennedy turned over to his successor a much more difficult problem in Vietnam than he had inherited from Eisenhower.

Kennedy Task Force May 1961 "Program of Action"

This program of action, recommended by a special task force
on Vietnam on May 8, 1961, became the basis for Kennedy's
spring 1961 escalation of the U.S. commitment to South Vietnam.

2. MILITARY

a The following military actions were approved by the NSC meeting
   of 29 April 1961:

   (1) Increase the MAAG as necessary to insure the effective imple-
       mentation of the military portion of the program including the
       training of a 20,000-man addition to the present G.V.N. armed
       forces of 150,000. Initial appraisal of new tasks assigned
       CHMAAG indicate that approximately 100 additional military
       personnel will be required immediately in addition to the pres-
       ent complement of 685.

   (2) Expand MAAG responsibilities to include authority to provide
       support and advice to the Self-Defense Corps with a strength
       of approximately 40,000.

   (3) Authorize MAP support for the entire Civil Guard force of
       68,000. MAP support is now authorized for 32,000; the re-
       maining 36,000 are not now adequately trained and equipped.

   (4) Install as a matter of priority a radar surveillance capability
       which will enable the G.V.N. to obtain warning of Communist
       overflights being conducted for intelligence or clandestine air
       supply purposes. Initially, this capability should be provided
       from U.S. mobile radar capability.

   (5) Provide MAP support for the Vietnamese Junk Force as a
       means of preventing Viet Cong clandestine supply and infil-
       tration into South Vietnam by water. MAP support, which was
       not provided in the Counter-Insurgency Plan, will include
       training of junk crews in Vietnam or at U.S. bases by U.S.
       Navy personnel.

b The following additional actions are considered necessary to assist
   the G.V.N. in meeting the increased security threat resulting from
   the new situation along the Laos-G.V.N. frontier:

   (1) Assist the G.V.N. armed forces to increase their border patrol
       and insurgency suppression capabilities by establishing an ef-
       fective border intelligence and patrol system, by instituting

regular aerial surveillance over the entire frontier area, and by applying modern technological area-denial techniques to control the roads and trails along Vietnam's borders. A special staff element (approximately 6 U.S. personnel) to concentrate upon solutions to the unique problems of Vietnam's borders, will be activated in MAAG, Vietnam, to assist a similar special unit in the RVNAF which the G.V.N. will be encouraged to establish; these two elements working as an integrated team will help the G.V.N. gain the support of nomadic tribes and other border inhabitants, as well as introduce advanced techniques and equipment to strengthen the security of South Vietnam's frontiers.

(2) Assist the G.V.N. to establish a Combat Development and Test Center in South Vietnam to develop, with the help of modern technology, new techniques for use against the Viet Cong forces. (Approximately 4 U.S. personnel.)

(3) Assist the G.V.N. forces with health, welfare and public work projects by providing U.S. Army civil action mobile training teams, coordinated with the similar civilian effort. (Approximately 14 U.S. personnel.)

(4) Deploy a Special Forces Group (approximately 400 personnel) to Nha Trang in order to accelerate G.V.N. Special Forces training. The first increment, for immediate deployment in Vietnam, should be a Special Forces company (52 personnel).

(5) Instruct JCS, CINCPAC, and MAAG to undertake an assessment of the military utility of a further increase in the G.V.N. forces from 170,000 to 200,000 in order to create two new division equivalents for deployment to the northwest border region. The parallel political and fiscal implications should be assessed. . . .

4. ECONOMIC

Objective: Undertake economic programs having both a short-term immediate impact as well as ones which contribute to the longer range economic viability of the country.

a   Undertake a series of economic projects designed to accompany the counter-insurgency effort, by the following action:

(1) Grant to ICA the authority and funds to move into a rural development–civil action program. Such a program would include short-range, simple, impact projects which would be undertaken by teams working in cooperation with local communities. This might cost roughly $3 to $5 million, most in lo-

cal currency. Directors of field teams should be given authority with respect to the expenditures of the funds, including use
of dollar instruments to purchase local currency on the spot.
b Assist Vietnam to make the best use of all available economic resources by the following action:
   (1) Having in mind that our chief objective is obtaining a full and
enthusiastic support by the G.V.N. in its fight against the
Communists, a high level team preferably headed by Assistant
Secretary of the Treasury John Leddy, with State and ICA
members, should be dispatched to Saigon to work out in conjunction with the Ambassador a plan whereby combined U.S.
and Vietnamese financial resources can best be utilized. This
group's terms of reference should cover the broad range of fiscal and economic problems. Authority should be given to
make concessions necessary to achieve our objectives and to
soften the blow of monetary reform. Ambassador Nolting and
perhaps the Vice President should notify Diem of the proposed
visit of this group stressing that their objective is clearly to
maximize the joint effort rather than to force the Vietnamese
into inequitable and unpalatable actions.
   (2) As a part of the foregoing effort, an assessment should be undertaken of the fiscal and other implications of a further force
increase from 170,000 to 200,000 (as noted in the Military
section above).
c Undertake the development of a long-range economic development
program as a means of demonstrating U.S. confidence in the economic and political future of the country by the following action:
   (1) Authorize Ambassador Nolting to inform the G.V.N. that the
U.S. is prepared to discuss a long-range joint five-year development program which would involve contributions and undertakings by both parties. . . .

5. PSYCHOLOGICAL

a Assist the G.V.N. to accelerate its public information program to
help develop a broad public understanding of the actions required to
help combat the Communist insurgents and to build public confidence in the G.V.N.'s determination and ability to deal with the
Communist threat.
b The U.S. Country Team, in coordination with the G.V.N. Ministry
of Defense, should compile and declassify for use of media representatives in South Vietnam and throughout the world, documented

facts concerning Communist infiltration and terrorists' activities and the measures being taken by the G.V.N. to counter such attacks.

c   In coordination with CIA and the appropriate G.V.N. Ministry, USIS will increase the flow of information about unfavorable conditions in North Vietnam to media representatives.

d   Develop agricultural pilot-projects throughout the country, with a view toward exploiting their beneficial psychological effects. This project would be accomplished by combined teams of Vietnamese Civic Action personnel, Americans in the Peace Corps, Filipinos in Operation Brotherhood, and other Free World nationals.

e   Exploit as part of a planned psychological campaign the rehabilitation of Communist Viet Cong prisoners now held in South Vietnam. Testimony of rehabilitated prisoners, stressing the errors of Communism, should be broadcast to Communist-held areas, including North Vietnam, to induce defections. This rehabilitation program would be assisted by a team of U.S. personnel including U.S. Army (Civil Affairs, Psychological Warfare and Counter-Intelligence), USIS, and USOM experts.

f   Provide adequate funds for an impressive U.S. participation in the Saigon Trade Fair of 1962.

6.   COVERT ACTIONS

a   Expand present operations in the field of intelligence, unconventional warfare, and political-psychological activities to support the U.S. objective as stated.

b   Initiate the communications intelligence actions, CIA and ASA personnel increases, and funding which were approved by the President at the NSC meeting of 29 April 1961.

c   Expand the communications intelligence actions by inclusion of 15 additional Army Security Agency personnel to train the Vietnamese Army in tactical COMINT operations. . . .

7.   FUNDING

a   As spelled out in the funding annex, the funding of the counter-insurgency plan and the other actions recommended in this program might necessitate increases in U.S. support of the G.V.N. budget for FY 61 of as much as $58 million, making up to a total of $192 million compared to $155 million for FY 60. The U.S. contribution for the G.V.N. Defense budget in FY 62 as presently estimated would total $161 million plus any deficiency in that Budget which the

G.V.N. might be unable to finance. The exact amount of U.S. contributions to the G.V.N. Defense budgets for FY 61 and FY 62 are subject to negotiation between the U.S. and the G.V.N.
b U.S. military assistance to G.V.N., in order to provide the support contemplated by the proposed program, would total $140 million, or $71 million more than now programmed for Vietnam in the U.S. current MAP budget for FY 62. . . . .

ANNEX 6

Covert Actions

a **Intelligence:** Expand current positive and counter-intelligence operations against Communist forces in South Vietnam and against North Vietnam. These include penetration of the Vietnamese Communist mechanism, dispatch of agents to North Vietnam and strengthening Vietnamese internal security services. Authorization should be given, subject to existing procedures, for the use in North Vietnam operations of civilian air crews of American and other nationality, as appropriate, in addition to Vietnamese. Consideration should be given for overflights of North Vietnam for photographic intelligence coverage, using American or Chinese Nationalist crews and equipment as necessary.

b **Communications Intelligence:** Expand the current program of interception and direction-finding covering Vietnamese Communist communications activities in South Vietnam, as well as North Vietnam targets. Obtain further USIB authority to conduct these operations on a fully joint basis, permitting the sharing of results of interception, direction finding, traffic analysis and cryptographic analysis by American agencies with the Vietnamese to the extent needed to launch rapid attacks on Vietnamese Communist communications and command installations.

This program should be supplemented by a program, duly coordinated, of training additional Vietnamese Army units in intercept and direction-finding by the U.S. Army Security Agency. Also, U.S. Army Security Agency teams could be sent to Vietnam for direct operations, coordinated in the same manner—Approved by the President at the NSC meeting of 29 April 1961.

c **Unconventional Warfare:** Expand present operations of the First Observation Battalion in guerrilla warfare areas of South Vietnam, under joint MAAG-CIA sponsorship and direction. This should be in full operational collaboration with the Vietnamese, using Vietnamese civilians recruited with CIA aid.

In Laos, infiltrate teams under light civilian cover to Southeast Laos to locate and attack Vietnamese Communist bases and lines of communications. These teams should be supported by assault units of 100 to 150 Vietnamese for use on targets beyond capability of teams. Training of teams could be a combined operation by CIA and U.S. Army Special Forces.

In North Vietnam using the foundation established by intelligence operations, form networks of resistance, covert bases and teams for sabotage and light harassment. A capability should be created by MAAG in the South Vietnamese Army to conduct Ranger raids and similar military actions in North Vietnam as might prove necessary or appropriate. Such actions should try to avoid any outbreak of extensive resistance or insurrection which could not be supported to the extent necessary to stave off repression.

Conduct overflights for dropping of leaflets to harass the Communists and to maintain morale of North Vietnamese population and increase gray broadcasts to North Vietnam for the same purposes.

d   **Internal South Vietnam:** Effect operations to penetrate political forces, government, armed services, and opposition elements to measure support of government, provide warning of any coup plans and identify individuals with potentiality of providing leadership in event of disappearance of President Diem.

Build up an increase in the population's participation in and loyalty to free government in Vietnam, through improved communication between the government and the people, and by strengthening independent or quasi-independent organizations of political, syndical or professional character. Support covertly the GVN in allied and neutral countries, with special emphasis on bringing out GVN accomplishments, to counteract tendencies toward a "political solution" while the Communists are attacking GVN. Effect, in support, a psychological program in Vietnam and elsewhere exploiting Communist brutality and aggression in North Vietnam.

e   **The expanded program** outlined above was estimated to require an additional 40 personnel for the CIA station and an increase in the CIA outlay for Vietnam of approximately $1.5 million for FY 62, partly compensated by the withdrawal of personnel from other areas. The U.S. Army Security Agency actions to supplement communications intelligence will require 78 personnel and approximately $1.2 million in equipment. The personnel and fund augmentations in this paragraph were approved by the President at the NSC meeting of 29 April 1961.

f   In order adequately to train the Vietnamese Army in tactical COMINT operations, the Army Security Agency estimates that an additional 15 personnel are required. This action has been approved by the U.S. Intelligence Board.

NSAM 52 May 1961 Program

National Security Action Memorandum (NSAM) 52, signed by
Kennedy's national security adviser, McGeorge Bundy, May
11, 1961, reaffirmed the continuing U.S. commitment to an independent, non-Communist South Vietnam and set forth a series of new measures designed to achieve the U.S. goal.

1 The U.S. objective and concept of operations stated in report
are approved: to prevent Communist domination of South Vietnam; to
create in that country a viable and increasingly democratic society, and
to initiate, on an accelerated basis, a series of mutually supporting actions of a military, political, economic, psychological and covert character designed to achieve this objective.

2 The approval given for specific military actions by the President at the National Security Council meeting on April 29, 1961, is
confirmed.

3 Additional actions listed at pages 4 and 5 of the Task Force
Report are authorized, with the objective of meeting the increased security threat resulting from the new situation along the frontier between
Laos and Vietnam. In particular, the President directs an assessment of
the military utility of a further increase in G.V.N. forces from 170,000
to 200,000, together with an assessment of the parallel political and fiscal implications.

4 The President directs full examination by the Defense Department, under the guidance of the Director of the continuing Task
Force on Vietnam, of the size and composition of forces which would
be desirable in the case of a possible commitment of U.S. forces to
Vietnam. The diplomatic setting within which this action might be
taken should also be examined.

5 The U.S. will seek to increase the confidence of President
Diem and his Government in the United States by a series of actions
and messages relating to the trip of Vice President [Lyndon B.] Johnson. The U.S. will attempt to strengthen President Diem's popular support within Vietnam by reappraisal and negotiations, under the direction of Ambassador [Frederick] Nolting. Ambassador Nolting is also
requested to recommend any necessary reorganization of the Country
Team for these purposes.

6 The U.S. will negotiate in appropriate ways to improve Vietnam's relationship with other countries, especially Cambodia, and its
standing in world opinion.

7 The Ambassador is authorized to begin negotiations looking toward a new bilateral arrangement with Vietnam, but no firm commitment will be made to such an arrangement without further review by the President.

8 The U.S. will undertake economic programs in Vietnam with a view to both short-term immediate impact and a contribution to the longer-range economic viability of the country, and the specific actions proposed on pages 12 and 13 of the Task Force Report are authorized.

9 The U.S. will strengthen its efforts in the psychological field as recommended on pages 14 and 15 of the Task Force Report.

10 The program for covert actions outlined on page 15 of the Task Force Report is approved.

11 These decisions will be supported by appropriate budgetary action, but the president reserves judgment on the levels of funding proposed on pages 15 and 16 of the Task Force Report and in the funding annex.

12 Finally, the President approves the continuation of a special Task Force on Vietnam, established in and directed by the Department of State under Sterling J. Cottrell as Director, and Chalmers B. Wood as Executive Officer.

LBJ May 1961 Report on Asian Trip

The following are excerpts from a memorandum, "Mission to Southeast Asia, India and Pakistan," written by Vice President Johnson upon his return to the United States, May 23, 1961. Johnson's rhetoric has often been ridiculed, but the ideas he expressed here did not differ fundamentally from those of the President and most of his other advisers.

. . . I took to Southeast Asia some basic convictions about the problems faced there. I have come away from the mission there—and to India and Pakistan—with many of those convictions sharpened and deepened by what I saw and learned. I have also reached certain other conclusions which I believe may be of value as guidance for those responsible in formulating policies.

These conclusions are as follows:

1   The battle against Communism must be joined in Southeast Asia
    with strength and determination to achieve success there—or the
    United States, inevitably, must surrender the Pacific and take up our
    defenses on our own shores. Asian Communism is compromised
    and contained by the maintenance of free nations on the subconti-
    nent. Without this inhibitory influence, the island outposts—Philip-
    pines, Japan, Taiwan—have no security and the vast Pacific be-
    comes a Red Sea.

2   The struggle is far from lost in Southeast Asia and it is by no means
    inevitable that it must be lost. In each country it is possible to build
    a sound structure capable of withstanding and turning the Commu-
    nist surge. The will to resist—while now the target of subversive at-
    tack—is there. The key to what is done by Asians in defense of
    Southeast Asia freedom is confidence in the United States.

3   There is no alternative to United States leadership in Southeast
    Asia. Leadership in individual countries—or the regional leadership
    and cooperation so appealing to Asians—rests on the knowledge
    and faith in United States power, will and understanding.

4   SEATO is not now and probably never will be the answer because
    of British and French unwillingness to support decisive action.
    Asian distrust of the British and French is outspoken. Success at
    Geneva [in the current negotiations on Laos] would prolong
    SEATO's role. Failure at Geneva would terminate SEATO's mean-
    ingfulness. In the latter event, we must be ready with a new ap-
    proach to collective security in the area.
        We should consider an alliance of all the free nations of the
    Pacific and Asia who are willing to join forces in defense of their
    freedom. Such an organization should:
    a   have a clear-cut command authority
    b   also devote attention to measures and programs of social jus-
        tice, housing, land reform, etc.

5   Asian leaders—at this time—do not want American troops involved
    in Southeast Asia other than on training missions. American combat
    troop involvement is not only not required, it is not desirable. Possi-
    bly Americans fail to appreciate fully the subtlety that recently-
    colonial peoples would not look with favor upon governments
    which invited or accepted the return this soon of Western troops. To
    the extent that fear of ground troop involvement dominates our po-
    litical responses to Asia in Congress or elsewhere, it seems most
    desirable to me to allay those paralyzing fears in confidence, on the
    strength of the individual statements made by leaders consulted on

this trip. This does not minimize or disregard the probability that open attack would bring calls for U.S. combat troops. But the present probability of open attack seems scant, and we might gain much needed flexibility in our policies if the spectre of combat troop commitment could be lessened domestically.

6 Any help—economic as well as military—we give less developed nations to secure and maintain their freedom must be a part of a mutual effort. These nations cannot be saved by United States help alone. To the extent the Southeast Asian nations are prepared to take the necessary measures to make our aid effective, we can be— and must be—unstinting in our assistance. It would be useful to enunciate more clearly than we have—for the guidance of these young and unsophisticated nations—what we expect or require of them.

7 In large measure, the greatest danger Southeast Asia offers to nations like the United States is not the momentary threat of Communism itself, rather that danger stems from hunger, ignorance, poverty and disease. We must—whatever strategies we evolve— keep these enemies the point of our attack, and make imaginative use of our scientific and technological capability in such enterprises.

8 Vietnam and Thailand are the immediate—and most important— trouble spots, critical to the U.S. These areas require the attention of our very best talents—under the very closest Washington direction—on matters economic, military and political.
    The basic decision in Southeast Asia is here. We must decide whether to help these countries to the best of our ability or throw in the towel in the area and pull back our defenses to San Francisco and a "Fortress America" concept. More important, we would say to the world in this case that we don't live up to treaties and don't stand by our friends. This is not my concept. I recommend that we move forward promptly with a major effort to help these countries defend themselves. I consider the key here is to get our best MAAG people to control, plan, direct and exact results from our military aid program. In Vietnam and Thailand, we must move forward together.
    a In Vietnam, Diem is a complex figure beset by many problems. He has admirable qualities, but he is remote from the people, is surrounded by persons less admirable and capable than he. The country can be saved—if we move quickly and wisely. We must decide whether to support Diem—or let Vietnam fall. We must have coordination of purpose in our country team, diplomatic

and military. The Saigon Embassy, USIS, MAAG and related operations leave much to be desired. They should be brought up to maximum efficiency. The most important thing is imaginative, creative, American management of our military aid program. The Vietnamese and our MAAG estimate that $50 million of U.S. military and economic assistance will be needed if we decide to support Vietnam. This is the best information available to us at the present time and if it is confirmed by the best Washington military judgment it should be supported. Since you proposed and Diem agreed to a joint economic mission, it should be appointed and proceed forthwith.

b   In Thailand, the Thais and our own MAAG estimate probably as much is needed as in Vietnam—about $50 million of military and economic assistance. Again, should our best military judgment concur, I believe we should support such a program. [Thai leader] Sarit is more strongly and staunchly pro-Western than many of his people. He is and must be deeply concerned at the consequence to his country of a communist-controlled Laos. If Sarit is to stand firm against neutralism, he must have—soon— concrete evidence to show his people of United States military and economic support. He believes that his armed forces should be increased to 150,000. His Defense Minister is coming to Washington to discuss aid matters.

The fundamental decision required of the United States—and time is of the greatest importance—is whether we are to attempt to meet the challenge of Communist expansion now in Southeast Asia by a major effort in support of the forces of freedom in the area or throw in the towel. This decision must be made in a full realization of the very heavy and continuing costs involved in terms of money, of effort and of United States prestige. It must be made with the knowledge that at some point we may be faced with the further decision of whether we commit major United States forces to the area or cut our losses and withdraw should our other efforts fail. We must remain master in this decision. What we do in Southeast Asia should be part of a rational program to meet the threat we face in the region as a whole. It should include a clear-cut pattern of specific contributions to be expected by each partner according to his ability and resources. I recommend we proceed with a clear-cut and strong program of action.

I believe that the mission—as you conceived it—was a success. I am grateful to the many who labored to make it so.

Maxwell Taylor Proposes U.S. Combat Troops for Vietnam

This cablegram sent to Kennedy by his personal chief of staff, General Maxwell Taylor, on November 1, 1961, after a visit to South Vietnam, proposed the drastic measure of dispatching U.S. combat troops to Vietnam under the guise of flood relief forces.

This message is for the purpose of presenting my reasons for recommending the introduction of a U.S. military force into SVN. I have reached the conclusion that this is an essential action if we are to reverse the present downward trend of events in spite of a full recognition of the following disadvantages:

   a   The strategic reserve of U.S. forces is presently so weak that we can ill afford any detachment of forces to a peripheral area of the Communist bloc where they will be pinned down for an uncertain duration.

   b   Although U.S. prestige is already engaged in SVN, it will become more so by the sending of troops.

   c   If the first contingent is not enough to accomplish the necessary results, it will be difficult to resist the pressure to reinforce. If the ultimate result sought is the closing of the frontiers and the clean-up of the insurgents within SVN, there is no limit to our possible commitment (unless we attack the source in Hanoi).

   d   The introduction of U.S. forces may increase tensions and risk escalation into a major war in Asia.

   On the other side of the argument, there can be no action so convincing of U.S. seriousness of purpose and hence so reassuring to the people and Government of SVN and to our other friends and allies in SEA as the introduction of U.S. forces into SVN. The views of indigenous and U.S. officials consulted on our trip were unanimous on this point. I have just seen Saigon 575 to State and suggest that it be read in connection with this message.

   The size of the U.S. force introduced need not be great to provide the military presence necessary to produce the desired effect on national morale in SVN and on international opinion. A bare token, however, will not suffice; it must have a significant value. The kinds of tasks which it might undertake which would have a significant value are suggested in Baguio [cablegram #] 0005. They are:

(a)   Provide a U.S. military presence capable of raising national morale and of showing to SEA the seriousness of the U.S. intent to resist a Communist takeover.

(b)   Conduct logistical operations in support of military and flood relief operations.

(c)   Conduct such combat operations as are necessary for self-defense and for the security of the area in which they are stationed.

(d)   Provide an emergency reserve to back up the Armed Forces of the GVN in the case of a heightened military crisis.

(e)   Act as an advance party of such additional forces as may be introduced if CINCPAC or SEATO contingency plans are invoked.

It is noteworthy that this force is not proposed to clear the jungles and forests of VC guerrillas. That should be the primary task of the Armed Forces of Vietnam for which they should be specifically organized, trained and stiffened with ample U.S. advisors down to combat battalion levels. However, the U.S. troops may be called upon to engage in combat to protect themselves, their working parties, and the area in which they live. As a general reserve, they might be thrown into action (with U.S. agreement) against large, formed guerrilla bands which have abandoned the forests for attacks on major targets. But in general, our forces should not engage in small-scale guerrilla operations in the jungle.

As an area for the operations of U.S. troops, SVN is not an excessively difficult or unpleasant place to operate. While the border areas are rugged and heavily forested, the terrain is comparable to parts of Korea where U.S. troops learned to live and work without too much effort. However, these border areas, for reasons stated above, are not the places to engage our forces. In the High Plateau and in the coastal plain where U.S. troops would probably be stationed, these jungle-forest conditions do not exist to any great extent. The most unpleasant feature in the coastal areas would be the heat and, in the Delta, the mud left behind by the flood. The High Plateau offers no particular obstacle to the stationing of U.S. troops.

The extent to which the Task Force would engage in flood relief activities in the Delta will depend upon further study of the problem there. As reported in Saigon [cablegram #] 537, I see considerable advantages in playing up this aspect of the TF mission. I am presently inclined to favor a dual mission, initially help to the flood area and subsequently use in any other area of SVN where its resources can be used effectively to give tangible support in the struggle against the VC. However, the possibility of emphasizing the humanitarian mission will wane if we wait long in moving in our forces or in linking our stated purpose with the emergency conditions created by the flood.

The risks of backing into a major Asian war by way of SVN are present but are not impressive. NVN is extremely vulnerable to conventional bombing, a weakness which should be exploited diplomatically in convincing Hanoi to lay off SVN. Both the D.R.V. and the Chicoms would face severe logistical difficulties in trying to maintain strong forces in the field in SEA, difficulties which we share but by no means to the same degree. There is no case for fearing a mass onslaught of Communist manpower into SVN and its neighboring states, particularly if our airpower is allowed a free hand against logistical targets. Finally, the starvation conditions in China should discourage Communist leaders there from being militarily venturesome for some time to come.

By the foregoing line of reasoning, I have reached the conclusion that the introduction of [word illegible] military Task Force without delay offers definitely more advantage than it creates risks and difficulties. In fact, I do not believe that our program to save SVN will succeed without it. If the concept is approved, the exact size and composition of the force should be determined by Sec Def in consultation with the JCS, the Chief MAAG and CINCPAC. My own feeling is that the initial size should not exceed about 8000, of which a preponderant number would be in logistical-type units. After acquiring experience in operating in SVN, this initial force will require reorganization and adjustment to the local scene.

As CINCPAC will point out, any forces committed to SVN will need to be replaced by additional forces to this area from the strategic reserve in the U.S. Also, any troops to SVN are in addition to those which may be required to execute SEATO Plan 5 in Laos. Both facts should be taken into account in current considerations of the FY 1963 budget which bear upon the permanent increase which should be made in the U.S. military establishment to maintain our strategic position for the long pull.

McNamara Response to Taylor Proposals

This memorandum for the President from Secretary of Defense Robert S. McNamara, November 8, 1961, raised warning signals about sending U.S. troops to Vietnam, supporting such a step only if the United States made an unqualified commitment to maintaining an independent, non-Communist South Vietnam.

The basic issue framed by the Taylor Report is whether the U.S. shall:

    a Commit itself to the clear objective of preventing the fall of South Vietnam to Communism, and

    b Support this commitment by necessary immediate military actions and preparations for possible later actions.

    The Joint Chiefs, Mr. [Roswell] Gilpatric [deputy secretary of defense] and I have reached the following conclusions:

1 The fall of South Vietnam to Communism would lead to the fairly rapid extension of Communist control, or complete accommodation to Communism, in the rest of mainland Southeast Asia and in Indonesia. The strategic implications worldwide, particularly in the Orient, would be extremely serious.

2 The chances are against, probably sharply against, preventing that fall by any measures short of the introduction of U.S. forces on a substantial scale. We accept General Taylor's judgment that the various measures proposed by him short of this are useful but will not in themselves do the job of restoring confidence and setting Diem on the way to winning his fight.

3 The introduction of a U.S. force of the magnitude of an initial 8,000 men in a flood relief context will be of great help to Diem. However, it will not convince the other side (whether the shots are called from Moscow, Peiping, or Hanoi) that we mean business. Moreover, it probably will not tip the scales decisively. We would be almost certain to get increasingly mired down in an inconclusive struggle.

4   The other side can be convinced we mean business only if we accompany the initial force introduction by a clear commitment to the full objective stated above, accompanied by a warning through some channel to Hanoi that continued support of the Viet Cong will lead to punitive retaliation against North Vietnam.

5   If we act in this way, the ultimate possible extent of our military commitment must be faced. The struggle may be prolonged and Hanoi and Peiping may intervene overtly. In view of the logistic difficulties faced by the other side, I believe we can assume that the maximum U.S. forces required on the ground in Southeast Asia will not exceed 6 divisions, or about 205,000 men (CINCPAC Plan 32–59, Phase IV). Our military posture is, or with the addition of more National Guard or regular Army divisions, can be made, adequate to furnish these forces without serious interference with our present Berlin plans.

6   To accept the stated objective is of course a most serious decision. Military force is not the only element of what must be a most carefully coordinated set of actions. Success will depend on factors many of which are not within our control—notably the conduct of Diem himself and other leaders in the area. Laos will remain a major problem. The domestic political implications of accepting the objective are also grave, although it is our feeling that the country will respond better to a firm initial position than to courses of action that lead us in only gradually, and that in the meantime are sure to involve casualties. The overall effect on Moscow and Peiping will need careful weighing and may well be mixed; however, permitting South Vietnam to fall can only strengthen and encourage them greatly.

7   In sum:

   a   We do not believe major units of U.S. forces should be introduced in South Vietnam unless we are willing to make an affirmative decision on the issue stated at the start of this memorandum.

   b   We are inclined to recommend that we do commit the U.S. to the clear objective of preventing the fall of South Vietnam to Communism and that we support this commitment by the necessary military actions.

   c   If such a commitment is agreed upon, we support the recommendations of General Taylor as the first steps toward its fulfillment.

State Department Pessimism on Vietnam

Kennedy rejected Taylor's proposals, opting for more cautious measures, and for a time these seemed to produce results. But this report of December 3, 1962, to Secretary Rusk from Roger Hilsman, director of the State Department's Bureau of Intelligence and Research, raised major doubts about progress in Vietnam and highlighted continuing serious problems.

. . . President Ngo Dinh Diem and other leading Vietnamese as well as many U.S. officials in South Vietnam apparently believe that the tide is now turning in the struggle against Vietnamese Communist (Viet Cong) insurgency and subversion. This degree of optimism is premature. At best, it appears that the rate of deterioration has decelerated with improvement, principally in the security sector, reflecting substantially increased U.S. assistance and GVN implementation of a broad counterinsurgency program.

The GVN has given priority to implementing a basic strategic concept featuring the strategic hamlet and systematic pacification programs. It has paid more attention to political, economic, and social counterinsurgency measures and their coordination with purely military measures. Vietnamese military and security forces—now enlarged and of higher quality—are significantly more offensive-minded and their counterguerilla tactical capabilities are greatly improved. Effective GVN control of the countryside has been extended slightly. In some areas where security has improved peasant attitudes toward the government appear also to have improved.

As a result, the Viet Cong has had to modify its tactics and perhaps set back its timetable. But the "national liberation war" has not abated nor has the Viet Cong been weakened. On the contrary, the Viet Cong has expanded the size and enhanced the capability and organization of its guerilla force—now estimated at about 23,000 in elite fighting personnel, plus some 100,000 irregulars and sympathizers. It still controls about 20 percent of the villages and about 9 percent of the rural population, and has varying degrees of influence among additional 47 percent of the villages. Viet Cong control and communication lines to the peasant have not been seriously weakened and the guerillas have thus been able to maintain good intelligence and a high degree of initiative, mobility, and striking power. Viet Cong influence has almost certainly improved in urban areas not only through subversion and terrorism but also because of its propaganda appeal to the increasingly frustrated non-Communist anti-Diem elements.

The internal political situation is considerably more difficult to assess. Diem has strengthened his control of the bureaucracy and the military establishment. He has delegated a little more authority than in the past, and has become increasingly aware of the importance of the peasantry to the counterinsurgency effort. Nevertheless, although there are fewer reports of discontent with Diem's leadership within official circles and the civilian elite, there are still many indications of continuing serious concern, particularly with Diem's direction of the counterinsurgency effort. There are also reports that important military and civilian officials continue to participate in coup plots. Oppositionists, critics, and dissenters outside the government appear to be increasingly susceptible to neutralist, pro-Communist, and possibly anti-U.S. sentiments. They are apparently placing increased reliance on clandestine activities.

The Viet Cong is obviously prepared for a long struggle and can be expected to maintain the present pace and diversity of its insurgent-subversive effort. During the next month or so, it may step up its military effort in reaction to the growing GVN-U.S. response. Hanoi can also be expected to increase its efforts to legitimatize its "National Front for the Liberation of South Vietnam" (NFLSV) and to prepare further groundwork for a "liberation government" in South Vietnam. On the present evidence, the Communists are not actively moving toward neutralization of South Vietnam in the Laos pattern, although they could seek to do so later. Elimination, even significant reduction, of the Communist insurgency will almost certainly require several years. In either case, a considerably greater effort by the GVN, as well as continuing U.S. assistance, is crucial. If there is continuing improvement in security conditions, Diem should be able to alleviate concern and boost morale within the bureaucracy and the military establishment. But the GVN will not be able to consolidate its military successes into permanent political gains and to evoke the positive support of the peasantry unless it gives more emphasis to non-military aspects of the counterinsurgency program, integrates the strategic hamlet program with an expanded systematic pacification program, and appreciably modifies military tactics (particularly those relating to large-unit actions and tactical use of air-power and artillery). Failure to do so might increase militant opposition among the peasants and their positive identification with the Viet Cong.

A coup could occur at any time, but would be more likely if the fight against the Communists goes badly, if the Viet Cong launches a series of successful and dramatic operations, or if Vietnamese army casualties increase appreciably over a protracted period. The coup most likely to succeed would be one with non-Communist leadership and support, involving middle and top echelon military and civilian officials. For a time at least, the serious disruption of government leadership resulting from a coup would probably halt and possibly reverse the momentum of the government's counterinsurgency effort. The role of the U.S. can be extremely important in restoring this momentum and in averting widespread fighting and a serious internal power struggle. . . .

Intelligence Assessment of 1963 Buddhist Protest

The following excerpts from Special National Intelligence Estimate 53–2–63, "The Situation in South Vietnam," July 10, 1963, note the threat posed to the Diem government by the Buddhist protest.

CONCLUSIONS

A The Buddhist crisis in South Vietnam has highlighted and intensified a widespread and long-standing dissatisfaction with the Diem regime and its style of government. If—as is likely—Diem fails to carry out truly and promptly the commitments he has made to the Buddhists, disorders will probably flare again and the chances of a coup or assassination attempts against him will become better than ever. . . .

B The Diem regime's underlying uneasiness about the extent of the U.S. involvement in South Vietnam has been sharpened by the Buddhist affair and the firm line taken by the U.S. This attitude will almost certainly persist and further pressure to reduce the U.S. presence in the country is likely. . . .

C Thus far, the Buddhist issue has not been effectively exploited by the Communists, nor does it appear to have had any appreciable effect on the counterinsurgency effort. We do not think Diem is likely to be overthrown by a Communist coup. Nor do we think the Communists would necessarily profit if he were overthrown by some combination of his non-Communist opponents. A non-Communist successor regime might be initially less effective against the Viet Cong, but, given continued support from the U.S. could provide reasonably effective leadership for the government and the war effort. . . .

Washington Moves toward Coup

This controversial cablegram from the State Department to Ambassador Henry Cabot Lodge in Saigon, August 24, 1963, was composed by lower-level officials while Kennedy and other top officials were away from Washington and was cleared with the President without extensive consultation and deliberation. It not only called for the removal of Nhu but also raised for the first time the possibility of getting rid of Diem.

It is now clear that whether military proposed martial law or whether Nhu tricked them into it, Nhu took advantage of its imposition to smash pagodas with police and Tung's Special Forces loyal to him, thus placing onus on military in eyes of world and Vietnamese people. Also clear that Nhu has maneuvered himself into commanding position.

U.S. Government cannot tolerate situation in which power lies in Nhu's hands. Diem must be given chance to rid himself of Nhu and his coterie and replace them with best military and political personalities available.

If, in spite of all of your efforts, Diem remains obdurate and refuses, then we must face the possibility that Diem himself cannot be preserved.

We now believe immediate action must be taken to prevent Nhu from consolidating his position further. Therefore, unless you in consultation with Harkins perceive overriding objections you are authorized to proceed along following lines:

(1) First we must press on appropriate levels of GVN following line:
  (a) USG cannot accept actions against Buddhists taken by Nhu and his collaborators under cover martial law.
  (b) Prompt dramatic actions redress situation must be taken, including repeal of decree 10, release of arrested monks, nuns, etc.

(2) We must at same time also tell key military leaders that U.S. would find it impossible to continue support GVN militarily and economically unless above steps are taken immediately which we recognize requires removal of Nhus from the scene. We wish give Diem reasonable opportunity to remove Nhus, but if he remains obdurate, then we are prepared to accept the obvious implications that we can no longer support Diem. You may also tell appropriate military commanders we will give them direct support in any interim period of breakdown central government mechanism.

(3) We recognize the necessity of removing taint on military for pagoda raids and placing blame squarely on Nhu. You are authorized to have such statements made in Saigon as you consider desirable to achieve this objective. We are prepared to take same line here and to have Voice of America make statement along lines contained in next numbered telegram whenever you give the word, preferably as soon as possible.

Concurrently, with above, Ambassador and country team should urgently examine all possible alternative leadership and make detailed plans as to how we might bring about Diem's replacement if this should become necessary.

Assume you will consult with General [Paul] Harkins [chief, U.S. MAAG] re any precautions necessary protect American personnel during crisis period.

You will understand that we cannot from Washington give you detailed instructions as to how this operation should proceed, but you will also know we will back you to the hilt on actions you take to achieve our objectives.

Needless to say we have held knowledge of this telegram to minimum essential people and assume you will take similar precautions to prevent premature leaks.

Ambassador Lodge Encourages Coup Planning

Lodge's response, dated August 25, 1963, moves a large step closer to the authorization of a coup against Diem.

Believe that chances of Diem's meeting our demands are virtually nil. At same time, by making them we give Nhu chance to forestall or block action by military. Risk, we believe, is not worth taking, with Nhu in control combat forces Saigon.

Therefore, propose we go straight to Generals with our demands, without informing Diem. Would tell them we prepared have Diem without Nhus but it is in effect up to them whether to keep him. Would also insist generals take steps to release Buddhist leaders and carry out June 16 agreement.

Request immediate modification instructions. However, do not propose move until we are satisfied with E and E plans. Harkins concurs. I present credentials President Diem tomorrow 11 A.M.

CIA Station Chief Assesses Coup Prospects

In this cable of August 28, 1963, John Richardson assessed the atmosphere in Saigon and the possibilities of a coup.

Situation here has reached point of no return. Saigon is armed camp. Current indications are that Ngo family have dug in for last ditch battle. It is our considered estimate that General officers cannot retreat now. Conein's meeting with Gen. Khiem (Saigon 0346) reveals that overwhelming majority of general officers, excepting Dinh and Cao, are united, having conducted prior planning, realize that they must proceed quickly and understand that they have no alternative but to go forward. Unless the generals are neutralized before being able to launch their operation, we believe they will act and that they have good chance to win. If General Dinh primarily and Tung secondly cannot be neutralized at outset, there may be widespread fighting in Saigon and serious loss of life.

We recognize the crucial stakes involved and have no doubt that the generals do also. Situation has changed drastically since 21 August. If the Ngo family wins now, they and Vietnam will stagger on to final defeat at the hands of their own people and the VC. Should a generals' revolt occur and be put down, GVN will sharply reduce American presence in SVN. Even if they did not do so, it seems clear that American public opinion and Congress, as well as world opinion, would force withdrawal or reduction of American support for VN under the Ngo administration.

Bloodshed can be avoided if the Ngo family would step down before the coming armed action. . . . It is obviously preferable that the generals conduct this effort without apparent American assistance. Otherwise, for a long time in the future, they will be vulnerable to charges of being American puppets, which they are not in any sense. Nevertheless, we all understand that the effort must succeed and that whatever needs to be done on our part must be done. If this attempt by the generals does not take place or if it fails, we believe it no exaggeration to say that VN runs serious risk of being lost over the course of time.

Lodge Scenario for Removal of Diem

This cablegram from Lodge to Rusk, August 29, 1963, proposes the steps to be taken to promote and ensure the success of a coup.

We are launched on a course from which there is no respectable turning back: the overthrow of the Diem government. There is no turning back in part because U.S. prestige is already publicly committed to this end in large measure and will become more so as the facts leak out. In a more fundamental sense, there is no turning back because there is no possibility, in my view, that the war can be won under a Diem administration, still less that Diem or any member of the family can govern the country in a way to gain the support of the people who count, i.e., the educated class in and out of government service, civil and military—not to mention the American people. In the last few months (and especially days) they have in fact positively alienated these people to an incalculable degree. So that I am personally in full agreement with the policy which I was instructed to carry out by last Sunday's telegram.

[Point 1 unavailable.]

2 The chance of bringing off a Generals' coup depends on them to some extent; but it depends at least as much on us.

3 We should proceed to make all-out effort to get Generals to move promptly. To do so we should have authority to do following:

    (a) That Gen. Harkins repeat to Generals personally message previously transmitted by CAS officers. This should establish their authenticity. Gen. Harkins should have order on this.

    (b) If nevertheless Generals insist on public statement that all U.S. aid to VN through Diem regime has been stopped, we would agree, on express understanding that Generals will have started at same time. (We would seek persuade Generals that it would be better to hold this card for use in event of stalemate. We hope it will not be necessary to do this at all.)

    (c) VNese Generals doubt that we have the will power, courage, and determination to see this thing through. They are haunted by the idea that we will run out on them even though we have told them pursuant to instructions, that the game had started.

[Point 4 unavailable.]

5 We must press on for many reasons. Some of these are:

    (a) Explosiveness of the present situation which may well lead to riots and violence if issue of discontent with regime is not met. Out of this could come a pro-Communist or at best a neutralist set of politicians.

    (b) The fact that war cannot be won with the present regime.

    (c) Our own reputation for steadfastness and our unwillingness to stultify ourselves.

    (d) If proposed action is suspended, I believe a body blow will be dealt to respect for us by VNese Generals. Also, all those who expect U.S. to straighten out this situation will feel let down. Our help to the regime in past years inescapably gives a responsibility which we cannot avoid.

6 I realize that this course involves a very substantial risk of losing VN. It also involves some additional risk to American lives. I would never propose it if I felt there was a reasonable chance of holding VN with Diem.

[Point 7 unavailable.]

8 Gen. Harkins thinks that I should ask Diem to get rid of the Nhus before starting the Generals' action. But I believe that such a step has no chance of getting the desired results and would have the very

serious effect of being regarded by the Generals as a sign of American indecision and delay. I believe this is a risk which we should not run. The Generals distrust us too much already. Another point is that Diem would certainly ask for time to consider such a far-reaching request. This would give the ball to Nhu.

9   With the exception of par. 8 above Gen. Harkins concurs in this telegram.

Washington Response to Lodge Proposals

This cablegram from Rusk to Lodge, August 29, 1963, followed a meeting of the National Security Council and laid out the guidelines to be followed in executing the coup.

1   Highest level meeting noon today reviewed your 375 and reaffirmed basic course. Specific decisions follow:

2   In response to your recommendation, General Harkins is hereby authorized to repeat to such Generals as you indicate the messages previously transmitted by CAS officers. He should stress that the USG supports the movement to eliminate the Nhus from the government, but that before arriving at specific understandings with the generals, General Harkins must know who are involved, resources available to them and overall plan for coup. The USG will support a coup which has good chance of succeeding but plans no direct involvement of U.S. armed forces. Harkins should state that he is prepared to establish liaison with the coup planners and to review plans, but will not engage directly in joint coup planning.

3   Question of last approach to Diem remains undecided and separate personal message from Secretary to you develops our concern and asks your comment.

4   On movement of U.S. forces, we do not expect to make any announcement or leak at present and believe that any later decision to publicize such movements should be closely connected to developing events on your side. We cannot of course prevent unauthorized disclosures or speculation, but we will in any event knock down any reports of evacuation.

5   You are hereby authorized to announce suspension of aid through Diem government at a time and under conditions of your choice. In deciding upon the use of this authority, you should consider

importance of timing and managing announcement so as to minimize appearance of collusion with Generals and also to minimize danger of unpredictable and disruptive reaction by existing government. We also assume that you will not in fact use this authority unless you think it essential, and we see it as possible that Harkins' approach and increasing process of cooperation may provide assurance Generals desire. Our own view is that it will be best to hold this authority for use in close conjunction with coup, and not for present encouragement of Generals, but decision is yours.

Unravelling of August Coup Plan

This cable from General Harkins to General Taylor, August 31, 1963, explains how the August coup plot came apart amidst confusion and mutual suspicion among plotters and government in Saigon.

(saw Khiem: he stated [General Duong Van] Big Minh had stopped planning at this time, and was working on other methods; others had called off planning also, himself and [General Nguyen] Khanh, following Minh. He knew Thao was making plans—but that few of military trusted him because of his VC background—and that he might still be working for the VC. The Generals were not ready as they did not have enough forces under their control compared to those under President and now in Saigon. He indicated they, the Generals, did not want to start anything they could not successfully finish.

. . . At a meeting yesterday, Mr. Nhu said he now went along with everything the U.S. wants to do, and even had the backing of Pres. Kennedy. I said this was news to me. Khiem said he wondered if Nhu was again trying to flush out the generals. He intimated the generals do not have too much trust in Nhu and that he's such a friend of Mr. Richardson the generals wonder if Mr. Nhu and Mme. Nhu were on the CIA payroll. . . .

. . . I asked if someone couldn't confront the Nhus with the fact that their absence from the scene was the key to the overall solution. He replied that for anyone to do that would be self-immolation—he also went on to say he doubted if the Nhus and Diem could be split.

. . . So we see we have an "organisation de confusion" with everyone suspicious of everyone else and none desiring to take any positive action as of right now. You can't hurry the East. . . .

Generals Renew Coup Plotting

This October 5, 1963, cable from Lodge to the State Department raises once again the possibility of a coup.

1 [CIA operative] Lt. Col. [Lucien] Conein met with Gen Duong Van Minh at Gen. Minh's Headquarters on Le Van Duyet for one hour and ten minutes morning of 5 Oct 63. This meeting was at the initiative of Gen Minh and had been specifically cleared in advance by Ambassador Lodge. No other persons were present. The conversation was conducted in French.

2 Gen. Minh stated that he must know American Government's position with respect to a change in the Government of Vietnam within the very near future. Gen. Minh added the Generals were aware the situation is deteriorating rapidly and that action to change the Government must be taken or the war will be lost to the Viet Cong because the Government no longer has the support of the people. Gen. Minh identified among the other Generals participating with him in this plan:

    Maj. Gen. Tran Van Don
    Brig. Gen. Tran Thien Khiem
    Maj. Gen. Tran Van Kim

3 Gen. Minh made it clear that he did not expect any specific American support for an effort on the part of himself and his colleagues to change the Government but he states he does need American assurances that the USG will not rpt not attempt to thwart this plan.

4 Gen. Minh also stated that he himself has no political ambitions nor do any of the other General Officers except perhaps, he said laughingly, Gen. Ton That Dinh. Minh insisted that his only purpose is to win the war. He added emphatically that to do this continuation of American Military and Economic Aid at the present level (he said one and one half million dollars per day) is necessary.

5   Gen. Minh outlined three possible plans for the accomplishment of
    the change of Government:
    a   Assassination of Ngo Dinh Nhu and Ngo Dinh Can keeping
        President Diem in Office. Gen Minh said this was the easiest
        plan to accomplish.
    b   The encirclement of Saigon by various military units particu-
        larly the unit at Ben Cat.
    c   Direct confrontation between military units involved in the
        coup and loyalist military units in Saigon. In effect, dividing
        the city of Saigon into sectors and cleaning it out pocket by
        pocket, Gen. Minh claims under the circumstances Diem and
        Nhu could count on the loyalty of 5,500 troops within the city
        of Saigon.
6   Conein replied to Gen. Minh that he could not answer specific
    questions as to USG non-interference nor could he give any advice
    with respect to tactical planning. He added that he could not ad-
    vise concerning the best of the three plans.
7   Gen. Minh went on to explain that the most dangerous men in
    South Viet-Nam are Ngo Dinh Nhu, Ngo Dinh Can and Ngo
    Trong Hieu. Minh stated that Hieu was formerly a Communist and
    still has Communist sympathies. When Col. Conein remarked that
    he had considered Col. Tung as one of the more dangerous indi-
    viduals, Gen. Minh stated "if I get rid of Nhu, Can and Hieu, Col.
    Tung will be on his knees before me."
8   Gen. Minh also stated that he was worried as to the role of Gen.
    Tran Thien Khiem since Khiem may have played a double role in
    August. Gen. Minh asked that copies of the documents previously
    passed to Gen. Khiem (plan of Camp Long Thanh and munitions
    inventory at that camp) be passed to Gen. Minh personally for
    comparison with papers passed by Khiem to Minh purportedly
    from CAS.
9   Minh further stated that one of the reasons they are having to act
    quickly was the fact that many regimental, battalion and company
    commanders are working on coup plans of their own which could
    be abortive and a "catastrophe."
10 Minh appeared to understand Conein's position of being unable to
    comment at the present moment but asked that Conein again meet
    with Gen. Minh to discuss the specific plan of operations which
    Gen. Minh hopes to put into action. No specific date was given for
    this next meeting. Conein was again noncommittal in his reply.
    Gen. Minh once again indicated his understanding and stated that
    he would arrange to contact Conein in the near future and hoped
    that Conein would be able to meet with him and give the assur-
    ance outlined above.

Washington Response to Minh Overture

The White House's vague response to Lodge, October 6, 1963, reflected its continuing interest in getting rid of Diem, its uncertainty how to proceed, and its fear of failure.

1   Believe CAP 63560 gives general guidance requested REFTEL. We have following additional general thoughts which have been discussed with President. While we do not wish to stimulate coup, we also do not wish to leave impression that U.S. would thwart a change of government or deny economic and military assistance to a new regime if it appeared capable of increasing effectiveness of military effort, ensuring popular support to win war and improving working relations with U.S. We would like to be informed on what is being contemplated but we should avoid being drawn into reviewing or advising on operational plans or any other act which might tend to identify U.S. too closely with change in government. We would, however, welcome information which would help us assess character of any alternate leadership.

2   With reference to specific problem of General Minh you should seriously consider having contact take position that in present state his knowledge he is unable present Minh's case to responsible policy officials with any degree of seriousness. In order to get responsible officials even to consider Minh's problem, contact would have to have detailed information clearly indicating that Minh's plans offer a high prospect of success. At present contact sees no such prospect in the information so far provided.

3   You should also consider with Acting Station Chief whether it would be desirable in order to preserve security and deniability in this as well as similar approaches to others whether appropriate arrangements could be made for follow-up contacts by individuals brought in especially from outside Vietnam. As we indicated in CAP 63560 we are most concerned about security problem and we are confining knowledge these sensitive matters in Washington to extremely limited group, high officials in White House, State, Defense and CIA with whom this message cleared.

Lodge Urges Support for Coup

Lodge's cable to Bundy, October 25, 1963, explains why the United States should not attempt to stop a coup and reveals the ambassador's own deep personal commitment to a change in government.

1 I appreciate the concern expressed by you in ref. a relative to the Gen. Don/Conein relationship, and also the present lack of firm intelligence on the details of the general's plot. I hope that ref. b will assist in clearing up some of the doubts relative to general's plans, and I am hopeful that the detailed plans promised for two days before the coup attempt will clear up any remaining doubts.

2 CAS has been punctilious in carrying out my instructions. I have personally approved each meeting between Gen. Don and Conein who has carried out my orders in each instance explicitly. While I share your concern about the continued involvement of Conein in this matter, a suitable substitute for Conein as the principal contact is not presently available. Conein, as you know, is a friend of some eighteen years standing with Gen. Don, and General Don has expressed extreme reluctance to deal with anyone else. I do not believe the involvement of another American in close contact with the generals would be productive. We are, however, considering the feasibility of a plan for the introduction of an additional officer as a cut-out between Conein and a designee of Gen. Don for communications purposes only. This officer is completely unwitting of any details of past or present coup activities and will remain so.

3 With reference to Gen. Harkins' comment to Gen. Don which Don reports to have referred to a presidential directive and the proposal for a meeting with me, this may have served the useful purposes of allaying the General's fears as to our interest. If this were a provocation, the GVN could have assumed and manufactured any variations of the same theme. As a precautionary measure, however, I of course refused to see Gen. Don. As to the lack of information as to General Don's real backing, and the lack of evidence that any real capabilities for action have been developed, ref. b provides only part of the answer. I feel sure that the reluctance of the generals to provide the U.S. with full details of their plans at this time, is a reflection of their own sense security and a lack of confidence that in the large American community present in Saigon their plans will not be prematurely revealed.

4 The best evidence available to the Embassy, which I grant you is not as complete as we would like it, is that Gen. Don and the other generals involved with him are seriously attempting to effect a change in the government. I do not believe that this is a provocation by Ngo Dinh Nhu, although we shall continue to assess the planning as well as possible. In the event that the coup aborts, or in the event that Nhu has masterminded a provocation, I believe that our involvement to date through Conein is still within the realm of plausible denial. CAS is perfectly prepared to have me disavow Conein at any time it may serve the national interest.

5 I welcome your reaffirming instructions contained in CAS Washington 74228. It is vital that we neither thwart a coup nor that we are even in a position where we do not know what is going on.

6 We should not thwart a coup for two reasons. First, it seems at least an even bet that the next government would not bungle and stumble as much as the present one has. Secondly, it is extremely unwise in the long range for us to pour cold water on attempts at a coup, particularly when they are just in their beginning stages. We should remember that this is the only way in which the people in Vietnam can possibly get a change of government. Whenever we thwart attempts at a coup, as we have done in the past, we are incurring very long lasting resentments, we are assuming an undue responsibility for keeping incumbents in office, and in general are setting ourselves in judgment over the affairs of Vietnam. Merely to keep in touch with this situation and a policy merely limited to "not thwarting" are courses both of which entail some risks but these are lesser risks than either thwarting all coups while they are stillborn or our not being informed of what is happening. All the above is totally distinct from not wanting U.S. military advisors to be distracted by matters which are not in their domain, with which I heartily agree. But obviously this does not conflict with a policy of not thwarting. In judging proposed coups, we must consider the effect on the war effort. It must also be said that the war effort has been interfered with already by the incompetence of the present government and the uproar which this has caused.

7 Gen. Don's intention to have no religious discrimination in a future government is commendable and I applaud his desire not to be a "vassal" of the U.S. But I do not think his promise of a democratic election is realistic. This country simply is not ready for that procedure. I would add two other requirements. First, that there be no wholesale purges of personnel in the government. Individuals who were particularly reprehensible could be dealt with later by the regular legal process. Then I would be impractical, but I am thinking of a government which might include Tri Quang and which certainly should include men of the stature of Mr. Buu, the labor leader.

8 Copy to Gen. Harkins.

Washington's Concern about Coup

Bundy's cable to Lodge, October 25, 1963, again expresses
the administration's fear of failure.

Your 1964 most helpful.

　　We will continue to be grateful for all additional information giving increased clarity to prospects of action by Don or others, and we
look forward to discussing with you the whole question of control and
cut-out on your return, always assuming that one of the D-Days does
not turn out to be real. We are particularly concerned about hazard that
an unsuccessful coup, however carefully we avoid direct engagement,
will be laid at our door by public opinion almost everywhere. Therefore, while sharing your view that we should not be in position of
thwarting coup, we would like to have option of judging and warning
on any plan with poor prospects of success. We recognize that this is a
large order, but President wants you to know of our concern.

Lodge Urges Proceeding with Plan

In a cable of October 30, 1963, Bundy had continued to press
Lodge to be certain of success before permitting a coup to
proceed. Lodge's response of the same date emphasized that
plans had reached the point of no return and there was no
choice but to go ahead. Lodge's deep personal commitment
to a change of government is evident in this cable.

　　1　We must, of course, get best possible estimate of chance of
coup's success and this estimate must color our thinking, but do not
think we have the power to delay or discourage a coup. Don has made
it clear many times that this is a Vietnamese affair. It is theoretically
possible for us to turn over the information which has been given to us
in confidence to Diem and this would undoubtedly stop the coup and
would make traitors out of us. For practical purposes therefore I would
say that we have very little influence on what is essentially a Viet-

namese affair. In addition, this would place the heads of the Generals, their civilian supporters, and lower military officers on the spot, thereby sacrificing a significant portion of the civilian and military leadership needed to carry the war against the VC to its successful conclusion. After our efforts not to discourage a coup and this change of heart, we would foreclose any possibility of change of the GVN for the better. Diem/Nhu have displayed no intentions to date of a desire to change the traditional methods of control through police action or take any repeat any actions which would undermine the power position or solidarity of the Ngo family. This, despite our heavy pressures directed DEPTEL 534. If our attempt to thwart this coup were successful, which we doubt, it is our firm estimate that younger officers, small groups of military, would then engage in an abortive action creating chaos ideally suited to VC objectives.

2   While we will attempt a combined assessment in a following message, time has not yet permitted substantive examination of this matter with General Harkins. My general view is that the U.S. is trying to bring this medieval country into the 20th Century and that we have made considerable progress in military and economic ways but to gain victory we must also bring them into the 20th Century politically and that can only be done by either a thoroughgoing change in the behavior of the present government or by another government. The Viet Cong problem is partly military but it is also partly psychological and political.

3   With respect to paragraph 3 Ref., I believe that we should continue our present position of keeping hands off but continue to monitor and press for more detailed information. CAS has been analyzing potential coup forces for some time and it is their estimate that the Generals have probably figured their chances pretty closely and probably also expect that once they begin to move, not only planned units, but other units will join them. We believe that Vietnam's best Generals are involved in directing this effort. If they can't pull it off, it is doubtful other military leadership could do so successfully. It is understandable that the Generals would be reticent to reveal full details of their plan for fear of leaks to the GVN.

4   Re para. 4, Ref., we expect that Conein will meet Don on the night of 30 Oct or early morning 31 Oct. We agree with Para. 4, Ref., that we should continue to press for details and question Don as to his estimate of the relative strengths of opposing forces. We do not believe, however, that we should show any signs of attempting to direct this affair ourselves or of giving the impression of second thoughts on this Vietnamese initiation. In the meantime, we will respond specifically to CAS Washington 79126. Please note that CAS Saigon 2059 corrects CAS Saigon 2023 and two regiments of the 7th Division are included in the coup forces.

5 Apparently Para. 5, Ref., overlooks CAS 1445, 5 Oct 1963 which gave an account of the face to face meeting of General "Big Minh" and Conein at Minh's instigation and through the specific arrangement of Gen Don. Minh specifically identified Gen Don as participating in a plan to change the government. Please note that Minh's remarks parallel in every way the later statements of Gen. Don. We believe that the limitation of contact to Don and Cein [sic] is an appropriate security measure consonant with our urging that the smallest number of persons be aware of these details.

6 We do not believe it wise to ask that "Big Minh" pass his plans to Gen. [Richard] Stilwell. The Vietnamese believe that there are members of the U.S. military who leak to the Government of Vietnam. I do not doubt that this is an unjust suspicion but it is a fact that this suspicion exists and there is no use in pretending that it does not.

7 I much appreciate your furnishing the berth-equipped military aircraft which I trust is a jet. I intend to tell Pan American that a jet has been diverted for my use and therefore I will no longer need their services. This will undoubtedly leak to the newspapers and the GVN may study this move with some suspicion. I will answer any inquiries on this score to the effect that I am most pleased by this attention and that this is obviously done as a measure to insure my comfort and save my time. To allay suspicions further, I will offer space on the aircraft to MACV for emergency leave cases, etc., and handle this in as routine fashion as possible. I wish to reserve comment as to my actual time of departure until I have some additional information, hopefully tomorrow.

8 Your para. 7 somewhat perplexes me. It does not seem sensible to have the military in charge of a matter which is so profoundly political as a change of government. In fact, I would say to do this would probably be the end of any hope for a change of government here. This is said impersonally as a general proposition, since Gen. Harkins is a splendid General and an old friend of mine to whom I would gladly entrust anything I have. I assume that the Embassy and MACV are able to handle normal activities under A, that CAS can continue coup contacts under B, and as regards C, we must simply do the very best we can in the light of events after the coup has started.

9 We appreciate the steps taken as outlined in para. 8. However, we should remember that the GVN is not totally inept in its foreign soundings and that these moves should be as discreet and security conscious as possible. I would, of course, call for these forces only in case of extreme necessity since my hope coincides with the Generals that this will be an all-Vietnamese affair.

10 We anticipate that at the outset of the coup, unless it moves with lightning swiftness, the GVN will request me or Gen. Harkins to use our influence to call it off. I believe our responsibilities should be that our influence certainly could not be superior to that of the President who is Commander-in-Chief and that if he is unable to call it off, we would certainly be unable to do so and would merely be risking American lives attempting to interfere in this Vietnamese problem. The Government might request aircraft. Helicopters, for the evacuation of key personalities that would have to be studied closely, but we would certainly not commit our planes and pilots between the battle lines of the opposing forces. We should, rather, state that we would be willing to act in this fashion during a truce in which both sides agree to the removal of key personalities. I believe that there would be immediate political problems in attempting to take these personalities to another neighboring country and probably we would be best served in depositing them in Saipan where the absence of press, communications, etc., would allow us some leeway to make a further decision as to their ultimate disposition. If senior Vietnamese personalities and their families requested asylum in the Embassy or other American installations, we would probably have to grant it in light of our previous action with respect to [Buddhist leader Thich] Tri Quang. This will undoubtedly present later problems but hopefully the new government might feel disposed to help us solve this problem. Naturally, asylum would be granted on the same basis as the Buddhists, i.e., physical presence at the Embassy or other location.

11   As to requests from the Generals, they may well have need of funds at the last moment with which to buy off potential opposition. To the extent that these funds can be passed discreetly, I believe we should furnish them, provided we are convinced that the proposed coup is sufficiently well organized to have a good chance of success. If they are successful, they will undoubtedly ask for prompt recognition and some assurance that military and economic aid will continue at normal level. We should be prepared to make these statements if the issue is clear-cut predicating our position on the President's stated desire to continue the war against the VC to final victory. VOA might be an important means of disseminating this message. Should the coup fail, we will have to pick up the pieces as best we can at that time. We have a commitment to the Generals from the August episode to attempt to help in the evacuation of their dependents. We should try to live up to this if conditions will permit. American complicity will undoubtedly be charged and there might be some acts taken against specific personalities which we should anticipate and make provision against as best we can. Should the coup prove indecisive and a protracted struggle is in progress, we should probably offer our good offices to help resolve the issue in the interest of the war against the VC. This might hold some benefit in terms of concessions by GVN. We will naturally incur some oppro-

brium from both sides in our role as mediator. However, this oppro-
brium would probably be less distasteful than a deadlock which would
open the door to the VC. We consider such a deadlock as the least
likely possibility of the three.

12 As regards your para. 10, I do not know what more proof can
be offered than the fact these men are obviously prepared to risk their
lives and that they want nothing for themselves. If I am any judge of
human nature, Don's face expressed of sincerity and determination on
the morning that I spoke to him. Heartily agree that a miscalculation
could jeopardize position in Southeast Asia. We also run tremendous
risks by doing nothing.

If we were convinced that the coup was going to fail, we would, of
course, do everything we could to stop it.

13 Gen. Harkins has read this and does not concur.

Bundy Outlines Contingency Plans

Bundy's final cable to Lodge (dated October 30, 1963) before
the coup actually began reflected the President's continuing
nervousness and the administration's persisting fear of failure.

1 Our reading your thoughtful 2063 leads us to believe a significant
difference of shading may exist on one crucial point (see next para.)
and on one or two lesser matters easily clarified.

2 We do not accept as a basis for U.S. policy that we have no power
to delay or discourage a coup. In your paragraph 12 you say that if
you were convinced that the coup was going to fail you would of
course do everything you could to stop it. We believe that on this
same basis you should take action to persuade coup leaders to stop
or delay any operation which, in your best judgment, does not
clearly give high prospect of success. We have not considered any
betrayal of generals to Diem, and our 79109 explicitly rejects that
course. We recognize the danger of appearing hostile to generals,
but we believe that our own position should be on as firm ground as
possible, hence we cannot limit ourselves to proposition implied in
your message that only conviction of certain failure justifies intervention. We believe that your standard for intervention should be
that stated above.

3 Therefore, if you should conclude that there is not clearly a high prospect of success, you should communicate this doubt to generals in a way calculated to persuade them to desist at least until chances are better. In such a communication you should use the weight of U.S. best advice and explicitly reject any implication that we oppose the effort of the generals because of preference for present regime. We recognize need to bear in mind generals' interpretation of U.S. role in 1960 coup attempt, and your agent should maintain clear distinction between strong and honest advice given as a friend and any opposition to their objectives.

We continue to be deeply interested in up-to-the-minute assessment of prospects and are sending this before reply to our CAS 79126. We want continuous exchange latest assessments on this topic. . . .

5 To clarify our intent, paragraph 7 of our 79109 is rescinded and we restate our desires as follows:

   a While you are in Saigon you will be Chief of Country Team in all circumstances and our only instruction is that we are sure it will help to have Harkins fully informed at all stages and to use advice from both him and Smith in framing guidance for coup contacts and assessment. We continue to be concerned that neither Conein nor any other reporting source is getting the clarity we would like with respect to alignment of forces and level of determination among generals.

   b When you leave Saigon and before there is a coup, [William] Truehart will be Chief of the Country Team. Our only modification of existing procedures is that in this circumstance we wish all instruction to Conein to be conducted in immediate consultation with Harkins and Smith so that all three know what is said to Conein. Any disagreement among the three on such instruction should be reported to Washington and held for our resolution, when time permits.

   c If you have left and a coup occurs, we believe that emergency situation requires, pending your return, that direction of country team be vested in most senior officer with experience of military decisions, and the officer in our view is Harkins. We do not intend that this switch in final responsibility should be publicized in any way, and Harkins will of course be guided in basic posture by our instructions, which follow in paragraph 6. We do not believe that this switch will have the effect suggested in your paragraph 8.

6 This paragraph contains our present standing instructions for U.S. posture in the event of a coup.

   a U.S. authorities will reject appeals for direct intervention from either side, and U.S.-controlled aircraft and other resources will not be committed between the battle lines or in support of either side, without authorization from Washington.

b In event of indecisive contest, U.S. authorities may in their discretion agree to perform any acts agreeable to both sides, such as removal of key personalities or relay of information. In such actions, however, U.S. authorities will strenuously avoid appearance of pressure on either side. It is not in the interest of USG to be or appear to be either instrument of existing government or instrument of coup.

c In the event of imminent or actual failure of coup, U.S. authorities may afford asylum in their discretion to those to whom there is any express or implied obligation of this sort. We believe however that in such a case it would be in our interest and probably in interest of those seeking asylum that they seek protection of other Embassies in addition to our own. This point should be made strongly if need arises.

d But once a coup under responsible leadership has begun, and within these restrictions, it is in the interest of the U.S. Government that it should succeed.

7 We have your message about return to Washington and we suggest that all public comment be kept as low-key and quiet as possible, and we also urge that if possible you keep open the exact time of your departure. We are strongly sensitive to great disadvantage of having you out of Saigon if this should turn out to be a week of decision, and if it can be avoided we would prefer not to see you pinned to a fixed hour of departure now.

Lodge's Phone Conversation with Diem

At 4:30 P.M. on November 1, 1963, with the coup under way, Diem telephoned Lodge to determine where the United States stood. The following poignant conversation, excerpted from Lodge's cable to the State Department on the same day, reveals Diem's fear and Lodge's cold standoffishness. Diem and Nhu subsequently fled to a Catholic church in the Cholon district of Saigon, where they were eventually apprehended and then brutally murdered.

Diem: Some units have made a rebellion and I want to know what is the attitude of the U.S.?

Lodge: I do not feel well enough informed to be able to tell you. I have heard the shooting, but am not acquainted with all the facts. Also it is 4:30 A.M. in Washington and the U.S. Government cannot possibly have a view.

Diem: But you must have some general ideas. After all, I am a Chief of State. I have tried to do my duty. I want to do now what duty and good sense require. I believe in duty above all.

Lodge: You have certainly done your duty. As I told you only this morning, I admire your courage and your great contributions to your country. No one can take away from you the credit for all you have done. Now I am worried about your physical safety. I have a report that those in charge of the current activity offer you and your brother safe conduct out of the country if you resign. Had you heard this?

Diem: No. (And then after a pause) You have my telephone number.

Lodge: Yes. If I can do anything for your physical safety, please call me.

Diem: I am trying to re-establish order.

Chapter 3

Graduated Response,
1963–1965

Between November 1963 and February 1965, the United States moved inexorably toward direct military involvement in the war in Vietnam.

The major cause of U.S. escalation was the gradual and increasingly drastic deterioration of the political and military situation in South Vietnam. The generals who assumed power with the overthrow of Diem could not agree among themselves on who should lead, much less what should be done, and coup followed coup, government followed government in revolving door fashion. With increased support from North Vietnam, the National Liberation Front took advantage of the chaos in Saigon, undermining what remained of Government of (South) Vietnam (GVN) authority in the countryside and mounting major attacks on ARVN forces.

The initial U.S. response to these unsettling events was carefully measured. American officials were deeply concerned with the instability in Saigon and even feared an outright GVN collapse. They were increasingly inclined to take action against North Vietnam as a substitute for effective action in the South. At the same time, however, they were quite reluctant to launch a wider war from such a weak base. In addition, Kennedy's successor, Lyndon Johnson, was up for election in his own right in 1964, and political exigencies required caution. The administration thus responded with a series of covert operations designed to stiffen the U.S.-South Vietnamese position and signal to North Vietnam U.S. unwillingness to accept defeat. In February 1964, the United States launched Operation Plan (OPLAN) 34A, a series of clandestine measures against North Vietnam including sabotage and commando raids against military installations along the coast. The United States also initiated air attacks against North Vietnamese forces in Laos, attacks that steadily increased in intensity and moved closer to the North Vietnamese border. A third element of the covert program was the sending of U.S. warships into the Gulf of Tonkin on so-called DeSoto patrols both as a show of force and as a way to collect intelligence information on North Vietnamese air defenses.

While taking these covert measures, U.S. officials also drafted plans for further escalation of the war. The covert operations had little perceptible impact on the war, and U.S. planners were more and more inclined to look north for solutions they seemed unable to find in the South. A crisis in Laos in May 1964 spurred top-level planning, and in spring and early summer U.S. officials worked up a full "scenario" of actions to be taken to avert disaster in Vietnam. To provide a solid domestic political basis for an expanded war, the administration would seek a congressional resolution. It would then launch full-scale air attacks against North Vietnamese port facilities, transportation networks, and military installations. Still cautious in view of the approaching elections, Johnson refused to go beyond planning at this point, agreeing only to send the Canadian diplomat Blair Seaborn to Hanoi to warn of U.S. resolve and to step up air operations in Laos.

In response to a series of incidents in the Gulf of Tonkin in early August, the administration implemented part of its scenario. On August 2, North Vietnamese gunboats attacked the *USS Maddox,* then engaged in DeSoto patrols in the Gulf. Two days later, the *Maddox* and the *USS Turner Joy* reported being under furious North Vietnamese attack. Although doubts subsequently developed (and have never been satisfactorily resolved) as to whether this second alleged attack actually took place, the administration seized the opportunity to retaliate. Claiming that U.S. ships had been the victims of unprovoked attacks in international waters, the Johnson administration launched a series of retaliatory air strikes against North Vietnamese naval bases. At the same time, the President guided through a near-unanimous Congress the so-called Tonkin Gulf Resolution, authorizing him to "take all necessary measures to repel any armed attack against the forces of the United States and to prevent further aggression," in effect giving him a blank check to escalate the war at his discretion.

In the six months after the Tonkin Gulf incidents, a consensus gradually developed among the President's top advisers in favor of the regularized bombing of North Vietnam. The situation in South Vietnam continued to deteriorate, and the National Liberation Front continued to gain ground. Until November, the election campaign put a premium on caution, and even after the election Johnson and his top advisers were wary of expanding the war until South Vietnam was stabilized. Thus even when the NLF attacked the U.S. air base at Bien Hoa on November 1, killing four Americans and destroying five aircraft, and attacked the Brinks' Hotel in Saigon on Christmas eve, killing two Americans and wounding fifty-eight the President refused to retaliate. By the end of January, however, he and his advisers agreed that the bombing of North Vietnam must soon be undertaken. The political crisis in Saigon persisted, and what had once been an argument against escalation now became an argument for it. There was wide disagreement among Johnson's advisers as to how the bombing should be carried out and what results might be expected from it, but there was general agreement that something must be done. By February 1, 1965, the United States was committed to a major escalation of the war.

McNamara's March 1964 Assessment of Situation in Vietnam

These excerpts from Secretary of Defense McNamara's memorandum to President Johnson, March 16, 1964, paint a generally gloomy picture of developments in South Vietnam and indicate the administration's growing inclination to take the war to North Vietnam.

I. U.S. OBJECTIVES IN SOUTH VIETNAM

We seek an independent non-Communist South Vietnam. We do not require that it serve as a Western base or as a member of a Western Alliance. Vietnam must be free, however, to accept outside assistance as required to maintain its security. This assistance should be able to take the form not only of economic and social pressures but also police and military help to root out and control insurgent elements.

Unless we can achieve this objective in South Vietnam, almost all of Southeast Asia will probably fall under Communist dominance (all of Vietnam, Laos, and Cambodia), accommodate to Communism so as to remove effective U.S. and anti-Communist influence (Burma), or fall under the domination of forces not now explicitly Communist but likely then to become so (Indonesia taking over Malaysia). Thailand might hold for a period with our help, but would be under grave pressure. Even the Philippines would become shaky, and the threat to India to the west, Australia and New Zealand to the south, and Taiwan, Korea, and Japan to the north and east would be greatly increased.

All these consequences would probably have been true even if the U.S. had not since 1954, and especially since 1961, become so heavily engaged in South Vietnam. However, that fact accentuates the impact of a Communist South Vietnam not only in Asia, but in the rest of the world, where the South Vietnam conflict is regarded as a test case of U.S. capacity to help a nation meet a Communist "war of liberation."

Thus, purely in terms of foreign policy, the stakes are high. They are increased by domestic factors.

II. PRESENT U.S. POLICY IN SOUTH VIETNAM

We are now trying to help South Vietnam defeat the Viet Cong, supported from the North, by means short of the unqualified use of U.S.

combat forces. We are not acting against North Vietnam except by a very modest "covert" program operated by South Vietnamese (and a few Chinese Nationalists)—a program so limited that it is unlikely to have any significant effect. In Laos, we are still working largely within the framework of the 1962 Geneva Accords. In Cambodia we are still seeking to keep [Prince Norodon] Sihanouk from abandoning whatever neutrality he may still have and fulfilling his threat of reaching an accommodation with Hanoi and Peking. As a consequence of these policies, we and the GVN have had to condone the extensive use of Cambodian and Laotian territory by the Viet Cong, both as a sanctuary and as infiltration routes.

III. THE PRESENT SITUATION IN SOUTH VIETNAM

The key elements in the present situation are as follows:

A   The military tools and concepts of the GVN-US efforts are generally sound and adequate.* Substantially more can be done in the effective employment of military forces and in the economic and civic action areas. These improvements may require some selective increases in the U.S. presence, but it does not appear likely that major equipment replacement and additions in U.S. personnel are indicated under current policy.

B   The U.S. policy of reducing existing personnel where South Vietnamese are in a position to assume the functions is still sound. Its application will not lead to any major reductions in the near future, but adherence to this policy as such has a sound effect in portraying to the U.S. and the world that we continue to regard the war as a conflict the South Vietnamese must win and take ultimate responsibility for. Substantial reductions in the numbers of U.S. military training personnel should be possible before the end of 1965. However, the U.S. should continue to reiterate that it will provide all the assistance and advice required to do the job regardless of how long it takes.

C   The situation has unquestionably been growing worse, at least since September:

    1   In terms of government control of the countryside, about 40% of the territory is under Viet Cong control or predominant in-

* Mr. McCone emphasizes that the GVN/US program can never be considered completely satisfactory so long as it permits the Viet Cong a sanctuary in Cambodia and a continuing uninterrupted and unmolested source of supply and reinforcement from NVN through Laos.

fluence. In 22 of the 43 provinces, the Viet Cong control 50% or more of the land area, including 80% of Phuoc Tuy; 90% of Binh Duong; 75% of Hau Nghia; 90% of Long An; 90% of Kien Tuong; 90% of Dinh Tuong; 90% of Kien Hoa and 85% of An Xuyen.

2 Large groups of the population are now showing signs of apathy and indifference, and there are some signs of frustration within the U.S. contingent. . . .

a The ARVN and paramilitary desertion rates, and particularly the latter, are high and increasing.

b Draft-dodging is high while the Viet Cong are recruiting energetically and effectively.

c The morale of the hamlet militia and of the Self Defense Corps, on which the security of the hamlets depends, is poor and failing.

3 In the last 90 days the weakening of the government's position has been particularly noticeable. . . .

4 The political control structure extending from Saigon down into the hamlets disappeared following the November coup. . . .

5 North Vietnamese support, always significant, has been increasing. . . .

D The greatest weakness in the present situation is the uncertain viability of the [Nguyen] Khanh government. Khanh himself is a very able man within his experience, but he does not yet have wide political appeal and his control of the army itself is uncertain. . . .

E On the positive side, we have found many reasons for encouragement in the performance of the Khanh Government to date. Although its top layer is thin, it is highly responsive to U.S. advice, and with a good grasp of the basic elements of rooting out the Viet Cong. . . .

IV. ALTERNATIVE PRESENT COURSES OF ACTION

A *Negotiate on the Basis of "Neutralization"*
While de Gaulle has not been clear on what he means by this—and is probably deliberately keeping it vague as he did in working toward an Algerian settlement—he clearly means not only a South Vietnam that would not be a Western base or part of an alliance structure (both of which we could accept) but also withdrawal of all external military assistance and specifically total U.S. withdrawal. To negotiate on this basis—indeed without specifically rejecting it—would simply mean a Communist take-over in South Vietnam. Only the U.S. presence after 1954 held the South together

under far more favorable circumstances, and enabled Diem to refuse to go through with the 1954 provision calling for nationwide "free" elections in 1956. Even talking about a U.S. withdrawal would undermine any chance of keeping a non-Communist government in South Vietnam, and the rug would probably be pulled before the negotiations had gone far.

B *Initiate GVN and U.S. Military Actions Against North Vietnam*
We have given serious thought to all the implications and ways of carrying out direct military action against North Vietnam in order to supplement the counterinsurgency program in South Vietnam. (The analysis of overt U.S. action is attached as Annex A.) In summary, the actions break down into three categories:

1 Border Control Actions. For example:
   a An expansion of current authority for Laotian overflights to permit low-level reconnaissance by aircraft when such flights are required to supplement the currently approved U-2 flights.
   b Vietnamese cross-border ground penetrations into Laos, without the presence of U.S. advisors or re-supply by U.S. aircraft.
   c Expansion of the patrols into Laos to include use of U.S. advisors and re-supply by U.S. aircraft.
   d Hot pursuit of VC forces moving across the Cambodian border and destruction of VC bases on the Vietnam/Cambodian line.
   e Air and ground strikes against selected targets in Laos by South Vietnamese forces.

2 Retaliatory Actions. For example:
   a Over high and/or low-level reconnaissance flights by U.S. or Farmgate aircraft over North Vietnam to assist in locating and identifying the sources of external aid to the Viet Cong.
   b Retaliatory bombing strikes and commando raids on a tit-for-tat basis by the GVN against NVN targets (communication centers, training camps, infiltration routes, etc.).
   c Aerial mining by the GVN aircraft (possibly with U.S. assistance) of the major NVN ports.

3 Graduated Overt Military Pressure by GVN and U.S. forces.
      This program would go beyond reacting on a tit-for-tat basis. It would include air attacks against military and possibly industrial targets. This program would utilize the combined resources of the GVN Air Force and the U.S. Farmgate Squadron, with the latter reinforced by three squadrons of B-57s presently in Japan. Before this program could be imple-

mented it would be necessary to provide some additional air defense for South Vietnam and to ready U.S. forces in the Pacific for possible escalation.

The analysis of the more serious of these military actions (from 2 (b) upward) revealed the extremely delicate nature of such operations, both from the military and political standpoints. There would be the problem of marshalling the case to justify such action, the problem of communist escalation, and the problem of dealing with the pressures for premature or "stacked" negotiations. We would have to calculate the effect of such military actions against a specified political objective. That objective, while being cast in terms of eliminating North Vietnamese control and direction of the insurgency, would in practical terms be directed toward collapsing the morale and the self-assurance of the Viet Cong cadres now operating in South Vietnam and bolstering the morale of the Khanh regime. We could not, of course, be sure that our objective could be achieved by any means within the practical range of our options. Moreover, and perhaps most importantly, unless and until the Khanh government has established its position and preferably is making significant progress in the South, an overt extension of operations into the North carries the risk of being mounted from an extremely weak base which might at any moment collapse and leave the posture of political confrontation worsened rather than improved.

The other side of the argument is that the young Khanh Government [two words illegible] reinforcement of some significant sources against the North and without [words illegible] in-country program, even with the expansion discussed in Section [words illegible] may not be sufficient to stem the tide.

[Words illegible] balance, except to the extent suggested in Section V below, I [words illegible] against initiation at this time of overt GVN and/or U.S. military [words illegible] against North Vietnam.

C   Initiate Measures to Improve the Situation in South Vietnam.

There were and are sound reasons for the limits imposed by present policy—the South Vietnamese must win their own fight; U.S. intervention on a larger scale, and/or GVN actions against the North, would disturb key allies and other nations; etc. In any case, it is vital that we continue to take every reasonable measure to assure success in South Vietnam. The policy choice is not an "either/or" between this course of action and possible pressures against the North; the former is essential without regard to our decision with respect to the latter. The latter can, at best, only reinforce the former.

The following are the actions we believe can be taken in order to improve the situation both in the immediate future and over a longer-term period. To emphasize that a new phase has begun, the measures to be taken by the Khanh government should be described by some term such as "South Vietnam's Program for National Mobilization."

Basic U.S. Posture

1   The U.S. at all levels must continue to make it emphatically clear that we are prepared to furnish assistance and support for as long as it takes to bring the insurgency under control.

2   The U.S. at all levels should continue to make it clear that we fully support the Khanh government and are totally opposed to any further coups. The Ambassador should instruct all elements, including the military advisors, to report intelligence information of possible coups promptly, with the decision to be made by the ambassador whether to report such information to Khanh. However, we must recognize that our chances would not be great of detecting and preventing a coup that had major military backing.

3   We should support fully the Pacification Plan now announced by Khanh (described in Annex B), and particularly the basic theory—now fully accepted both on the Vietnamese and U.S. sides—of concentrating on the more secure areas and working out from these through military operations to provide security, followed by necessary civil and economic actions to make the presence of the government felt and to provide economic improvements. . . .

V. POSSIBLE LATER ACTIONS

If the Khanh government takes hold vigorously—inspiring confidence, whether or not noteworthy progress has been made—or if we get hard information of significantly stepped-up VC arms supply from the North, we may wish to mount new and significant pressures against North Vietnam. We should start preparations for such a capability now. (See Annex C for an analysis of the situation in North Vietnam and Communist China.) Specifically, we should develop a capability to initiate within 72 hours the "Border Control"* and "Retaliatory Actions" referred to on pages 5 and 6, and we should achieve a capability to ini-

---

* Authority should be granted immediately for covert Vietnamese operations into Laos, for the purposes of border control and of "hot pursuit" into Laos. Decision on "hot pursuit" into Cambodia should await further study of our relations with that country.

tiate with 30 days' notice the program of "Graduated Overt Military Pressure." The reasoning behind this program of preparations for initiating action against North Vietnam is rooted in the fact that, even with progress in the pacification plan, the Vietnamese Government and the population in the South will still have to face the prospect of a very lengthy campaign based on a war-weary nation and operating against Viet Cong cadres who retain a great measure of motivation and assurance.

In this connection, General Khanh stated that his primary concern is to establish a firm base in the South. He favors continuation of covert activities against North Vietnam, but until such time as "rear-area security" has been established, he does not wish to engage in overt operations against the North.

In order to accelerate the realization of pacification and particularly in order to denigrate the morale of the Viet Cong forces, it may be necessary at some time in the future to put demonstrable retaliatory pressure on the North. Such a course of action might proceed according to the scenario outlined in Annex D. . . .

VII.   RECOMMENDATIONS

I recommend that you instruct the appropriate agencies of the U.S. Government:

1   To make it clear that we are prepared to furnish assistance and support to South Vietnam for as long as it takes to bring the insurgency under control.

2   To make it clear that we fully support the Khanh government and are opposed to further coups.

3   To support a Program for National Mobilization (including a national service law) to put South Vietnam on a war footing.

4   To assist the Vietnamese to increase the armed forces (regular plus paramilitary) by at least 50,000 men.

5   To assist the Vietnamese to create a greatly enlarged Civil Administrative Corps for work at province, district and hamlet levels.

6   To assist the Vietnamese to improve and reorganize the paramilitary forces and increase their compensation.

7   To assist the Vietnamese to create an offensive guerrilla force.

8   To provide the Vietnamese Air Force 25 A-1H aircraft in exchange for the present T-28s.

9   To provide the Vietnamese Army additional M-113 armored personnel carriers (withdrawing the M-114s there), additional river boats, and approximately $5–10 million of other additional material.

   10   To announce publicly the Fertilizer Program and to expand it with a view within two years to trebling the amount of fertilizer made available.

   11   To authorize continued high-level U.S. overflights of South Vietnam's borders and to authorize "hot pursuit" and South Vietnamese ground operations over the Laotian line for the purpose of border control. More ambitious operations into Laos involving units beyond battalion size should be authorized only with the approval of Souvanna Phouma. Operations across the Cambodian border should depend on the state of relations with Cambodia.

   12   To prepare immediately to be in a position on 72 hours' notice to initiate the full range of Laotian and Cambodian "Border Control" actions (beyond those authorized in Paragraph 11 above) and the "Retaliatory Actions" against North Vietnam, and to be in a position on 30 days' notice to initiate the program of "Graduated Overt Military Pressure" against North Vietnam.

NSAM 288 Plans for Retaliation

National Security Action Memorandum 288, approved March 17, 1964, reaffirmed in ringing language the U.S. commitment in Vietnam and set forth the plan of action followed in the spring of that year. The following excerpts from NSAM 288 come from the body of the Pentagon study. The italicized words in brackets are those of the study. The paragraph in italics is a paraphrase by a writer of the study.

[*The United States' policy is*] to prepare immediately to be in a position on 72 hours' notice to initiate the full range of Laotian and Cambodian "Border Control actions" . . . and the "Retaliatory Actions" against North Vietnam, and to be in a position on 30 days' notice to initiate the program of "Graduated Overt Military Pressure" against North Vietnam. . . .

   We seek an independent non-Communist South Vietnam. We do not require that it serve as a Western base or as a member of a Western Alliance. South Vietnam must be free, however, to accept outside assistance as required to maintain its security. This assistance should be able to take the form not only of economic and social measures but also police and military help to root out and control insurgent elements.

Unless we can achieve this objective in South Vietnam, almost all of Southeast Asia will probably fall under Communist dominance (all of Vietnam, Laos, and Cambodia), accommodate to Communism so as to remove effective U.S. and anti-Communist influence (Burma), or fall under the domination of force not now explicitly Communist but likely then to become so (Indonesia taking over Malaysia). Thailand might hold for a period without help, but would be under grave pressure. Even the Philippines would become shaky, and the threat to India on the West, Australia and New Zealand to the South, and Taiwan, Korea, and Japan to the North and East would be greatly increased.

All of these consequences would probably have been true even if the U.S. had not since 1954, and especially since 1961, become so heavily engaged in South Vietnam. However, that fact accentuates the impact of a Communist South Vietnam not only in Asia but in the rest of the world, where the South Vietnam conflict is regarded as a test case of U.S. capacity to help a nation to meet the Communist "war of liberation."

Thus, purely in terms of foreign policy, the stakes are high. . . .

We are now trying to help South Vietnam defeat the Viet Cong, supported from the North, by means short of the unqualified use of U.S. combat forces. We are not acting against North Vietnam except by a modest "covert" program operated by South Vietnamese (and a few Chinese Nationalists)—a program so limited that it is unlikely to have any significant effect. . . .

There were and are some sound reasons for the limits imposed by the present policy—the South Vietnamese must win their own fight; U.S. intervention on a larger scale, and/or GVN actions against the North, would disturb key allies and other nations; etc. In any case, it is vital that we continue to take every reasonable measure to assure success in South Vietnam. The policy choice is not an "either/or" between this course of action and possible pressure against the North; the former is essential and without regard to our decision with respect to the latter. The latter can, at best, only reinforce the former. . . .

Many of the actions described in the succeeding paragraphs fit right into the framework of the [pacification] plan as announced by Khanh. Wherever possible, we should tie our urgings of such actions to Khanh's own formulation of them, so that he will be carrying out a Vietnamese plan and not one imposed by the United States. . . .

*Among the alternatives considered, but rejected for the time being
. . . were overt military pressure on North Vietnam, neutralization, return of U.S. dependents, furnishing of a U.S. combat unit to secure the
Saigon area, and a full takeover of the command in South Vietnam by
the U.S. With respect to this last proposal, it was said that*

. . . the judgment of all senior people in Saigon, with which we
concur, was that the possible military advantages of such action would
be far outweighed by adverse psychological impact. It would cut across
the whole basic picture of the Vietnamese winning their own war and
lay us wide open to hostile propaganda both within South Vietnam and
outside.

U.S. Warnings to North Vietnam

This U.S. note was delivered to the Canadian Embassy in
Washington on August 8, 1964, for transmission to J. Blair
Seaborn, Canadian member of the International Control Com-
mission. Seaborn was to visit Hanoi at the behest of the
United States to convey to the North Vietnamese U.S. deter-
mination to stand firm in Vietnam.

Canadians are urgently asked to have Seaborn during August 10 visit
make following points (as having been conveyed to him by U.S. Government since August 6):
A   Re Tonkin Gulf actions, which almost certainly will come up:
    1   The DRV has stated that Hon Ngu and Hon Me islands were
       attacked on July 30. It should be noted that the USS MADDOX
       was all of that day and into the afternoon of the next day, over
       100 miles south of those islands, in international waters near
       the 17th parallel, and that the DRV attack on the MADDOX
       took place on August 2nd, more than two days later. Neither
       the MADDOX or any other destroyer was in any way associ-
       ated with any attack on the DRV islands.
    2   Regarding the August 4 attack by the DRV on the two U.S. de-
       stroyers, the Americans were and are at a complete loss to un-
       derstand the DRV motive. They had decided to absorb the Au-
       gust 2 attack on the grounds that it very well might have been
       the result of some DRV mistake or miscalculation. The August

4 attack, however—from the determined nature of the attack as indicated by the radar, sonar, and eye witness evidence both from the ships and from their protecting aircraft—was, in the American eyes, obviously deliberate and planned and ordered in advance. In addition, premeditation was shown by the evidence that the DRV craft were waiting in ambush for the destroyers. The attack did not seem to be in response to any action by the South Vietnamese nor did it make sense as a tactic to further any diplomatic objective. Since the attack took place at least 60 miles from nearest land, there could have been no question about territorial waters. About the only reasonable hypothesis was that North Vietnam was intent either upon making it appear that the United States was a "paper tiger" or upon provoking the United States.

3 The American response was directed solely to patrol craft and installations acting in direct support of them. As President Johnson stated: "Our response for the present will be limited and fitting."

4 In view of uncertainty aroused by the deliberate and unprovoked DRV attacks this character, U.S. has necessarily carried out precautionary deployments of additional air power to SVN and Thailand.

B Re basic American position:

5 Mr. Seaborn should again stress that U.S. policy is simply that North Vietnam should contain itself and its ambitions within the territory allocated to its administration by the 1954 Geneva Agreements. He should stress that U.S. policy in South Vietnam is to preserve the integrity of that state's territory against guerrilla subversion.

6 He should reiterate that the U.S. does not seek military bases in the area and that the U.S. is not seeking to overthrow the Communist regime in Hanoi.

7 He should repeat that the U.S. is fully aware of the degree to which Hanoi controls and directs the guerrilla action in South Vietnam and that the U.S. holds Hanoi directly responsible for that action. He should similarly indicate U.S. awareness of North Vietnamese control over the Pathet Lao movement in Laos and the degree of North Vietnamese involvement in that country. He should specifically indicate U.S. awareness of North Vietnamese violations of Laotian territory along the infiltration route into South Vietnam.

8 Mr. Seaborn can again refer to the many examples of U.S. policy in tolerance of peaceful coexistence with Communist

regimes, such as Yugoslavia, Poland, etc. He can hint at the economic and other benefits which have accrued to those countries because their policy of Communism has confirmed itself to the development of their own national territories and has not sought to expand into other areas.

9 Mr. Seaborn should conclude with the following new points:

   a That the events of the past few days should add credibility to the statement made last time, that "U.S. public and official patience with North Vietnamese aggression is growing extremely thin."

   b That the U.S. Congressional Resolution was passed with near unanimity, strongly re-affirming the unity and determination of the U.S. Government and people not only with respect to any further attacks on U.S. military forces but more broadly to continue to oppose firmly, by all necessary means, DRV efforts to subvert and conquer South Vietnam and Laos.

   c That the U.S. has come to the view that the DRV role in South Vietnam and Laos is critical. If the DRV persists in its present course, it can expect to continue to suffer the consequences.

   d That the DRV knows what it must do if the peace is to be restored.

   e That the U.S. has ways and means of measuring the DRV's participation in, and direction and control of, the war on South Vietnam and in Laos and will be carefully watching the DRV's response to what Mr. Seaborn is telling them.

September 1964 Proposals for Escalation

This memorandum from the assistant secretary of state for Far Eastern affairs, William P. Bundy, for President Johnson, September 8, 1964, reveals the administration's persisting caution. The memorandum was entitled "Courses of Action for South Vietnam."

This memorandum records the consensus reached in discussions between Ambassador [Maxwell] Taylor and Secretary Rusk, Secretary McNamara and General [Earle] Wheeler [chairman, Joint Chiefs of Staff] for review and decision by the President.

THE SITUATION

1 Khanh will probably stay in control and may make some headway in the next two–three months in strengthening the Government (GVN). The best we can expect is that he and the GVN will be able to maintain order, keep the pacification program ticking over (but not progressing markedly) and give the appearance of a valid Government.

2 Khanh and the GVN leaders are temporarily too exhausted to be thinking much about moves against the North. However, they do need to be reassured that the U.S. continues to mean business, and as Khanh goes along in his Government efforts, he will probably want more U.S. effort visible, and some GVN role in external actions.

3 The GVN over the next 2–3 months will be too weak for us to take any major deliberate risks of escalation that would involve a major role for, or threat to, South Vietnam. However, escalation arising from and directed against U.S. action would tend to lift GVN morale at least temporarily.

4 The Communist side will probably avoid provocative action against the U.S., and it is uncertain how much they will step up VC activity. They do need to be shown that we and the GVN are not simply sitting back after the Gulf of Tonkin.

COURSES OF ACTION

We recommend in any event:

1 U.S. naval patrols in the Gulf of Tonkin should be resumed immediately (about September 12). They should operate initially beyond the 12-mile limit and be clearly dissociated from 34A maritime operations. The patrols would comprise 2–3 destroyers and would have air cover from carriers; the destroyers would have their own ASW capability.

2 34A operations by the GVN should be resumed immediately thereafter (next week). The maritime operations are by far the most important. North Vietnam is likely to publicize them, and at this point we should have the GVN ready to admit that they are taking place and to justify and legitimize them on the basis of the facts on VC infiltration by sea. 34A air drop and leaflet operations should also be resumed but are secondary in importance. We should not consider air strikes under 34A for the present.

3 Limited GVN air and ground operations into the corridor areas of Laos should be undertaken in the near future, together with Lao air strikes as soon as we can get [Prince] Souvanna's [Phouma] permission. We should not consider air strikes under 34A for the present.

4 We should be prepared to respond on a tit-for-tat basis against the DRV in the event of any attack on U.S. units or any special DRV / VC action against SVN. The response for an attack on U.S. units should be along the lines of the Gulf of Tonkin attacks, against specific and related targets. The response to special action against SVN should likewise be aimed at specific and comparable targets.

The main further question is the extent to which we should add elements to the above actions that would tend deliberately to provoke a DRV reaction, and consequent retaliation by us. Example of actions to be considered would be running U.S. naval patrols increasingly close to the North Vietnamese coast and / or associating them with 34A operations. We believe such deliberately provocative elements should not be added in the immediate future while the GVN is still struggling to its feet. By early October, however, we may recommend such actions depending on GVN progress and Communist reaction in the meantime, especially to U.S. naval patrols.

The aim of the above actions, external to South Vietnam, would be to assist morale in SVN and show the Communists we still mean business, while at the same time seeking to keep the risks low and under our control at each stage.

Further actions within South Vietnam are not covered in this memorandum. We believe that there are a number of immediate-impact actions we can take, such as pay raises for the police and civil administrators and spot projects in the cities and selected rural areas. These actions would be within current policy and will be refined for decision during Ambassador Taylor's visit. We are also considering minor changes in the U.S. air role within South Vietnam, but these would not involve decisions until November.

McNaughton Proposals, November 1964

This second draft of a paper, "Action for South Vietnam," by
Assistant Secretary of Defense John McNaughton, November
6, 1964, reflects the emerging consensus among the President's top advisers that the United States must soon escalate
the war with direct attacks on North Vietnam.

1   U.S. aims:
   (a)   To protect U.S. reputation as a counter-subversion guarantor.
   (b)   To avoid domino effect especially in Southeast Asia.
   (c)   To keep South Vietnamese territory from Red hands.
   (d)   To emerge from crisis without unacceptable taint from meth-
         ods.
2   Present situation:
   The situation in South Vietnam is deteriorating. Unless new actions
   are taken, the new government will probably be unstable and inef-
   fectual, and the VC will probably continue to extend their hold over
   the population and territory. It can be expected that, soon (6
   months? two years?), (a) government officials at all levels will adjust their behavior to an eventual VC take-over, (b) defections of
   significant military forces will take place, (c) whole integrated re-
   gions of the country will be totally denied to the GVN, (d) neutral
   and / or left-wing elements will enter the government, (e) a popular
   front regime will emerge which will invite the U.S. out, and (f) fundamental concessions to the VC and accommodations to the DRV
   will put South Vietnam behind the Curtain.
3   Urgency:
   [The NLF attack on] "Bien Hoa" having passed, no urgent decision
   is required regarding military action against the DRV, but (a) such a
   decision, related to the general deteriorating situation in South Vietnam, should be made soon, and (b) in the event of another VC or
   DRV "spectacular," a decision (for at least a reprisal) would be urgently needed.
4   Inside South Vietnam:
   Progress inside SVN is important, but it is unlikely despite our best
   ideas and efforts (and progress, if made, will take at least several
   months). Nevertheless, whatever other actions might be taken, great
   efforts should be made within South Vietnam: (a) to strengthen the
   government, its bureaucracy, and its civil-military coordination and
   planning, (b) to dampen ethnic, religious, urban and civil-military

strife by a broad and positive GVN program designed (with U.S. Team help) to enlist the support of important groups, and (c) to press the pacification program in the countryside.

5   **Action against DRV:**
Action against North Vietnam is to some extent a substitute for strengthening the government in South Vietnam. That is, a less active VC (on orders from DRV) can be matched by a less efficient GVN. We therefore should consider squeezing North Vietnam.

6   **Options open to us:**
We have three options open to us (all envision reprisals in the DRV for DRV / VC "spectaculars" against GVN as well as U.S. assets in South Vietnam).

OPTION A. Continue present policies. Maximum assistance within SVN and limited external actions in Laos and by the GVN covertly against North Vietnam. The aim of any reprisal actions would be to deter and punish large VC actions in the South, but not to a degree that would create strong international negotiating pressures. Basic to this option is the continued rejection of negotiating in the hope that the situation will improve.

OPTION B. Fast full squeeze. Present policies plus a systematic program of military pressures against the north, meshing at some point with negotiation, but with pressure actions to be continued at a fairly rapid pace and without interruption until we achieve our central present objectives.

OPTION C. Progressive squeeze-and-talk. Present policies plus an orchestration of communications with Hanoi and a crescendo of additional military moves against infiltration targets, first in Laos and then in the DRV, and then against other targets in North Vietnam. The scenario would be designed to give the U.S. the option at any point to proceed or not, to escalate or not, and to quicken the pace or not. The decision in these regards would be made from time to time in view of all relevant factors.

7   **Analysis of OPTION A**
    (To be provided)

8   **Analysis of OPTION B**
    (To be provided)

9   **Analysis of OPTION C**
    (a)   Military actions. Present policy, in addition to providing for reprisals in DRV for DRV actions against the U.S., envisions (1) 34A Airops and Marops, (2) deSoto patrols, for intelligence purposes, (3) South Vietnamese shallow ground actions in Laos when practicable, and (4) T28 strikes against infiltration-associated targets in Laos. Additional actions should be:

PHASE ONE (in addition to reprisals in DRV for VC "spectaculars" in South Vietnam): (5) U.S. strikes against infiltration-associated targets in Laos.

PHASE TWO (in addition to reprisals in DRV against broader range of VC actions): (6) Low-level reconnaissance in southern DRV, (7) U.S. / VNAF strikes against infiltration-associated targets in southern DRV.

PHASE THREE: Either continue only the above actions or add one or more of the following, making timely deployment of U.S. forces: (8) Aerial mining of DRV ports, (9) Naval quarantine of DRV, and (10) U.S./VNAF, in "crescendo," strike additional targets on "94 target list."

South Vietnamese forces should play a role in any action taken against the DRV.

(b)   Political actions. Establish immediately a channel for bilateral U.S.-DRV communication. This could be in Warsaw or via Seaborn in Hanoi. Hanoi should be told that we do not seek to destroy North Vietnam or to acquire a colony or base, but that North Vietnam must:

   (1)   Stop training and sending personnel to wage war in SVN and Laos.
   (2)   Stop sending arms and supplies to SVN and Laos.
   (3)   Stop directing and controlling military actions in SVN and Laos.
   (4)   Order the VC and PL to stop their insurgencies and military actions.
   (5)   Remove VM forces and cadres from SVN and Laos.
   (6)   Stop propaganda broadcasts to South Vietnam.
   [(7)   See that VC and PL stop attacks and incidents in SVN and Laos?]
   [(8)   See that VC and PL cease resistance to government forces?]
   [(9)   See that VC and PL turn in weapons and relinquish bases?]
   [(10)   See that VC and PL surrender for amnesty of expatriation?]

U.S. demands should be accompanied by offers (1) to arrange a rice-barter deal between two halves of Vietnam and (2) to withdraw U.S. forces from South Vietnam for so long as the terms are complied with.

We should not seek wider negotiations—in the UN, in Geneva, etc.—but we should evaluate and pass on each negotiating opportunity as it is pressed on us.

(c)   Information actions. The start of military actions against the

DRV will have to be accompanied by a convincing world-wide public information program. (The information problem will be easier if the first U.S. action against the DRV is related in time and kind to a DRV or VC outrage or "spectacular," preferably against SVN as well as U.S. assets.)

(d) VS/DRV/Chicom-USSR reactions. (To be elaborated later.) The DRV and China will probably not invade South Vietnam, Laos or Burma, nor is it likely that they will conduct air strikes on these countries. The USSR will almost certainly confine herself to political actions. If the DRV or China strike or invade South Vietnam, U.S. forces will be sufficient to handle the problem.

(e) GVN reactions. Military action against the DRV could be counterproductive in South Vietnam because (1) the VC could step up its activities, (2) the South Vietnamese could panic, (3) they could resent our striking their "brothers," and (4) they could tire of waiting for results. Should South Vietnam disintegrate completely beneath us, we should try to hold it together long enough to permit us to try to evacuate our forces and to convince the world to accept the uniqueness (and congenital impossibility) of the South Vietnamese case.

(f) Allied and neutral reactions. (To be elaborated later.) (1) Even if OPTION C failed, it would, by demonstrating U.S. willingness to go to the mat, tend to bolster allied confidence in the U.S. as an ally. (2) U.S. military action against the DRV will probably prompt military actions elsewhere in the world—e.g., Indonesia against Malaysia or Timor, or Turkey against Cyprus.

Ambassador Taylor's Meeting with South Vietnamese Generals

These excerpts from a Saigon airgram to the State Department, December 24, 1964, as provided in the body of the Pentagon study, report a meeting of Ambassador Taylor and his deputy, U. Alexis Johnson, with the so-called Young Turk leaders, among them Generals Nguyen Cao Ky, Nguyen Van Thieu and Nguyen Chanh Thi and an admiral identified as Cang, after the latest Saigon coup. This classic document speaks volumes about U.S. interaction with the South Vietnamese during this period.

. . . *Ambassador Taylor:* Do all of you understand English? (Vietnamese officers indicated they did, although the understanding of General Thi was known to be weak.) I told you all clearly at General Westmoreland's dinner we Americans were tired of coups. Apparently I wasted my words. Maybe this is because something is wrong with my French because you evidently didn't understand. I made it clear that all the military plans which I know you would like to carry out are dependent on governmental stability. Now you have made a real mess. We cannot carry you forever if you do things like this. Who speaks for this group? Do you have a spokesman?

General Ky: I am not the spokesman for the group but I do speak English. I will explain why the Armed Forces took this action last night.

We understand English very well. We are aware of our responsibilities, we are aware of the sacrifices of our people over twenty years. We know you want stability, but you cannot have stability until you have unity. . . . But still there are rumors of coups and doubts among groups. We think these rumors come from the HNC, not as an organization but from some of its members. Both military and civilian leaders regard the presence of these people in the HNC as divisive of the Armed Forces due to their influence.

Recently the Prime Minister showed us a letter he had received from the Chairman of the HNC. This letter told the Prime Minister to beware of the military, and said that maybe the military would want to come back to power. Also the HNC illegally sought to block the retirement of the generals that the Armed Forces Council unanimously recommended be retired in order to improve unity in the Armed Forces.

General Thieu: The HNC cannot be bosses because of the Constitution. Its members must prove that they want to fight.

General Ky: It looks as though the HNC does not want unity. It does not want to fight the Communists.

It has been rumored that our action of last night was an intrigue of Khanh against Minh, who must be retired. Why do we seek to retire these generals? Because they had their chance and did badly. . . .

Yesterday we met, twenty of us, from 1430 to 2030. We reached agreement that we must take some action. We decided to arrest the bad members of the HNC, bad politicians, bad student leaders, and the leaders of the Committee of National Salvation, which is a Communist organization. We must put the trouble-making organizations out of action and ask the Prime Minister and the Chief of State to stay in office.

After we explain to the people why we did this at a press conference, we would like to return to our fighting units. We have no political
ambitions. We seek strong, unified, and stable Armed Forces to support
the struggle and a stable government. Chief of State Suu agrees with us.
General Khanh saw Huong who also agreed.

We did what we thought was good for this country; we tried to
have a civilian government clean house. If we have achieved it, fine.
We are now ready to go back to our units.

Ambassador Taylor: I respect the sincerity of you gentlemen. Now
I would like to talk to you about the consequences of what you have
done. But first, would any of the other officers wish to speak?

Admiral Cang: It seems that we are being treated as though we
were guilty. What we did was good and we did it only for the good of
the country.

Ambassador Taylor: Now let me tell you how I feel about it, what
I think the consequences are: first of all, this is a military coup that has
destroyed the government-making process that, to the admiration of the
whole world, was set up last fall largely through the statesman-like acts
of the Armed Forces.

You cannot go back to your units, General Ky. You military are
now back in power. You are up to your neck in politics.

Your statement makes it clear that you have constituted yourselves
again substantially as a Military Revolutionary Committee. The dissolution of the HNC was totally illegal. Your decree recognized the Chief
of State and the Huong Government but this recognition is something
that you could withdraw. This will be interpreted as a return of the military to power. . . .

Ambassador Taylor: Who commands the Armed Forces? General
Khanh?

General Ky: Yes, sir. . . .

General Thieu: In spite of what you say, it should be noted that
the Vietnamese Commander-in-Chief is in a special situation. He therefore needs advisors. We do not want to force General Khanh; we advise
him. We will do what he orders. . . .

Ambassador Taylor: Would your officers be willing to come into
a government if called upon to do so by Huong? I have been impressed
by the high quality of many Vietnamese officers. I am sure that many
of the most able men in this country are in uniform. Last fall when the
HNC and Huong Government was being formed, I suggested to General Khanh there should be some military participation, but my sugges-

tions were not accepted. It would therefore be natural for some of them now to be called upon to serve in the government. Would you be willing to do so? . . .

General Ky: Nonetheless, I would object to the idea of the military going back into the government right away. People will say it is a military coup.

Ambassador Taylor and *Ambassador Johnson:* (together) People will say it anyway. . . .

Ambassador Taylor: You have destroyed the Charter. The Chief of State will still have to prepare for elections. Nobody believes that the Chief of State has either the power or the ability to do this without the HNC or some other advisory body. If I were the Prime Minister, I would simply overlook the destruction of the HNC. But we are preserving the HNC itself. You need a legislative branch and you need this particular step in the formation of a government with National Assembly. . . .

Ambassador Taylor: It should be noted that Prime Minister Huong has not accepted the dissolution of the HNC. . . .

General Thieu: What kind of concession does Huong want from us?

Ambassador Taylor again noted the need for the HNC function.

General Thieu: After all, we did not arrest all the members of the HNC. Of nine members we detained only five. These people are not under arrest. They are simply under controlled residence. . . .

Ambassador Taylor: Our problem now, gentlemen, is to organize our work for the rest of the day. For one thing, the government will have to issue a communiqué.

General Thieu: We will still have a press conference this afternoon but only to say why we acted as we did.

Ambassador Taylor: I have real troubles on the U.S. side. I don't know whether we will continue to support you after this. Why don't you tell your friends before you act? I regret the need for my blunt talk today but we have lots at stake. . . .

Ambassador Taylor: And was it really all that necessary to carry out the arrests that very night? Couldn't this have been put off a day or two? . . .

In taking a friendly leave, Ambassador Taylor said: You people have broken a lot of dishes and now we have to see how we can straighten out this mess.

Chapter 4

America Goes to War, 1965

The spring-summer of 1965 may be the most crucial single period in the history of U.S. escalation of the war in Vietnam. During that time, the United States mounted a sustained, regular bombing campaign against North Vietnam, one that eventually reached enormous proportions. In the months that followed, the Johnson administration, carefully concealing or deliberately downplaying the importance of its moves, drastically increased the level of U.S. ground forces and authorized them to take offensive actions against North Vietnamese and Vietcong units. By the end of July 1965, the United States was committed to all-out war in Vietnam.

The bombing of North Vietnam began in February. For some time, top administration officials had agreed that regular bombing should be started. The appropriate time came in early February after the Vietcong had attacked an American base at Pleiku in the Central Highlands. The United States responded immediately with reprisal raids, Operation Flaming Dart. Within less than a month, the reprisal raids had shifted to regular bombing attacks, code-named Rolling Thunder. Officials disagreed among themselves on what the bombing might accomplish. Some saw it as a way to boost morale in South Vietnam; others saw it as a way to persuade North Vietnam to cease supporting the insurgency in the South. All saw it as a substitute for more drastic U.S. action.

These hopes were quickly dashed, and the air war became in time a reason for more drastic action. Additional ground forces were required to protect the air bases against enemy attack, and in early March a sizable detachment of marines—the first combat unit committed to the war—waded ashore at Danang. Within less than a month, these troops were authorized to take offensive action against NLF/NVA forces. As it became evident, moreover, that the bombing would not quickly achieve the goals set for it, if indeed it would achieve them at all, the military command in Saigon, supported by the Joint Chiefs of Staff, pressed for additional ground forces.

The crucial decisions came in July. General William C. Westmoreland had requested an additional forty-four battalions, including major units of the U.S. Army, and after nearly a month of intensive internal deliberations the President approved his request. South Vietnam again seemed on the verge of collapse. Internal division continued to mark the Saigon government, and the army suffered defeat after defeat at the hands of the enemy. The bombing was having limited effect. In these pressing circumstances, only the undersecretary of state, George Ball, and the personal adviser to the President, Clark Clifford, advocated a face-saving withdrawal. The President's other advisers, including most importantly Secretary of Defense McNamara, pressed for escalation as a way of upholding the U.S. commitment in Vietnam. The President eventually concurred, and on July 28, 1965, he announced what in retrospect appears to have been a decision for war in Vietnam.

Bundy Urges "Sustained Reprisal"

Bundy's memorandum to Johnson, dated February 7, 1965, was drafted aboard the President's plane, Air Force One, on a return flight from Vietnam and formally recommended what U.S. officials had long believed was needed: a full-scale bombing campaign against North Vietnam.

I. INTRODUCTORY

We believe that the best available way of increasing our chance of success in Vietnam is the development and execution of a policy of *sustained reprisal* against North Vietnam—a policy in which air and naval action against the North is justified by and related to the whole Viet Cong campaign of violence and terror in the South.

While we believe that the risks of such a policy are acceptable, we emphasize that its costs are real. It implies significant U.S. air losses even if no full air war is joined, and it seems likely that it would eventually require an extensive and costly effort against the whole air defense system of North Vietnam.

Yet measured against the costs of defeat in Vietnam, this program seems cheap. And even if it fails to turn the tide—as it may—the value of the effort seems to us to exceed its cost.

II. OUTLINE OF THE POLICY

In partnership with the Government of Vietnam, we should develop and exercise the option to retaliate against *any* VC act of violence to persons or property. . . .

2   In practice, we may wish at the outset to relate our reprisals to those acts of relatively high visibility such as the Pleiku incident. Later, we might retaliate against the assassination of a province chief, but not necessarily the murder of a hamlet official; we might retaliate against a grenade thrown into a crowded cafe in Saigon, but not necessarily to a shot fired into a small shop in the countryside.

3   Once a program of reprisals is clearly underway, it should not be necessary to connect each specific act against North Vietnam to a particular outrage in the South. It should be possible, for example, to publish weekly lists of outrages in the South and to have it clearly un-

derstood that these outrages are the cause of such action against the
North as may be occurring in the current period. Such a more general-
ized pattern of reprisal would remove much of the difficulty involved in
finding precisely matching targets in response to specific atrocities.
Even in such a more general pattern, however, it would be important to
insure that the general level of reprisal action remained in close corre-
spondence with the level of outrages in the South. We must keep it
clear at every stage both to Hanoi and to the world, that our reprisals
will be reduced or stopped when outrages in the South are reduced or
stopped—and that we are *not* attempting to destroy or conquer North
Vietnam.

4 In the early3 stages of such a course, we should take the appropriate occasion to make clear our firm intent to undertake reprisals on
any further acts, major or minor, that appear to us and the GVN as indicating Hanoi's support. We would announce that our two governments
have been patient and forebearing in the hope that Hanoi would come
to its senses without the necessity of our having to take further action;
but the outrages continue and now we must react against those who are
responsible; we will not provoke; we will not use our force indiscrimi-
nately; but we can no longer sit by in the face of repeated acts of terror
and violence for which the DRV is responsible.

5 Having once made this announcement, we should execute our
reprisal policy with as low a level of public noise as possible. It is to
our interest that our acts should be seen—but we do not wish to boast
about them in ways that make it hard for Hanoi to shift its ground. We
should instead direct maximum attention to the continuing acts of violence which are the cause of our continuing reprisals.

6 This reprisal policy should begin at a low level. Its level of
force and pressure should be increased only gradually—and as indicated above should be decreased if VC terror visibly decreased. The
object would not be to "win" an air war against Hanoi, but rather to influence the course of the struggle in the South.

7 At the same time it should be recognized that in order to maintain the power of reprisal without risk of excessive loss, an "air war"
may in fact be necessary. We should therefore be ready to develop a
separate justification for energetic flak suppression and if necessary for
the destruction of Communist air power. The presence of such an explanation should be that these actions are intended solely to insure the
effectiveness of a policy of reprisal, and in no sense represent any intent to wage offensive war against the North. These distinctions should
not be difficult to develop.

8 It remains quite possible, however, that this reprisal policy
would get us quickly into the level of military activity contemplated in

the so-called Phase II of our December planning. It may even get us beyond this level with both Hanoi and Peiping, if there is Communist counter-action. We and the GVN should also be prepared for a spurt of VC terrorism, especially in urban areas, that would dwarf anything yet experienced. These are the risks of any action. They should be carefully reviewed—but we believe them to be acceptable.

9 We are convinced that the political values of reprisal require a *continuous* operation. Episodic responses geared on a one-for-one basis to "spectacular" outrages would lack the persuasive force of sustained pressure. More important still, they would leave it open to the Communists to avoid reprisal entirely by giving up only a small element of their own program. The Gulf of Tonkin affair produced a sharp upturn in morale in South Vietnam. When it remained an isolated episode, however, there was a severe relapse. It is the great merit of the proposed scheme that to stop it the Communists would have to stop enough of their activity in the South to permit the probable success of a determined pacification effort.

III. EXPECTED EFFECT OF SUSTAINED REPRISAL POLICY

1 We emphasize that our primary target in advocating a reprisal policy is the improvement of the situation in *South* Vietnam. Action against the North is usually urged as a means of affecting the will of Hanoi to direct and support the VC. We consider this an important but longer-range purpose. The immediate and critical targets are in the South—in the minds of the South Vietnamese and in the minds of the Viet Cong cadres.

2 Predictions of the effect of any given course of action upon the states of mind of people are difficult. It seems very clear that if the United States and the Government of Vietnam join in a policy of reprisal, there will be a sharp immediate increase in optimism in the South, among nearly all articulate groups. The Mission believes—and our own conversations confirm—that in all sectors of Vietnamese opinion there is a strong belief that the United States could do much more if it would, and that they are suspicious of our failure to use more of our obviously enormous power. At least in the short run, the reaction to reprisal policy would be very favorable.

3 This favorable reaction should offer opportunity for increased American influence in pressing for a more effective government—at least in the short run. Joint reprisals would imply military planning in which the American role would necessarily be controlling, and this new relation should add to our bargaining power in other military efforts—

and conceivably on a wider plane as well if a more stable government is formed. We have the whip hand in reprisals as we do not in other fields.

4 The Vietnamese increase in hope could well increase the readiness of Vietnamese factions themselves to join together in forming a more effective government.

5 We think it plausible that effective and sustained reprisals, even in a low key, would have a substantial depressing effect upon the morale of Viet Cong cadres in South Vietnam. This is the strong opinion of CIA Saigon. It is based upon reliable reports of the initial Viet Cong reaction to the Gulf of Tonkin episode, and also upon the solid general assessment that the determination of Hanoi and the apparent timidity of the mighty United States are both major items in Viet Cong confidence.

6 The long-run effect of reprisals in the South is far less clear. It may be that like other stimulants, the value of this one would decline over time. Indeed the risk of this result is large enough so that we ourselves believe that a very major effort all along the line should be made in South Vietnam to take full advantage of the immediate stimulus of reprisal policy in its early stages. Our object should be to use this new policy to effect a visible upward turn in pacification, in governmental effectiveness, in operations against the Viet Cong, and in the whole U.S./GVN relationship. It is changes in these areas that can have enduring long-term effects.

7 While emphasizing the importance of reprisals in the South, we do not exclude the impact on Hanoi. We believe, indeed, that it is of great importance that the level of reprisal be adjusted rapidly and visibly to both upward and downward shifts in the level of Viet Cong offenses. We want to keep before Hanoi the carrot of our desisting as well as the stick of continued pressure. We also need to conduct the application of force so that there is always a prospect of worse to come.

8 We cannot assert that a policy of sustained reprisal will succeed in changing the course of the contest in Vietnam. It may fail, and we cannot estimate the odds of success with any accuracy—they may be somewhere between 25% and 75%. What we can say is that even if it fails, the policy will be worth it. At a minimum it will damp down the charge that we did not do all that we could have done, and this charge will be important in many countries, including our own. Beyond that, a reprisal policy—to the extent that it demonstrates U.S. willingness to employ this new norm in counter-insurgency—will set a higher price for the future upon all adventures of guerrilla warfare, and it should therefore somewhat increase our ability to deter such adventures. We must recognize, however, that that ability will be gravely weakened if there is failure for any reason in Vietnam.

IV. PRESENT ACTION RECOMMENDATIONS

1 This general recommendation was developed in intensive discussions in the days just before the attacks on Pleiku. These attacks and our reaction to them have created an ideal opportunity for the prompt development and execution of sustained reprisals. Conversely, if no such policy is now developed, we face the grave danger that Pleiku, like the Gulf of Tonkin, may be a short-run stimulant and a long-term depressant. We therefore recommend that the necessary preparations be made for continuing reprisals. The major necessary steps to be taken appear to us to be the following:

(1) We should complete the evacuation of dependents.

(2) We should quietly start the necessary westward deployments of [word illegible] contingency forces.

(3) We should develop and refine a running catalogue of Viet Cong offenses which can be published regularly and related clearly to our own reprisals. Such a catalogue should perhaps build on the foundation of an initial White Paper.

(4) We should initiate joint planning with the GVN on both the civil and military level. Specifically, we should give a clear and strong signal to those now forming a government that we will be ready for this policy when they are.

(5) We should develop the necessary public and diplomatic statements to accompany the initiation and continuation of this program.

(6) We should insure that a reprisal program is matched by renewed public commitment to our family of programs in the South, so that the central importance of the southern struggle may never be neglected.

(7) We should plan quiet diplomatic communication of the precise meaning of what we are and are not doing, to Hanoi, to Peking and to Moscow.

(8) We should be prepared to defend and to justify this new policy by concentrating attention in every forum upon its cause—the aggression in the South.

(9) We should accept discussion on these terms in any forum, but we should *not* now accept the idea of negotiations of any sort except on the basis of a stand down of Viet Cong violence. A program of sustained reprisal, with its direct link to Hanoi's continuing aggressive actions in the South, will not involve us in nearly the level of international recrimination which would be precipitated by a go-North program which was not so connected. For this reason the international pressures for negotiation should be quite manageable.

Washington Approves Rolling Thunder

These excerpts from a State Department cablegram to Ambassador Taylor, February 13, 1965, as provided in the body of the Pentagon study, indicate the President's decision to launch the Rolling Thunder bombing program. The words in brackets are also those of the study.

The President today approved the following program for immediate future actions in follow-up decisions he reported to you in Deptel 1653. [The first FLAMING DART reprisal decision.]

1   We will intensify by all available means the program of pacification within SVN.
2   We will execute a program of measured and limited air action jointly with GVN against selected military targets in DRV, remaining south of 19th parallel until further notice.

    FYI. Our current expectation is that these attacks might come about once or twice a week and involve two or three targets on each day of operation. END FYI.
3   We will announce this policy of measured action in general terms and at the same time, we will go to UN Security Council to make clear case that aggressor is Hanoi. We will also make it plain that we are ready and eager for "talks" to bring aggression to an end.
4   We believe that this 3-part program must be concerted with SVN, and we currently expect to announce it by Presidential statement directly after next authorized air action. We believe this action should take place as early as possible next week.
5   You are accordingly instructed to seek immediate GVN agreement on this program. You are authorized to emphasize our conviction that announcement of readiness to talk is stronger diplomatic position than awaiting inevitable summons to Security Council by third parties. We would hope to have appropriate GVN concurrence by Monday [Feb. 14th] if possible here.

    In presenting above to GVN, you should draw fully, as you see fit, on following arguments:
    a   We are determined to continue with military actions regardless of Security Council deliberations and any "talks" or negotiations when [words illegible]. [Beginning of sentence illegible] that they cease [words illegible] and also the activity they are directing in the south.

b We consider the UN Security Council initiative, following another strike, essential if we are to avoid being faced with really damaging initiatives by the USSR or perhaps by such powers as India, France, or even the UN.

c At an early point in the UN Security Council initiative, we would expect to see calls for the DRV to appear in the UN. If they failed to appear, as in August, this will make doubly clear that it is they who are refusing to desist, and our position in pursuing military actions against the DRV would be strengthened. For same reason we would now hope GVN itself would appear at UN and work closely with U.S.

d With or without Hanoi, we have every expectation that any "talks" that may result from our Security Council initiative would in fact go on for many weeks or perhaps months and would above all focus constantly on the cessation of military action against the DRV. We further anticipate that any detailed discussions about any possible eventual form of agreement returning to the essentials of the 1954 Accords would be postponed and would be subordinated to the central issue. . . .

McNaughton's March 1965 Proposals

This "Plan for Action for South Vietnam," appended to a memorandum from John T. McNaughton, assistant secretary of defense for international security affairs, to Secretary of Defense McNamara, March 24, 1965, outlines at great length the "trilemma" facing the United States at this time and the various options being considered. The opening statement of U.S. "aims" is often cited as typifying the mind-set of this period.

1 U.S. aims:

70%—To avoid a humiliating U.S. defeat (to our reputation as a guarantor).

20%—To keep SVN (and the adjacent) territory from Chinese hands.

10%—To permit people of SVN to enjoy a better, freer way of life.

ALSO—To emerge from crisis without unacceptable taint from methods used.

NOT—to "help a friend," although it would be hard to stay in if asked out.

2 The situation: The situation in general is bad and deteriorating. The VC have the initiative. Defeatism is gaining among the rural population, somewhat in the cities, and even among the soldiers—especially those with relatives in rural areas. The Hop Tac [pacification] area around Saigon is making little progress; the Delta stays bad; the country has been severed in the north. GVN control is shrinking to the enclaves, some burdened with refugees. In Saigon we have a remission: Quat is giving hope on the civilian side, the Buddhists have calmed, and the split generals are in uneasy equilibrium. . . .

Evaluation: It is essential—however badly SEA may go over the next 1–3 years—that U.S. emerge as a "good doctor." We must have kept promises, been tough, taken risks, gotten bloodied, and hurt the enemy very badly. We must avoid harmful appearances which will affect judgments by, and provide pretexts to, other nations regarding how the U.S. will behave in future cases of particular interest to those nations—regarding U.S. policy, power, resolve and competence to deal with their problems. In this connection, the relevant audiences are the Communists (who must feel strong pressures), the South Vietnamese (whose morale must be buoyed), our allies (who must trust us as "underwriters") and the U.S. public (which must support our risk-taking with U.S. lives and prestige).

Urgency: If the strike-North program (para 7) is not altered: we will reach the MIG/Phuc Yen flash point in approximately one month. If the program is altered only to stretch out the crescendo: up to 3 months may be had before that flash point, at the expense of a less persuasive squeeze. If the program is altered to "plateau" or dampen the strikes: much of their negotiating value will be lost. (Furthermore, there is now a hint of flexibility on the Red side: the Soviets are struggling to find a Gordian knot-cutter; the Chicoms may be wavering (Paris 5326).)

POSSIBLE COURSE

(1) Redouble efforts inside SVN (get better organized for it).
(2) Prepare to deploy U.S. combat troops in phases, starting with one Army division at Pleiku and a Marine MEF at Danang.
(3) Stretch out strike-North program, postponing Phuc Yen until June (exceed flash points only in specific retaliations).

(4)   Initiate talks along the following lines, bearing in mind that formal partition, or even a "Laos" partition, is out in SVN; we must
break the VC back or work out an accommodation.

PHASE ONE TALKS:
(A)   When: Now, before an avoidable flash point.
(B)   Who: U.S.-USSR, perhaps also U.S.-India. (Not with China
or Liberation Front; not through UK or France or [UN Secretary General] U Thant; keep alert to possibility that GVN
officials are talking under the table.)
(C)   How: With GVN consent, private, quiet (refuse formal
talks).
(D)   What:
  (1)   Offer to stop strikes on DRV and withhold deployment of large U.S. forces in trade for DRV stoppage
  of infiltration, communications to VC, and VC attacks, sabotage and terrorism, and for withdrawal of
  named units in SVN.
  (2)   Compliance would be policed unilaterally. If as is
  likely, complete compliance by the DRV is not forthcoming, we would carry out occasional strikes.
  (3)   We make clear that we are not demanding cessation
  of Red propaganda nor a public renunciation by
  Hanoi of its doctrines.
  (4)   Regarding "defensive" VC attacks—i.e., VC defending VC-held areas from encroaching ARVN forces—
  we take the public position that ARVN forces must be
  free to operate throughout SVN, especially in areas
  where amnesty is offered (but in fact, discretion will
  be exercised).
  (5)   Terrorism and sabotage, however, must be dampened
  markedly throughout the country, and civilian administrators must be free to move and operate freely, certainly in so-called contested areas (and perhaps even
  in VC base areas).

PHASE TWO TALKS:
(A)   When: At the end of Phase One.
(B)   Who: All interested nations.
(C)   How: Publicly in large conference.
(D)   What:
  (1)   Offer to remove U.S. combat forces from South Viet-
  nam in exchange for repatriation (or regroupment?) of
  DRV infiltrators for erection of international machin-

ery to verify the end of infiltration and communication.

(2)   Offer to seek to determine the will of the people under international supervision, with an appropriate reflection of those who favor the VC.

(3)   Any recognition of the Liberation Front would have
to be accompanied by disarming the VC and at least
avowed VC independence from DRV control.

PHASE THREE TALKS: Avoid any talks regarding the
future of all of Southeast Asia. Thailand's future should not
be up for discussion; and we have the 1954 and 1962
Geneva Accords covering the rest of the area. . . .

Special Points:

(1)   Play on DRV's fear of China.
(2)   To show good will, suspend strikes on North for a few days if requested by Soviets during efforts to mediate.
(3)   Have a contingency plan prepared to evacuate U.S. personnel in
case a para-9-type situation arises.
(4)   If the DRV will not "play" the above game, we must be prepared
(a) to risk passing some flash points, in the Strike-North program,
(b) to put more U.S. troops into SVN, and / or (c) to reconsider
our minimum acceptable outcome.

CIA Assessment of Air War

CIA Director John A. McCone's memo to Rusk, McNamara,
Bundy, and Taylor, April 2, 1965, as provided in the body of
the Pentagon study, raised major questions about the nature
of the bombing program and the change of mission of ground
forces. Paragraphs in italics are the study's paraphrase or explanation.

*McCone did not inherently disagree with the change in the U.S.
ground-force role, but felt that it was inconsistent with the decision to
continue the air strike program at the feeble level at which it was then
being conducted. McCone developed his argument as follows:*

I have been giving thought to the paper that we discussed in yesterday's meeting, which unfortunately I had little time to study, and also to the decision made to change the mission of our ground forces in South Vietnam from one of advice and static defense to one of active combat operations against the Viet Cong guerrillas.

I feel that the latter decision is correct only if our air strikes against the North are sufficiently heavy and damaging really to hurt the North Vietnamese. The paper we examined yesterday does not anticipate the type of air operation against the North necessary to force the NVN to reappraise their policy. On the contrary, it states, "We should continue roughly the present slowly ascending tempo of ROLLING THUNDER operations—," and later, in outlining the types of targets, states, "The target systems should continue to avoid the effective GCI range of MIG's," and these conditions indicate restraints which will not be persuasive to the NVN and would probably be read as evidence of a U.S. desire to temporize.

I have reported that the strikes to date have not caused a change in the North Vietnamese policy of directing Viet Cong insurgency, infiltrating cadres and supplying material. If anything, the strikes to date have hardened their attitude.

I have now had a chance to examine the 12-week program referred to by General Wheeler and it is my personal opinion that this program is not sufficiently severe and [words illegible] the North Vietnamese to [words illegible] policy.

On the other hand, we must look with care to our position under a program of slowly ascending tempo of air strikes. With the passage of each day and each week, we can expect increasing pressure to stop the bombing. This will come from various elements of the American public, from the press, the United Nations and world opinion. Therefore time will run against us in this operation and I think the North Vietnamese are counting on this.

Therefore I think what we are doing is starting on a track which involves ground force operations, which, in all probability, will have limited effectiveness against guerrillas, although admittedly will restrain some VC advances. However, we can expect requirements for an ever-increasing commitment of U.S. personnel without materially improving the chances of victory. I support and agree with this decision but I must point out that in my judgment, forcing submission of the VC can only be brought about by a decision in Hanoi. Since the contemplated actions against the North are modest in scale, they will not impose unacceptable damage on it, nor will they threaten the DRV's vital interests. Hence, they will not present them with a situation with which they cannot live, though such actions will cause the DRV pain and inconvenience.

I believe our proposed track offers great danger of simply encouraging Chinese Communists and Soviet support of the DRV and VC cause, if for no other reason than the risk for both will be minimum. I envision that the reaction of the NVN and Chinese Communists will be to deliberately, carefully, and probably gradually, build up the Viet Cong capabilities by covert infiltration of North Vietnamese and, possibly, Chinese cadres and thus bring an ever-increasing pressure on our forces. In effect, we will find ourselves mired down in combat in the jungle in a military effort that we cannot win, and from which we will have extreme difficulty in extracting ourselves.

Therefore it is my judgment that if we are to change the mission of the ground forces, we must also change the ground rules of the strikes against North Vietnam. We must hit them harder, more frequently, and inflict greater damage. Instead of avoiding the MIG's, we must go in and take them out. A bridge here and there will not do the job. We must strike their airfields, their petroleum resources, power stations and their military compounds. This, in my opinion, must be done promptly and with minimum restraint.

If we are unwilling to take this kind of a decision now, we must not take the actions concerning the mission of our ground forces for the reasons I have mentioned [words illegible].

NSAM 328 Enlarges Ground Forces and Changes Mission

National Security Action Memorandum 328, dated April 6, 1965, signed by McGeorge Bundy, and addressed to the secretary of state, the secretary of defense and the director of central intelligence, increased U.S. ground forces, changed their mission, and in section 11 called for these steps to be taken in ways that would disguise their significance.

On Thursday, April 1, the President made the following decisions with respect to Vietnam:

1 Subject to modifications in light of experience, to coordination and direction both in Saigon and in Washington, the President approved the 41-point program of non-military actions submitted by Ambassador Taylor in a memorandum dated March 31, 1965.

2 The President gave general approval to the recommendations submitted by Mr. [Carl] Rowan [head of the U.S. Information Agency] in his report dated March 16, with the exception that the President withheld approval of any request for supplemental funds at this time—it is his decision that this program is to be energetically supported by all agencies and departments and by the reprogramming of available funds as necessary within USIA.

3 The President approved the urgent exploration of the 12 suggestions for covert and other actions submitted by the Director of Central Intelligence under date of March 31.

4 The President repeated his earlier approval of the 21-point program of military actions submitted by [army Chief of Staff] General Harold K. Johnson under date of March 14 and re-emphasized his desire that aircraft and helicopter reinforcements under this program be accelerated.

5 The President approved an 18–20,000 man increase in U.S. military support forces to fill out existing units and supply needed logistic personnel.

6 The President approved the deployment of two additional Marine Battalions and one Marine Air Squadron and associated headquarters and support elements.

7 The President approved a change of mission for all Marine Battalions deployed to Vietnam to permit their more active use under conditions to be established and approved by the Secretary of Defense in consultation with the Secretary of State.

8 The President approved the urgent exploration, with the Korean, Australian, and New Zealand Governments, of the possibility of rapid deployment of significant combat elements from their armed forces in parallel with the additional Marine deployment approved in paragraph 6.

9 Subject to continuing review, the President approved the following general framework of continuing action against North Vietnam and Laos:

We should continue roughly the present slowly ascending tempo of ROLLING THUNDER operations being prepared to add strikes in response to a higher rate of VC operations, or conceivably to slow the pace in the unlikely event VC slacked off sharply for what appeared to be more than a temporary operational lull.

The target systems should continue to avoid the effective GCI range of MIGs. We should continue to vary the types of targets, stepping up attacks on lines of communication in the near future, and possibly moving in a few weeks to attacks on the rail lines north and northeast of Hanoi.

Leaflet operations should be expanded to obtain maximum practicable psychological effect on North Vietnamese population.

Blockade or aerial mining of North Vietnamese ports needs further study and should be considered for future operations. It would have major political complications, especially in relation to the Soviets and other third countries, but also offers many advantages.

Air operation in Laos, particularly route blocking operations in the Panhandle area should be stepped up to the maximum remunerative rate.

10   Ambassador Taylor will promptly seek the reactions of the South Vietnamese Government to appropriate sections of this program and their approval as necessary, and in the event of disapproval or difficulty at that end, these decisions will be appropriately reconsidered. In any event, no action into Vietnam under paragraphs 6 and 7 above should take place without GVN approval or further Presidential authorization.

11   The President desires that with respect to the actions in paragraphs 5 through 7, premature publicity be avoided by all possible precautions. The actions themselves should be taken as rapidly as practicable, but in ways that should minimize any appearance of sudden changes in policy, and official statements on these troop movements will be made only with the direct approval of the Secretary of Defense, in consultation with the Secretary of State. The President's desire is that these movements and changes should be understood as being gradual and wholly consistent with existing policy.

George Ball Opposes Escalation

Undersecretary of State George W. Ball consistently opposed the escalation of the war in 1964 and 1965. His July 1, 1965, memo to the President, "A Compromise Solution in South Vietnam," eloquently argued against the commitment of additional ground forces and urged that the United States cut its losses and get out of Vietnam.

(1)   A Losing War: The South Vietnamese are losing the war to the Viet Cong. No one can assure you that we can beat the Viet Cong or even force them to the conference table on our terms, no matter

how many hundred thousand *white,* foreign (U.S.) troops we deploy.

No one has demonstrated that a white ground force of whatever size can win a guerrilla war—which is at the same time a civil war between Asians—in jungle terrain in the midst of a population that refuses cooperation to the white forces (and the South Vietnamese) and thus provides a great intelligence advantage to the other side. Three recent incidents vividly illustrate this point: (a) the sneak attack on the Da Nang Air Base which involved penetration of a defense perimeter guarded by 9,000 Marines. This raid was possible only because of the cooperation of the local inhabitants; (b) the B52 raid that failed to hit the Viet Cong who had obviously been tipped off; (c) the search and destroy mission of the 173rd Air Borne Brigade which spent three days looking for the Viet Cong, suffered 23 casualties, and never made contact with the enemy who had obviously gotten advance word of their assignment.

(2) The Question to Decide: Should we limit our liabilities in South Vietnam and try to find a way out with minimal long-term costs?

The alternative—no matter what we may wish it to be—is almost certainly a protracted war involving an open-ended commitment of U.S. forces, mounting U.S. casualties, no assurance of a satisfactory solution, and a serious danger of escalation at the end of the road.

(3) Need for a Decision Now: So long as our forces are restricted to advising and assisting the South Vietnamese, the struggle will remain a civil war between Asian peoples. Once we deploy substantial numbers of troops in combat it will become a war between the U.S. and a large part of the population of South Vietnam, organized and directed from North Vietnam and backed by the resources of both Moscow and Peiping.

The decision you face now, therefore, is crucial. Once large numbers of U.S. troops are committed to direct combat, they will begin to take heavy casualties in a war they are ill-equipped to fight in a non-cooperative if not downright hostile countryside.

Once we suffer large casualties, we will have started a well-nigh irreversible process. Our involvement will be so great that we cannot—without national humiliation—stop short of achieving our complete objectives. *Of the two possibilities I think humiliation would be more likely than the achievement of our objectives—even after we have paid terrible costs.*

(4) Compromise Solution: Should we commit U.S. manpower and prestige to a terrain so unfavorable as to give a very large advan-

tage to the enemy—or should we seek a compromise settlement which achieves less than our stated objectives and thus cut our losses while we still have the freedom of maneuver to do so.

(5) Costs of Compromise Solution: The answer involves a judgment as to the cost to the U.S. of such a compromise settlement in terms of our relations with the countries in the area of South Vietnam, the credibility of our commitments, and our prestige around the world. In my judgment, if we act before we commit substantial U.S. troops to combat in South Vietnam we can, by accepting some short-term costs, avoid what may well be a long-term catastrophe. I believe we tended grossly to exaggerate the costs involved in a compromise settlement. An appreciation of probable costs is contained in the attached memorandum.

(6) With these considerations in mind, I strongly urge the following program:

(a) Military Program
   (1) Complete all deployments already announced—15 battalions—but decide not to go beyond a total of 72,000 men represented by this figure.
   (2) Restrict the combat role of the American forces to the June 19 announcement, making it clear to General Westmoreland that this announcement is to be strictly construed.
   (3) Continue bombing in the North but avoid the Hanoi-Haiphong area and any targets nearer to the Chinese border than those already struck.

(b) Political Program
   (1) In any political approaches so far, we have been the prisoners of whatever South Vietnamese government that was momentarily in power. If we are ever to move toward a settlement, it will probably be because the South Vietnamese government pulls the rug out from under us and makes its own deal or because we go forward quietly without advance prearrangement with Saigon.
   (2) So far we have not given the other side a reason to believe there is *any* flexibility in our negotiating approach. And the other side has been unwilling to accept what *in their terms* is complete capitulation.
   (3) Now is the time to start some serious diplomatic feelers looking towards a solution based on some application of a self-determination principle.
   (4) I would recommend approaching Hanoi rather than any of the other probable parties, the NLF—or Peiping.

Hanoi is the only one that has given any signs of interest in discussion. Peiping has been rigidly opposed. Moscow has recommended that we negotiate with Hanoi. The NLF has been silent.

(5)   There are several channels to the North Vietnamese but I think the best one is through their representative in Paris, Mai Van Bo. Initial feelers of Bo should be directed toward a discussion both of the four points we have put forward and the four points put forward by Hanoi as a basis for negotiation. We can accept all but one of Hanoi's four points, and hopefully we should be able to agree on some ground rules for serious negotiation—including no preconditions.

(6)   If the initial feelers lead to further secret, exploratory talks, we can inject the concept of self-determination that would permit the Viet Cong some hope of achieving some of their political objectives through local elections or some other device.

(7)   The contact on our side should be handled through a non-governmental cut-out (possibly a reliable newspaper man who can be repudiated).

(8)   If progress can be made at this level a basis can be laid for a multinational conference. At some point, obviously, the government of South Vietnam will have to be brought on board, but I would postpone this step until after a substantial feeling out of Hanoi.

(7)   Before moving to any formal conference we should be prepared to agree once the conference is started:

(a)   The U.S. will stand down its bombing of the North

(b)   The South Vietnamese will initiate no offensive operations in the South, and

(c)   The DRV will stop terrorism and other aggressive action against the South.

(8)   The negotiations at the conference should aim at incorporating our understanding with Hanoi in the form of a multi-national agreement guaranteed by the U.S., the Soviet Union and possibly other parties, and providing for an international mechanism to supervise its execution.

PROBABLE REACTIONS TO THE CUTTING OF OUR LOSSES IN SOUTH VIETNAM

We have tended to exaggerate the losses involved in a complete settlement in South Vietnam. There are three aspects to the problem that should be considered. First, the local effect of our action on nations in or near Southeast Asia. Second, the effect of our action on the credibility of our commitments around the world. Third, the effect on our position of world leadership.

A   Free Asian Reactions to a Compromise Settlement in South Vietnam Would Be Highly Parochial.

With each country interpreting the event primarily in terms of (a) its own immediate interest, (b) its sense of vulnerability to Communist invasion or insurgency, and (c) its confidence in the integrity of our commitment to its own security based on evidence other than that provided by our actions in South Vietnam.

Within this framework the following groupings emerge:

(1)   The Republic of China and Thailand: staunch allies whose preference for extreme U.S. actions including a risk of war with Communist China sets them apart from all other Asian nations;

(2)   The Republic of Korea and the Philippines: equally staunch allies whose support for strong U.S. action short of a war with Communist China would make post-settlement reassurance a pressing U.S. need;

(3)   Japan: it would prefer wisdom to valor in an area remote from its own interests where escalation could involve its Chinese or Eurasian neighbors or both;

(4)   Laos: a friendly neutral dependent on a strong Thai-U.S. guarantee of support in the face of increased Vietnamese and Laos pressures.

(5)   Burma and Cambodia: suspicious neutrals whose fear of antagonizing Communist China would increase their leaning toward Peiping in a conviction that the U.S. presence is not long for Southeast Asia; and

(6)   Indonesia: whose opportunistic marriage of convenience of both Hanoi and Peiping would carry it further in its overt aggression against Malaysia, convinced that foreign imperialism is a fast fading entity in the region.

Japan

Government cooperation [words illegible] essential in making the following points to the Japanese people:

(1)   U.S. support was given in full measure as shown by our casualties, our expenditures and our risk taking;

(2)   The U.S. record in Korea shows the credibility of our commitment so far as Japan is concerned.

The government as such supports our strong posture in Vietnam but stops short of the idea of a war between the U.S. and China.

Thailand

Thai commitments to the struggle within Laos and South Vietnam are based upon a careful evaluation of the regional threat to Thailand's security. The Thais are confident they can contain any threats from Indochina alone. They know, however, they cannot withstand the massive power of Communist China without foreign assistance. Unfortunately, the Thai view of the war has seriously erred in fundamental respects. They believe American power can do anything, both militarily and in terms of shoring up the Saigon regime. They now assume that we really could take over in Saigon and win the war if we felt we had to. If we should fail to do so, the Thais would initially see it as a failure of U.S. will. Yet time is on our side, providing we employ it effectively. Thailand is an independent nation with a long national history, and unlike South Vietnam, an acute national consciousness. It has few domestic Communists and none of the instability that plagues its neighbors, Burma and Malaysia. Its one danger area in the northeast is well in hand so far as preventive measures against insurgency are concerned. Securing the Mekong Valley will be critical in any long-run solution, whether by the partition of Laos with Thai-U.S. forces occupying the western half or by some [word illegible] arrangement. Providing we are willing to make the effort, Thailand can be a foundation of rock and not a bed of sand in which to base our political/military commitment to Southeast Asia.

—With the exception of the nations in Southeast Asia, a compromise settlement in South Vietnam should not have a major impact on the credibility of our commitments around the world. . . . Chancellor [Ludwig] Erhard [of West Germany] has told us privately that the people of Berlin would be concerned by a compromise settlement of South Vietnam. But this was hardly an original thought, and I suspect he was telling us what he believed we would like to hear. After all, the confidence of the West Berliners will depend more on what they see on the spot than on [word illegible] news or events halfway around the world. In my observation, the principal anxiety of our NATO Allies is that we have become too preoccupied with an area which seems to them an irrelevance and may be tempted in neglect to our NATO responsibilities. Moreover, they have a vested interest in an easier relationship between Washington and Moscow. By and large, therefore, they will be inclined to regard a compromise solution in South Vietnam more as new evidence of American maturity and judgment than of American loss of face. . . . On balance, I believe we would more seriously undermine the effectiveness of our world leadership by continuing the war and deepening our involvement than by pursuing a carefully plotted course toward a compromise solution. In spite of the number of powers that have—in response to our pleading—given verbal support from feeling of loyalty and dependence, we cannot ignore the fact that the war is vastly unpopular and that our role in it is perceptively eroding the respect and confidence with which other nations regard us. We have not persuaded either our friends or allies that our further involvement is essential to the defense of freedom in the cold war. Moreover, the [more] men we deploy in the jungles of South Vietnam, the more we contribute to a growing world anxiety and mistrust.

[Words illegible] the short run, of course, we could expect some catcalls from the sidelines and some vindictive pleasure on the part of Europeans jealous of American power. But that would, in my view, be a transient phenomenon with which we could live without sustained anguish. Elsewhere around the world I would see few unhappy implications for the credibility of our commitments. No doubt the Communists will [try] to gain propaganda value in Africa, but I cannot seriously believe that the Africans care too much about what happens in Southeast Asia. Australia and New Zealand are, of course, special cases since they feel lonely in the far reaches of the Pacific. Yet even their concern is far greater with Malaysia than with South Vietnam, and the degree of their anxiety would be conditioned largely by expressions of our support for Malaysia.

[Words illegible] Quite possibly President [Charles] de Gaulle [of France] will make propaganda about perfidious Washington, yet even he will be inhibited by his much-heralded disapproval of our activities in South Vietnam.

South Korea—As for the rest of the Far East the only serious point of concern might be South Korea. But if we stop pressing the Koreans for more troops to Vietnam (the Vietnamese show no desire for additional Asian forces since it affronts their sense of pride) we may be able to cushion Korean reactions to a compromise in South Vietnam by the provision of greater military and economic assistance. In this regard, Japan can play a pivotal role now that it has achieved normal relations with South Korea.

McNamara Urges Major Expansion of Ground Forces

Ultimately, McNamara, rather than Ball, carried the day. These excerpts from his memorandum to President Johnson, drafted on July 1, 1965, and revised on July 20, as provided in the body of the Pentagon's study, developed the rationale for the administration's major decisions to sharply increase the number of ground forces and adopt an aggressive, search-and-destroy strategy. Paragraphs in italics are the study's paraphrase or explanation.

In a memorandum to the President drafted on 1 July and then revised on 20 July, immediately following his return from a week-long visit to Vietnam, he recommended an immediate decision to increase the U.S.-Third Country presence from the current 16 maneuver battalions (15 U.S., one Australian), and a change in the mission of these forces from one of providing support and reinforcement for the ARVN to one which soon became known as "search and destroy"—as McNamara put it, they were "by aggressive exploitation of superior military forces . . . to gain and hold the initiative . . . pressing the fight against VC-DRV main force units in South Vietnam to run them to ground and destroy them.". . .

His specific recommendations, he noted, were concurred in by General Wheeler and Ambassador-designate Lodge, who accompanied him on his trip to Vietnam, and by Ambassador Taylor, Ambassador Johnson, Admiral Sharp and General Westmoreland, with whom he conferred there. The rationale for his decisions was supplied by the CIA, whose assessment he quoted with approval in concluding that 1 July version of his memorandum. It stated:

Over the longer term we doubt if the Communists are likely to change their basic strategy in Vietnam (i.e., aggressive and steadily mounting insurgency) unless and until two conditions prevail: (1) they are forced to accept a situation in the war in the South which offers them no prospect of an early victory and no grounds for hope that they can simply outlast the U.S. and (2) North Vietnam itself is under continuing and increasingly damaging punitive attack. So long as the Communists think they scent the possibility of an early victory (which is probably now the case), we believe that they will persevere and accept

extremely severe damage to the North. Conversely, if North Vietnam
itself is not hurting, Hanoi's doctrinaire leaders will probably be ready
to carry on the Southern struggle almost indefinitely. If, however, both
of the conditions outlined above should be brought to pass, we believe
Hanoi probably would, at least for a period of time, alter its basic strategy and course of action in South Vietnam.

*McNamara's memorandum of 20 July did not include this quota-
tion, although many of these points were made elsewhere in the paper.
Instead, it concluded with an optimistic forecast:*

The overall evaluation is that the course of action recommended in
this memorandum—if the military and political moves are properly integrated and executed with continuing vigor and visible determination—stands a good chance of achieving an acceptable outcome within
a reasonable time in Vietnam.

*Never again while he was Secretary of Defense would McNamara
make so optimistic a statement about Vietnam—except in public.*

*This concluding paragraph of McNamara's memorandum spoke
of political, as well as military, "vigor" and "determination." Earlier
in the paper, under the heading "Expanded political moves," he had
elaborated on this point, writing:*

Together with the above military moves, we should take political
initiatives in order to lay a groundwork for a favorable political settlement by clarifying our objectives and establishing channels of communications. At the same time as we are taking steps to turn the tide in
South Vietnam, we would make quiet moves through diplomatic channels (a) to open a dialogue with Moscow and Hanoi, and perhaps the
VC, looking first toward disabusing them of any misconceptions as to
our goals and second toward laying the groundwork for a settlement
when the time is ripe; (b) to keep the Soviet Union from deepening its
military [sic] in the world until the time when settlement can be
achieved; and (c) to cement support for U.S. policy by the U.S. public,
allies and friends, and to keep international opposition at a manageable
level. Our efforts may be unproductive until the tide begins to turn, but
nevertheless they should be made.

*Here was scarcely a program for drastic political action. McNa-
mara's essentially procedural (as opposed to substantive) recommendations amounted to little more than saying that the United States
should provide channels for the enemy's discreet and relatively face-
saving surrender when he decided that the game had grown too costly.
This was, in fact, what official Washington (again with the exception of*

Ball) meant in mid-1965 when it spoke of a "political settlement." (As McNamara noted in a footnote, even this went too far for Ambassador-designate Lodge, whose view was that "any further initiative by us now [before we are strong] would simply harden the Communist resolve not to stop fighting." In this view Ambassadors Taylor and Johnson concurred, except that they would maintain "discreet contacts with the Soviets.")

McNamara's concluding paragraph spoke of "an acceptable outcome." Previously in his paper he had listed "nine fundamental elements" of a favorable outcome. These were:

(a)   VC stop attacks and drastically reduce incidents of terror and sabotage.

(b)   DRV reduces infiltration to a trickle, with some reasonably reliable method of our obtaining confirmation of this fact.

(c)   U.S./GVN stop bombing of North Vietnam.

(d)   GVN stays independent (hopefully pro-U.S., but possibly genuinely neutral).

(e)   GVN exercises governmental functions over substantially all of South Vietnam.

(f)   Communists remain quiescent in Laos and Thailand.

(g)   DRV withdraws PAVN forces and other North Vietnamese infiltrators (not regroupees) from South Vietnam.

(h)   VC/NLF transform from a military to a purely political organization.

(i)   U.S. combat forces (not advisors or AID) withdraw.

Chapter 5

Stalemate, 1965–1966

The open-ended commitment of July 1965 led over the next eighteen months to steady escalation of both the ground and air wars. By the end of 1966, the United States had close to 400,000 ground troops in Vietnam, and General Westmoreland was waging an aggressive and relentless campaign against North Vietnamese and Vietcong main-force units. After a brief bombing pause in early 1966, the administration again expanded the bombing, attacking North Vietnamese petroleum, oil, and lubricant (POL) resources in June and in the ensuing months moving closer and closer to the major cities of Hanoi and Haiphong and the Chinese border.

As with earlier escalations, expansion of the war in 1965–1966 did not produce the desired results. On the ground, the North Vietnamese matched each U.S. escalation with one of their own. In a series of battles in the Ia Drang Valley in November 1965, U.S. forces engaged North Vietnamese regulars, inflicting huge losses but incurring heavy casualties themselves. In the months that followed, the North Vietnamese and Vietcong retained the strategic initiative, fighting when the situation favored them, retreating into sanctuaries in

Laos, Cambodia, or across the demilitarized zone when it did not. Most U.S. officials also agreed that the bombing had not worked, a conclusion borne out in a number of gloomy assessments in 1966. The military argued that it needed to be expanded; fearful of provoking Soviet and Chinese intervention, McNamara and other civilian advisers increasingly concluded that it was doing more harm than good.

More and more aware that they were caught up in a bloody and very costly stalemate, Johnson and his advisers grappled for alternatives. The military insistently pressed for mobilizing the reserves, expanding the bombing, and enlarging ground forces, in short for all-out war. McNamara and other civilians feared the implications of the military's proposals and sought other methods. The President and the secretary of defense looked toward what was called "pacification," economic, political, and military programs to win the rural population over to the Saigon government, as a means of succeeding while limiting costs to the United States. McNamara also pressed, as an alternative to the bombing, for construction of an electronic barrier to limit North Vietnamese infiltration into South Vietnam, a concept the military came to scorn as "McNamara's Line." The stage was set for a major debate on policy and strategy in 1967.

McNamara's November 1965 Assessment of the War

These excerpts from a McNamara memorandum for President Johnson, written on November 30, 1965, after the secretary's return from Vietnam, reveal for the first time doubts on McNamara's part that the war could be won. Despite these doubts, he recommended that the United States continue on its present course.

. . . The [Nguyen Cao] Ky "government of generals" is surviving, but not acquiring wide support or generating actions; pacification is thoroughly stalled, with no guarantee that security anywhere is permanent and no indications that able and willing leadership will emerge in the absence of that permanent security. (Prime Minister Ky estimates that his government controls only 25% of the population today and reports that his pacification chief hopes to increase that to 50% two years from now.)

The dramatic recent changes in the situation are on the military side. They are the increased infiltration from the North and the increased willingness of the Communist forces to stand and fight, even in large-scale engagements. The Ia Drang River Campaign of early November is an example. The Communists appear to have decided to increase their forces in SVN both by heavy recruitment in the South (especially in the Delta) and by infiltration of regular NVN forces from the North. . . . The enemy can be expected to enlarge his present strength of 110 battalion equivalents to more than 150 battalion equivalents by the end of calendar 1966, when hopefully his losses can be made to equal his input.

As for the Communist ability to supply this force, it is estimated that, even taking account of interdiction of routes by air and sea, more than 200 tons of supplies a day can be infiltrated—more than enough, allowing for the extent to which the enemy lives off the land, to support the likely PAVN/VC force at the likely level of operations.

To meet this possible—and in my view likely—Communist buildup, the presently contemplated Phase I forces will not be enough (approx 220,000 Americans, almost all in place by end of 1965). Bearing in mind the nature of the war, the expected weighted combat force ratio of less than 2-to-1 will not be good enough. Nor will the originally contemplated Phase II addition of 28 more U.S. battalions (112,000

men) be enough; the combat force ratio, even with 32 new SVNese battalions, would still be little better than 2-to-1 at the end of 1966. The
initiative which we have held since August would pass to the enemy;
we would fall far short of what we expected to achieve in terms of population control and disruption of enemy bases and lines of communications. Indeed, it is estimated that with the contemplated Phase II addition of 28 U.S. battalions, we would be able to hold our present
geographical positions. . . .

3   We have but two options, it seems to me. One is to go now for
a compromise solution (something substantially less than the "favorable outcome" I described in my memo of Nov. 3) and hold further deployments to a minimum. The other is to stick with our stated objectives and with the war, and provide what it takes in men and materiel. If
it is decided not to move now toward a compromise, I recommend that
the U.S. both send a substantial number of additional troops and very
gradually intensify the bombing of NVN. Amb. Lodge, Wheeler, Sharp
and Westmoreland concur in this prolonged course of action, although
Wheeler and Sharp would intensify the bombing of the North more
quickly.

(recommend up to 74 battalions by end-66: total to approx
400,000 by end-66.) And it should be understood that further deployments (perhaps exceeding 200,000) may be needed in 1967.) Bombing
of NVN. . . . over a period of the next six months we gradually enlarge
the target system in the northeast (Hanoi-Haiphong) quadrant until, at
the end of the period, it includes "controlled" reconnaissance of lines of
comm throughout the area, bombing of petroleum storage facilities and
power plants, and mining of the harbors. (Left unstruck would be population targets, industrial plants, locks and dams.)

4   Pause in bombing NVN. It is my belief that there should be a
three- or four-week pause in the program of bombing the North before
we either greatly increase our troop deployments to VN or intensify our
strikes against the North. (My recommendation for a "pause" is not
concurred in by Lodge, Wheeler or Sharp.) The reasons for this belief
are, first, that we must lay a foundation in the minds of the American
public and in world opinion for such an enlarged phase of the war and
second, we should give NVN a face-saving chance to stop the aggression. I am not seriously concerned about the risk of alienating the SV-
Nese, misleading Hanoi, or being "trapped" in a pause; if we take reasonable precautions, we can avoid these pitfalls. I am seriously
concerned about embarking on a markedly higher level of war in VN
without having tried, through a pause, to end the war or at least having
made it clear to our people that we did our best to end it.

5   Evaluation. We should be aware that deployments of the kind I

have recommended will not guarantee success. U.S. killed-in-action can be expected to reach 1000 a month, and the odds are even that we will be faced in early 1967 with a "no-decision" at an even higher level. My over-all evaluation, nevertheless, is that the best chance of achieving our stated objectives lies in a pause followed, if it fails, by the deployments mentioned above.

McNamara's Early Doubts

These excerpts from McNamara's December 7, 1965, memorandum for the President reaffirmed the doubts expressed on November 30 and reiterated the recommendations.

. . . We believe that, wheth er or not major new diplomatic initiatives are made, the U.S. must send a substantial number of additional forces to VN if we are to avoid being defeated there. (30 Nov program; concurred in by JCS)

IV Prognosis assuming the recommended deployments

Deployments of the kind we have recommended will not guarantee success. Our intelligence estimate is that the present Communist policy is to continue to prosecute the war vigorously in the South. They continue to believe that the war will be a long one, that time is their ally, and that their own staying power is superior to ours. They recognize that the U.S. reinforcements of 1965 signify a determination to avoid defeat, and that more U.S. troops can be expected. Even though the Communists will continue to suffer heavily from GVN and U.S. ground and air action, we expect them, upon learning of any U.S. intentions to augment its forces, to boost their own commitment and to test U.S. capabilities and will to persevere at higher level of conflict and casualties (U.S. KIA with the recommended deployments can be expected to reach 1000 a month).

If the U.S. were willing to commit enough forces—perhaps 600,000 men or more—we could ultimately prevent the DRV/VC from sustaining the conflict at a significant level. When this point was reached, however, the question of Chinese intervention would become critical. (We are generally agreed that the Chinese Communists will intervene with combat forces to prevent destruction of the Communist regime in the DRV. It is less clear whether they would intervene to prevent a DRV/VC defeat in the South.) The intelligence estimate is that the chances are a little better than even that, at this stage, Hanoi and Peiping would choose to reduce the effort in the South and try to salvage their resources for another day; but there is an almost equal chance that they would enlarge the war and bring in large numbers of Chinese forces (they have made certain preparations which could point in this direction).

It follows, therefore, that the odds are about even that, even with the recommended deployments, we will be faced in early 1967 with a military standoff at a much higher level, with pacification still stalled, and with any prospect of military success marred by the chances of an active Chinese intervention.

(memo of 24 jan 66: JCS believe that "the evaluation set forth in Par. 7 is on the pessimistic side in view of the constant and heavy military pressure which our forces in SEA will be capable of employing. While admittedly the following factors are to a degree imponderables, they believe that greater weight should be given to the following:

a   The cumulative effect of our air campaign against the DRV on morale and DRV capabilities to provide and move men and materiel from the DRV to SVN.

b   The effects of constant attack and harassment on the ground and from the air upon the growth of VC forces and on the morale and combat effectiveness of VC / PAVN forces.

c   The effect of destruction of VC base areas on the capabilities of VC/PAVN forces to sustain combat operations over an extended period of time.

d   The constancy of will of the Hanoi leaders to continue a struggle which they realize they cannot win in the face of progressively greater destruction of their country.")

McNaughton Hints at Compromise

These excerpts from a McNaughton memo, "Some Paragraphs on Vietnam," third draft, January 19, 1966, as provided in the body of the Pentagon study, hinted at the possibility of a compromise peace but in general recommended a continuation of existing policies. Paragraphs in italics are the analysis paraphrase or explanation.

McNaughton prepared a second memorandum complementing and partially modifying the one on bombing. It concerned the context for the decision. Opening with a paragraph which warned, "We . . . have in Vietnam the ingredients of an enormous miscalculation," it sketched the dark outlines of the Vietnamese scene:

. . . The ARVN is tired, passive and accommodation-prone. . . . The PAVN/VC are effectively matching our deployments. . . . The bombing of the North . . . may or may not be able effectively to interdict infiltration (partly because the PAVN/VC can simply refuse to do battle if supplies are short). . . . Pacification is stalled despite effort and hopes. The GVN political infrastructure is moribund and weaker than the VC infrastructure among most of the rural population. . . . South Vietnam is near the edge of inflation and economic chaos.

The situation might alter for the better, McNaughton conceded. "Attrition—save Chinese intervention—may push the DRV 'against the stops' by the end of 1966." Recent RAND motivation and morale studies showed VC spirit flagging and their grip on the peasantry growing looser. "The Ky government is coming along, not delivering its promised 'revolution' but making progress slowly and gaining experience and stature each week." Though McNaughton termed it "doubtful that a meaningful ceiling can be put on the infiltration," he said "there is no doubt that the cost of infiltration can . . . be made very high and that the flow of supplies can be reduced substantially below what it would otherwise be." Possibly bombing, combined with other pressures, could bring the DRV to consider terms after "a period of months, not of days or even weeks."

The central point of McNaughton's memorandum, following from its opening warning, was that the United States, too, should consider coming to terms. He wrote:

C   The present U.S. objective in Vietnam is to avoid humiliation. The reasons why we *went into* Vietnam to the present depth are varied; but they are now largely academic. Why we have *not withdrawn* from Vietnam is, by all odds, *one* reason: (1) to preserve our reputation as a guarantor, and thus to preserve our effectiveness in the rest of the world. We have not hung on (2) to save a friend, or (3) to deny the Communists the added acres and heads (because the dominoes don't fall for that reason in this case), or even (4) to prove that "wars of national liberation" won't work (except as our reputation is involved). At each decision point we have gambled; at each point, to avoid the damage to our effectiveness of defaulting on our commitment, we have upped the ante. We have not defaulted, and the ante (and commitment) is now very high. It is important that we behave so as to protect our reputation. At the same time, since it is our *reputation* that is at stake, it is important that we not construe our obligation to be more than do the countries whose opinions of us *are* our reputation.

D **We are in an escalating military stalemate.** There is an honest difference of judgment as to the success of the present military efforts in the South. There is no question that the U.S. deployments thwarted the VC hope to achieve a quick victory in 1965. But there is a serious question whether we are now defeating the VC / PAVN main forces and whether planned U.S. deployments will more than hold our position in the country. Population and area control has not changed significantly in the past year; and the best judgment is that, even with the Phase IIA deployments, we will probably be faced in early 1967 with a continued stalemate at a higher level of forces and casualties. . . .

   2 **U.S. commitment to SVN.** Some will say that we have defaulted if we end up, at any point in the relevant future, with anything less than a Western-oriented, non-Communist, independent government, exercising effective sovereignty over all of South Vietnam. This is not so. As stated above, the U.S. end is solely to preserve our reputation as a guarantor. It follows that the "softest" credible formulation of the U.S. commitment is the following:
   a DRV does not take over South Vietnam by force. This does not *necessarily* rule out:
   b A coalition government including Communists.
   c A free decision by the South to succumb to the VC or to the North.
   d A neutral (or even anti-U.S.) government in SVN.
   e A live-and-let-live "reversion to 1959." Furthermore, we must recognize that even if we fail in achieving this "soft" formulation, we could over time come out with minimum damage:

f   If the reason was GVN gross wrongheadedness or apathy.
g   If victorious North Vietnam "went Titoist."
h   If the Communist take-over was fuzzy and very slow.

Current decisions, McNaughton argued, should reflect awareness that the U.S. commitment could be fulfilled with something considerably short of victory. "It takes time to make hard decisions," he wrote, "It took us almost a year to take the decision to bomb North Vietnam; it took us weeks to decide on a pause; it could take us months (and could involve lopping some white as well as brown heads) to get us in position to go for a compromise. We should not expect the enemy's molasses to pour any faster than ours. And we should 'tip the pitchers' now if we want them to 'pour' a year from now."

But the strategy following from this analysis more or less corresponded over the short term to that recommended by the Saigon mission and the military commands: More effort for pacification, more push behind the Ky government, more battalions for MACV, and intensive interdiction bombing roughly as proposed by CINCPAC. The one change introduced in this memorandum, prepared only one day after the other, concerned North Vietnamese ports. Now McNaughton advised that the ports not be closed.

The argument which coupled McNaughton's political analysis with his strategic recommendations appeared at the end of the second memorandum:

The dilemma. We are in a dilemma. It is that the situation may be "polar." That is, it may be that while going for victory we have the strength for compromise, but if we go for compromise we have the strength only for defeat—this because a revealed lowering of sights from victory to compromise (a) will unhinge the GVN and (b) will give the DRV the "smell of blood." The situation therefore requires a thoroughly loyal and disciplined U.S. team in Washington and Saigon and great care in what is said and done. It also requires a willingness to escalate the war if the enemy miscalculates, misinterpreting our willingness to compromise as implying we are on the run. The risk is that it may be that the "coin must come up heads or tails, not on edge."

Proposal for an Anti-Infiltration Barrier

The notion of an anti-infiltration barrier was first raised in these excerpts from a McNaughton memorandum, given to McNamara on March 22, 1966, as provided in the body of the Pentagon study. Entitled "A Barrier Strategy," the document was based on a January 3, 1966, draft memo, "A Barrier Strategy," by Prof. Roger D. Fisher of Harvard Law School.

B. PRESENT MILITARY SITUATION IN NORTH VIETNAM

1 Physical consequences of bombing
a The DRV has suffered some physical hardship and pain, raising the cost to it of supporting the VC.
b Best intelligence judgment is that:
(1) Bombing may or may not—by destruction or delay—have resulted in net reduction in the flow of men or supplies to the forces in the South;
(2) Bombing has failed to reduce the limit on the capacity of the DRV to aid the VC to a point below VC needs;
(3) Future bombing of North Vietnam cannot be expected physically to limit the military support given the VC by the DRV to a point below VC needs.

2 Influence consequences of bombing
a There is no evidence that bombings have made it more likely the DRV will decide to back out of the war.
b Nor is there evidence that bombings have resulted in an increased DRV resolve to continue the war to an eventual victory. [Fisher's draft had read "There is some evidence that bombings. . . ."]

C. FUTURE OF A BOMBING STRATEGY

Although bombings of North Vietnam improve GVN morale and provide a counter in eventual negotiations (should they take place) there is no evidence that they meaningfully reduce either the capacity or the will for the DRV to support the VC. The DRV knows that we cannot force them to stop by bombing and that we cannot, without an unacceptable risk of a major war with China or Russia or both, force them to stop by conquering them or "blotting them out." Knowing that if they are not influenced we cannot stop them, the DRV will remain difficult to influence. With continuing DRV support, victory in the South may remain forever beyond our reach.

Having made the case against bombing, the memo then spelled out the case for an anti-infiltration barrier:

II. SUBSTANCE OF THE BARRIER PROPOSAL

A That the U.S. and GVN adopt the concept of physically cutting off DRV support to the VC by an on-the-ground barrier across the Ho Chi Minh Trail in the general vicinity of the 17th Parallel and Route 9. To the extent necessary the barrier would run from the sea across Vietnam and Laos to the Mekong, a straightline distance of about 160 miles.

B That in Laos an "interdiction and verification zone," perhaps 10 miles wide, be established and legitimated by such measures as leasing, international approval, compensation, etc.

C That a major military and engineering effort be directed toward constructing a physical barrier of minefields, barbed wire, walls, ditches and military strong points flanked by a defoliated strip on each side.

D That such bombing in Laos and North Vietnam as takes place be narrowly identified with interdiction and with the construction of the barrier by

    1 Being within the 10-mile-wide interdiction zone in Laos, or

    2 Being in support of the construction of the barrier, or

    3 Being interdiction bombing pending the completion of the barrier.

E That, of course, intensive interdiction continues at sea and from Cambodia.

(It might be stated that all bombings of North Vietnam will stop as soon as there is no infiltration and no opposition to the construction of the verification barrier.)

Johnson Presses for "Coonskins on the Wall"

Among all the programs in Vietnam, President Johnson was most deeply committed to pacification. These excerpts from his remarks to senior U.S. and South Vietnamese officials at a conference in Honolulu, February 9, 1966, represent a rallying cry to get long-stalled programs moving. The paragraph in italics is the study's explanation.

(The Vietnamese then thanked the Americans for the conference, and in turn some of the senior members of the American delegation—in order, Admiral Sharp, Leonard Marks, General Wheeler, Ambassador Lodge, Ambassador [Averell] Harriman—made brief statements about the meaning of the conference. The President then made his final statement:

. . . Preserve this communiqué, because it is one we don't want to forget. It will be a kind of bible that we are going to follow. When we come back here 90 days from now, or six months from now, we are going to start out and make reference to the announcements that the President, the Chief of State and the Prime Minister made in paragraph 1, and what the leaders and advisors reviewed in paragraph 2. . . . You men who are responsible for these departments, you ministers, and the staffs associated with them in both governments, bear in mind we are going to give you an examination and the finals will be on just what you have done.

In paragraph 5; how have you built democracy in the rural areas? How much of it have you built, when and where? Give us dates, times, numbers.

In paragraph 2; larger outputs, more efficient production to improve credit, handicraft, light industry, rural electrification—are those just phrases, high-sounding words, or have you coonskins on the wall. . . .

Next is health and education, Mr. Gardner. We don't want to talk about it; we want to do something about it. "The President pledges he will dispatch teams of experts." Well, we better do something besides dispatching. They should get out there. We are going to train health personnel. How many? You don't want to be like the fellow who was playing poker and when he made a big bet they called him and said "what have you got?" He said "aces" and they asked "how many" and he said "one aces.". . .

Next is refugees. That is just as hot as a pistol in my country. You don't want me to raise a white flag and surrender so we have to do something about that. . . .

Growing military effectiveness: we have not gone in because we don't want to overshadow this meeting here with bombs, with mortars, with hand grenades, with "Masher" movements. I don't know who names your operations, but "Masher." I get kind of mashed myself. But we haven't gone into the details of growing military effectiveness for two or three reasons. One, we want to be able honestly and truthfully to say that this has not been a military build-up conference of the world here in Honolulu. We have been talking about building a society following the outlines of the Prime Minister's speech yesterday.

Second, this is not the place, with 100 people sitting around, to build a military effectiveness.

Third, I want to put it off as long as I can, having to make these crucial decisions. I enjoy this agony. . . . I don't want to come out of this meeting that we have come up here and added on X divisions and Y battalions or Z regiments or D dollars, because one good story about how many billions are going to be spent can bring us more inflation that we are talking about in Vietnam. We want to work those out in the quietness of the Cabinet Room after you have made your recommendations, General Wheeler, Admiral Sharp, when you come to us. . . .

Walt Rostow on POL Bombing

Walt W. Rostow replaced McGeorge Bundy as presidential assistant for national security in the spring of 1966. Certain that carefully measured bombing could be decisive, he developed in this memo to Rusk and McNamara, May 6, 1966, the case for striking North Vietnam's POL resources. Paragraphs in italics are the study's paraphrase or explanation.

Rostow developed his argument for striking the petroleum reserves on the basis of U.S. experience in the World War II attacks on German oil supplies and storage facilities. His reasoning was as follows:

From the moment that serious and systematic oil attacks started, front line single engine fighter strength and tank mobility were affected. The reason was this: It proved much more difficult, in the face of general oil shortage, to allocate from less important to more important uses than the simple arithmetic of the problem would suggest. Oil moves in various logistical channels from central sources. When the central sources began to dry up the effects proved fairly prompt and widespread. What look like reserves statistically are rather inflexible commitments to logistical pipelines.

The same results might be expected from heavy and sustained attacks on the North Vietnamese oil reserves.

With an understanding that simple analogies are dangerous, I nevertheless feel it is quite possible the military effects of a systematic and sustained bombing of POL in North Vietnam may be more prompt and direct than conventional intelligence analysis would suggest.

I would underline, however, the adjectives "systematic and sustained." If we take this step we must cut clean through the POL system—and hold the cut—if we are looking for decisive results. . . .

JCS Order POL Attacks

In this cablegram to Admiral U. S. Grant Sharp, commander in chief of Pacific forces, June 22, 1966, the Joint Chiefs ordered attacks on North Vietnam's POL.

Strikes to commence with initial attacks against Haiphong and Hanoi POL on same day if operationally feasible. Make maximum effort to attain operational surprise. Do not conduct initiating attacks under marginal weather conditions but reschedule when weather assures success. Follow-on attacks authorized as operational and weather factors dictate.

At Haiphong, avoid damage to merchant shipping. No attacks authorized on craft unless U.S. aircraft are first fired on and then only if clearly North Vietnamese. Piers servicing target will not be attacked if tanker is berthed off end of pier.

Decision made after SecDef and CJCS were assured every feasible step would be taken to minimize civilian casualties would be small [sic]. If you do not believe you can accomplish objective while destroying targets and protecting crews, do not initiate program. Take the following measures; maximum use of most experienced ROLLING THUNDER personnel, detailed briefing of pilots stressing need to avoid civilians, execute only when weather permits visual identification of targets and improved strike accuracy, select best axis of attack to avoid populated areas, maximum use of ECM to hamper SAM and AAA fire control, in order to limit pilot distraction and improve accuracy, maximum use of weapons of high precision delivery consistent with mission objectives, and limit SAM and AAA suppression to sites located outside populated areas.

Take special precautions to insure security. If weather or operational considerations delay initiation of strikes, do not initiate on Sunday, 26 June.

McNamara Seeks to Limit Ground Forces

Throughout much of the war, McNamara engaged in a running battle with the military over the number of ground forces required to achieve U.S. objectives. This August 5, 1966, memorandum to the Joint Chiefs, "CINCPAC CY 1966 Adjusted Requirements & CY 1967," reveals his determination to limit forces to what was "truly essential."

As you know, it is our policy to provide the troops, weapons, and supplies requested by General Westmoreland at the times he desires them, to the greatest possible degree. The latest revised CINCPAC requirements, submitted on 18 June 1966, subject as above, are to be accorded the same consideration: valid requirements for SVN and related tactical air forces in Thailand will be deployed on a schedule as close as possible to CINCPAC/COMUSMACV's requests.

Nevertheless, I desire and expect a detailed, line-by-line analysis of these requirements to determine that each is truly essential to the carrying out of our war plan. We must send to Vietnam what is needed, but only what is needed. Excessive deployments weaken our ability to win by undermining the economic structure of the RVN and by raising doubts concerning the soundness of our planning.

In the course of your review of the validity of the requirements, I would like you to consider the attached Deployment Issue Papers which were prepared by my staff. While there may be sound reasons for deploying the units questioned, the issues raised in these papers merit your detailed attention and specific reply. They probably do not cover all questionable units, particularly for proposed deployments for the PACOM area outside of SVN. I expect that you will want to query CINCPAC about these and other units for which you desire clarification.

I appreciate the time required to verify the requirements and determine our capability to meet them, but decisions must be made on a timely basis if units are to be readied and equipment and supplies procured. Therefore I would appreciate having your recommended deployment plan, including your comments on each of the Deployment Issue Papers, no later than 15 September 1965.

Westmoreland Asks for Additional Troops

Noting the enemy's commitment to a protracted war of attrition, General Westmoreland in this August 10, 1966, cable to General Wheeler, chairman of the Joint Chiefs of Staff, and Admiral U. S. Grant Sharp, commander in chief of Pacific forces, raises the need for further increments of ground forces.

These and other facts support earlier predictions and suggest that the enemy intends to continue a protracted war of attrition. We must not underestimate the enemy nor his determination.

If, contrary to current indication, Hanoi decides not to escalate further, some modification of the forces which I have requested probably could be made. Under such circumstances, I conceive of a carefully balanced force that is designed to fight an extended war of attrition and sustainable without national mobilization.

I recognize the possibility that the enemy may not continue to follow the pattern of infiltration as projected. Accordingly, my staff is currently conducting a number of studies with the objective of placing this command and the RVN in a posture that will permit us to retain the initiative regardless of the course the enemy chooses to pursue. These include:

A A study which considers possible courses of action by the enemy on our force posture and counteractions to maintain our superiority.

B An analysis of our requirements to determine a balanced U.S. force that can be employed and sustained fully and effectively in combat on an indefinite basis without national mobilization.

C A study to determine the evolutionary steps to be taken in designing an ultimate GVN security structure.

D A study to determine the optimum RVNAF force structure which can be attained and supported in consideration of recent experience and our estimate of the manpower pool.

REF B [The CINCPAC submission] establishes and justifies minimal force requirements, emphasizing the requirement for a well balanced, sustainable force in SVN for an indefinite period. Consequently, at this point in time I cannot justify a reduction in requirements submitted.

IDA Assessment of the Bombing

This Institute for Defense Analyses report, "The Effects of U.S. Bombing on North Vietnam's Ability to Support Military Operations in South Vietnam: Retrospect and Prospect," August 29, 1966, was one of a series of independent analyses of the air war that raised doubts about its effectiveness and caused McNamara and other civilians to consider changes in policy. Paragraphs in italics are the Pentagon study's paraphrase or explanation.

1 As of July 1966 the U.S. bombing of North Vietnam (NVN) had had no measurable direct effect on Hanoi's ability to mount and support military operations in the South at the current level.

Although the political constraints seem clearly to have reduced the effectiveness of the bombing program, its limited effect on Hanoi's ability to provide such support cannot be explained solely on that basis. The countermeasures introduced by Hanoi effectively reduced the impact of U.S. bombing. More fundamentally, however, North Vietnam has basically a subsistence agricultural economy that presents a difficult and unrewarding target system for air attack.

The economy supports operations in the South mainly by functioning as a logistic funnel and by providing a source of manpower. The industrial sector produces little of military value. Most of the essential military supplies that the VC/NVN forces in the South require from external sources are provided by the USSR and Communist China. Furthermore, the volume of such supplies is so low that only a small fraction of the capacity of North Vietnam's rather flexible transportation network is required to maintain the flow. The economy's relatively underemployed labor force also appears to provide an ample manpower reserve for internal military and economic needs including repair and reconstruction and for continued support of military operations in the South.

2 Since the initiation of the ROLLING THUNDER program the damage to facilities and equipment in North Vietnam has been more than offset by the increased flow of military and economic aid, largely from the USSR and Communist China.

The measurable costs of the damage sustained by North Vietnam are estimated by intelligence analysts to have reached approximately $86 million by 15 July 1966. In 1965 alone, the value of the military and economic aid that Hanoi received from the USSR and Communist China is estimated to have been on the order of $250–400 million, of which about $100–150 million was economic, and they have continued to provide aid, evidently at an increasing rate, during the current year. Most of it has been from the USSR, which had virtually cut off aid during the 1962–64 period. There can be little doubt, therefore, that Hanoi's Communist backers have assumed the economic costs to a degree that has significantly cushioned the impact of U.S. bombing.

3 The aspects of the basic situation that have enabled Hanoi to continue its support of military operations in the South and to neutralize the impact of U.S. bombing by passing the economic costs to other Communist countries are not likely to be altered by reducing the present geographic constraints, mining Haiphong and the principal harbors in North Vietnam, increasing the number of armed reconnaissance sorties and otherwise expanding the U.S. air offensive along the lines now contemplated in military recommendations and planning studies.

An expansion of the bombing program along such lines would

make it more difficult and costly for Hanoi to move essential military supplies through North Vietnam to the VC/NVN forces in the South. The low volume of supplies required, the demonstrated effectiveness of the countermeasures already undertaken by Hanoi, the alternative options that the NVN transportation network provides and the level of aid the USSR and China seem prepared to provide, however, make it quite unlikely that Hanoi's capability to function as a logistic funnel would be seriously impaired. Our past experience also indicates that an intensified air campaign in NVN probably would not prevent Hanoi from infiltrating men into the South at the present or a higher rate, if it chooses. Furthermore there would appear to be no basis for assuming that the damage that could be inflicted by an intensified air offensive would impose such demands on the North Vietnamese labor force that Hanoi would be unable to continue and expand its recruitment and training of military forces for the insurgency in the South.

4 While conceptually it is reasonable to assume that some limit may be imposed on the scale of military activity that Hanoi can maintain in the South by continuing the ROLLING THUNDER program at the present, or some higher level of effort, there appears to be no basis for defining that limit in concrete terms or, for concluding that the present scale of VC/NVN activities in the field have approached that limit.

The available evidence clearly indicates that Hanoi has been infiltrating military forces and supplies into South Vietnam at an accelerated rate during the current year. Intelligence estimates have concluded that North Vietnam is capable of substantially increasing its support.

5 The indirect effects of the bombing on the will of the North Vietnamese to continue fighting and on their leaders' appraisal of the prospective gains and costs of maintaining the present policy have not shown themselves in any tangible way. Furthermore, we have not discovered any basis for concluding that the indirect punitive effects of bombing will prove decisive in these respects.

It may be argued on a speculative basis that continued or increased bombing must eventually affect Hanoi's will to continue, particularly as a component of the total U.S. military pressures being exerted throughout Southeast Asia. However, it is not a conclusion that necessarily follows from the available evidence; given the character of North Vietnam's economy and society, the present and prospective low levels of casualties and the amount of aid available to Hanoi. It would appear to be equally logical to assume that the major influences on Hanoi's will to continue are most likely to be the course of the war in the South and the degree to which the USSR and China support the policy of continuing the war and that the punitive impact of U.S. bombing may have but a marginal effect in the broader context.

In the body of the report these summary formulations were elabo-rated in more detail. For instance, in assessing the military and eco-nomic effect of the bombing on North Vietnam's capacity to sustain the war, the report stated:

The economic and military damage sustained by Hanoi in the first year of the bombing was moderate and the cost could be (and was) passed along to Moscow and Peiping.

The major effect of the attack on North Vietnam was to force Hanoi to cope with disruption to normal activity, particularly in trans-portation and distribution. The bombing hurt most in its disruption of the roads and rail nets and in the very considerable repair effort which became necessary. The regime, however, was singularly successful in overcoming the effects of the U.S. interdiction effort.

Much of the damage was to installations that the North Viet-namese did not need to sustain the military effort. The regime made no attempt to restore storage facilities and little to repair damage to power stations, evidently because of the existence of adequate excess capacity and because the facilities were not of vital importance. For somewhat similar reasons, it made no major effort to restore military facilities, but merely abandoned barracks and dispersed materiel usually stored in de-pots.

The major essential restoration consisted of measures to keep traf-fic moving, to keep the railroad yards operating, to maintain communi-cations, and to replace transport equipment and equipment for radar and SAM sites.

A little further on the report examined the political effects of the bombing on Hanoi's will to continue the war, the morale of the popula-tion, and the support of its allies.

The bombing through 1965 apparently had not had a major effect in shaping Hanoi's decision on whether or not to continue the war in Vietnam. The regime probably continued to base such decisions mainly on the course of the fighting in the South and appeared willing to suffer even stepped-up bombing so long as prospects of winning the South ap-peared to be reasonably good.

Evidence regarding the effect of the bombing on the morale of the North Vietnamese people suggests that the results were mixed. The bombing clearly strengthened popular support of the regime by engen-dering patriotic and nationalistic enthusiasm to resist the attacks. On the other hand, those more directly involved in the bombing underwent personal hardships and anxieties caused by the raids. Because the air strikes were directed away from urban areas, morale was probably damaged less by the direct bombing than by its indirect effects, such as evacuation of the urban population and the splitting of families.

Hanoi's political relations with its allies were in some respects strengthened by the bombing. The attacks had the effect of encouraging greater material and political support from the Soviet Union than might otherwise have been the case. While the Soviet aid complicated Hanoi's relationship with Peking, it reduced North Vietnam's dependence on China and thereby gave Hanoi more room for maneuver on its own behalf.

This report's concluding chapter was entitled "Observations" and contained some of the most lucid and penetrating analysis of air war produced to that date, or this! It began by reviewing the original objectives the bombing was initiated to achieve:

. . . Reducing the ability of North Vietnam to support the Communist insurgencies in South Vietnam and Laos, and . . . increasing progressively the pressure on NVN to the point where the regime would decide that it was too costly to continue directing and supporting the insurgency in the South.

After rehearsing the now familiar military failure of the bombing to halt the infiltration, the report crisply and succinctly outlined the bombing's failure to achieve the critical second objective—the psychological one:

. . . Initial plans and assessments for the ROLLING THUNDER program clearly tended to overestimate the persuasive and disruptive effects of the U.S. air strikes and, correspondingly, to underestimate the tenacity and recuperative capabilities of the North Vietnamese. This tendency, in turn, appears to reflect a general failure to appreciate the fact, well-documented in the historical and social scientific literature, that a direct, frontal attack on a society tends to strengthen the social fabric of the nation, to increase popular support of the existing government, to improve the determination of both the leadership and the populace to fight back, to induce a variety of protective measures that reduce the society's vulnerability to future attack, and to develop an increased capacity for quick repair and restoration of essential functions. The great variety of physical and social counter-measures that North Vietnam has taken in response to the bombing is now well documented in current intelligence reports, but the potential effectiveness of these counter-measures was not stressed in the early planning or intelligence studies.

Perhaps the most trenchant analysis of all, however, was reserved for last as the report attacked the fundamental weakness of the air war strategy—our ability to relate operations to objectives:

In general, current official thought about U.S. objectives in bombing NVN implicitly assumes two sets of causal relationships:

1 That by increasing the damage and destruction of resources in NVN, the U.S. is exerting pressure to cause the DRV to stop their support of the military operations in SVN and Laos; and

2 That the combined effect of the total military effort against NVN—including the U.S. air strikes in NVN and Laos, and the land, sea, and air operations in SVN—will ultimately cause the DRV to perceive that its probable losses accruing from the war have become greater than its possible gains and, on the basis of this net evaluation, the regime will stop its support of the war in the South.

These two sets of interrelationships are assumed in military planning, but it is not clear that they are systematically addressed in current intelligence estimates and assessments. Instead, the tendency is to encapsulate the bombing of NVN as one set of operations and the war in the South as another set of operations, and to evaluate each separately; and to tabulate and describe data on the physical, economic, and military effects of the bombing, but not to address specifically the relationship between such effects and the data relating to the ability and will of the DRV to continue its support of the war in the South.

The fragmented nature of current analyses and the lack of adequate methodology for assessing the net effects of a given set of military operations leaves a major gap between the quantifiable data on bomb damage effects, on the one hand, and policy judgments about the feasibility of achieving a given set of objectives on the other. Bridging this gap still requires the exercise of broad political-military judgments that cannot be supported or rejected on the basis of systematic intelligence indicators. It must be concluded, therefore, that there is currently no adequate basis for predicting the levels of U.S. military effort that would be required to achieve the stated objectives—indeed, there is no firm basis for determining if there is *any* feasible level of effort that would achieve these objectives.

The critical impact of this study on the Secretary's thinking is revealed by the fact that many of its conclusions and much of its analysis

would find its way into McNamara's October trip report to the President.

Having submitted a stinging condemnation of the bombing, the Study Group was under some obligation to offer constructive alternatives and this they did, seizing, not surprisingly, on the very idea McNamara had suggested—the anti-infiltration barrier. The product of their summer's work was a reasonably detailed proposal for a multi-system barrier across the DMZ and the Laotian panhandle that would make extensive use of recently innovated mines and sensors. The central portion of their recommendation follows:

The barrier would have two somewhat different parts, one designed against foot traffic and one against vehicles. The preferred location for the anti-foot-traffic barrier is in the region along the southern edge of the DMZ to the Laotian border and then north of Tchepone to the vicinity of Muong Sen, extending about 100 by 20 kilometers. This area is virtually unpopulated, and the terrain is quite rugged, containing mostly V-shaped valleys in which the opportunity for alternate trails appears lower than it is elsewhere in the system. The location of choice for the anti-vehicle part of the system is the area, about 100 by 40 kilometers, now covered by Operation Cricket. In this area the road network tends to be more constricted than elsewhere, and there appears to be a smaller area available for new roads. An alternative location for the anti-personnel system is north of the DMZ to the Laotian border and then north along the crest of the mountains dividing Laos from North Vietnam. It is less desirable economically and militarily because of its greater length, greater distance from U.S. bases, and greater proximity to potential North Vietnamese counter-efforts.

The air-supported barrier would, if necessary, be supplemented by a manned "fence" connecting the eastern end of the barrier to the sea.

The construction of the air-supported barrier could be initiated using currently available or nearly available components, with some necessary modifications, and could perhaps be installed by a year or so from go-ahead. However, we anticipate that the North Vietnamese would learn to cope with a barrier built this way after some period of time which we cannot estimate, but which we fear may be short. Weapons and sensors which can make a much more effective barrier, only some of which are now under development, are not likely to be available in less than 18 months to 2 years. Even these, it must be expected, will eventually be overcome by the North Vietnamese, so that further improvements in weaponry will be necessary. Thus we envisage a dynamic "battle of the barrier," in which the barrier is repeatedly improved and strengthened by the introduction of new components, and which will hopefully permit us to keep the North Vietnamese off balance by continually posing new problems for them. . . .

The anti-troop infiltration system (which would also function against supply porters) would operate as follows. There would be a constantly renewed mine field of non-sterilizing Gravel (and possibly button bomb-lets), distributed in patterns covering interconnected valleys and slopes (suitable for alternate trails) over the entire barrier region. The actual mined area would encompass the equivalent of a strip about 100 by 5 kilometers. There would also be a pattern of acoustic detectors to listen for mine explosions indicating an attempted penetration. The mine field is intended to deny opening of alternate routes for troop infiltrators and should be emplaced first. On the trails and bivouacs currently used, from which mines may—we tentatively assume—be cleared without great difficulty, a more dense pattern of sensors would be designed to locate groups of infiltrators. Air strikes using Gravel and SADEYES would then be called against these targets. The sensor patterns would be monitored 24 hours a day by patrol aircraft. The struck areas would be reseeded with new mines.

The anti-vehicle system would consist of acoustic detectors distributed every mile or so along all truckable roads in the interdicted area, monitored 24 hours a day by patrol aircraft, with vectored strike aircraft using SADEYE to respond to signals that trucks or truck convoys are moving. The patrol aircraft would distribute self-sterilizing Gravel over parts of the road net at dusk. The self-sterilizing feature is needed so that road-watching and mine-planting teams could be used in this area. Photo-reconnaissance aircraft would cover the entire area each few days to look for the development of new truckable roads, to see if the transport of supplies is being switched to porters, and to identify any other change in the infiltration system. It may also be desirable to use ground teams to plant larger anti-truck mines along the roads, as an interim measure pending the development of effective air-dropped anti-vehicle mines.

The cost of such a system (both parts) has been estimated to be about $800 million per year, of which by far the major fraction is spent for Gravel and SADEYES. The key requirements would be (all numbers are approximate because of assumptions which had to be made regarding degradation of system components in field use, and regarding the magnitude of infiltration): 20 million Gravel mines per month; possibly 25 million button bomblets per month. . . .

Apart from the tactical counter-measures against the barrier itself, one has to consider strategic alternatives available to the North Vietnamese in case the barrier is successful. Among these are: a move into the Mekong Plain; infiltration from the sea either directly to SVN or through Cambodia; and movement down the Mekong from Thakhek (held by the Pathet Lao–North Vietnamese) into Cambodia.

Finally, it will be difficult for us to find out how effective the barrier is in the absence of clearly visible North Vietnamese responses, such as end runs through the Mekong Plain. Because of supplies already stored in the pipeline, and because of the general shakiness of our quantitative estimates of either supply or troop infiltration, it is likely to be some time before the effect of even a wholly successful barrier becomes noticeable. A greatly stepped-up intelligence effort is called for, including continued road-watch activity in the areas of the motorcade roads, and patrol and reconnaissance activity south of the anti-personnel barrier.

Chapter 6

The 1967 Policy Debate

In the spring of 1967, U.S. strategy in Vietnam sparked a major debate within the Johnson administration. To a large extent, the debate pitted the military against civilians, although there were important differences within each group as well. The fundamental issue was whether to continue to escalate or to stabilize the ground and air wars at their existing levels and shift the emphasis to pacification and negotiations.

For months, Westmoreland and the Joint Chiefs had sought to enlarge the war, and they mounted a major campaign toward this end in early 1967. The Joint Chiefs pressed for an unrestricted bombing effort against North Vietnam to help bring the war to a close. Arguing that his ground strategy was working and could achieve results if expanded, Westmoreland asked for major increments of additional troops and for authority to attack the North Vietnamese/Vietcong forces in their sanctuaries in Laos, Cambodia, and across the demilitarized zone in North Vietnam. The Joint Chiefs supported his proposal and once again urged mobilization of the reserves to provide the forces necessary to fight the war in Vietnam and meet other commitments.

To an extent they had not before, civilians in the Defense and State Departments mobilized in the spring of 1967 to head off what they perceived as a highly dangerous military move to expand the war. Increasingly persuaded that the bombing was not effective and might even be counterproductive, some civilians urged that it be stabilized at its present level, cut back sharply, or even terminated altogether. Sensitive to growing frustration with the war in the United States, the civilians also increasingly opposed General Westmoreland's search-and-destroy ground strategy, which, they said, was unlikely to work and which incurred high casualties that turned Americans against the war. They proposed putting a ceiling on the forces given Westmoreland and shifting to a population security strategy that would be less costly. In a May 19 draft presidential memorandum that the authors of the Pentagon study properly labeled "radical," McNamara went a step further, recommending that the United States scale back its objectives in Vietnam and seek a compromise peace.

Johnson refused to resolve or even face directly the increasingly heated debate among his advisers. Fearful that expanding the war might provoke Chinese or Soviet intervention and thus bring about a much wider war, perhaps even a nuclear confrontation, he rejected the military's major proposals, approving only modest increases in ground forces and the addition of a handful of new bombing targets. At the same time, he rejected McNamara's major proposals, fearing that their adoption might provoke a military revolt, supported by conservatives in Congress. Toward the end of the year he eased McNamara out of government. At a time when the administration and the nation were becoming increasingly polarized by the war, Johnson clung to the shrinking center. The only new approach he adopted in the summer of 1967 was to launch a public relations campaign designed to solidify his domestic base by convincing a skeptical public that the United States was in fact winning the war.

McNamara Opposes Escalation

McNamara's draft presidential memorandum of October 14, 1966, "Actions Recommended for Vietnam," an important milepost in his gradual disillusionment with the war that had once been called "McNamara's War," expressed pessimism with the progress made in Vietnam and opposed further escalation. The secretary called for a "long-haul" strategy that included stabilizing the bombing program, leveling off the number of ground troops, building the electronic barrier to check infiltration, and intensifying the pacification program.

1 **Evaluation of the situation.** In the report of my last trip to Vietnam almost a year ago, I stated that the odds were about even that, even with the then-recommended deployments, we would be faced in early 1967 with a military stand-off at a much higher level of conflict and with "pacification" still stalled. I am a little less pessimistic now in one respect. We have done somewhat better militarily than I anticipated. We have by and large blunted the communist military initiative—any military victory in South Vietnam the Viet Cong may have had in mind 18 months ago has been thwarted by our emergency deployments and actions. And our program of bombing the North has exacted a price.

My concern continues, however, in other respects. This is because I see no reasonable way to bring the war to an end soon. Enemy morale has not broken—he apparently has adjusted to our stopping his drive for military victory and has adopted a strategy of keeping us busy and waiting us out (a strategy of attriting our national will). He knows that we have not been, and he believes we probably will not be, able to translate our military success into the "end products"—broken enemy morale and political achievements by the GVN.

The one thing demonstrably going for us in Vietnam over the past year has been the large number of enemy killed-in-action resulting from the big military operations. Allowing for possible exaggeration in reports, the enemy must be taking losses—deaths in and after battle—at the rate of more than 60,000 a year. The infiltration routes would seem to be one-way trails to death for the North Vietnamese. Yet there is no sign of an impending break in enemy morale and it appears that he can more than replace his losses by infiltration from North Vietnam and recruitment in South Vietnam.

Pacification is a bad disappointment. We have good grounds to be pleased by the recent elections [for a National Assembly], by Ky's 16 months in power, and by the faint signs of development of national political institutions and of a legitimate civil government. But none of this has translated itself into political achievements at Province level or below. Pacification has if anything gone backward. As compared with two, or four, years ago, enemy full-time regional forces and part-time guerrilla forces are larger; attacks, terrorism and sabotage have increased in scope and intensity; more railroads are closed and highways cut; the rice crop expected to come to market is smaller; we control little, if any, more of the population; the VC political infrastructure thrives in most of the country, continuing to give the enemy his enormous intelligence advantage; full security exists nowhere (not even behind the U.S. Marines' lines and in Saigon); in the countryside, the enemy almost completely controls the night.

Nor has the ROLLING THUNDER program of bombing the North either significantly affected infiltration or cracked the morale of Hanoi. There is agreement in the intelligence community on these facts (see the attached Appendix).

In essence, we find ourselves—from the point of view of the important war (for the complicity of the people)—no better, and if anything worse off. This important war must be fought and won by the Vietnamese themselves. We have known this from the beginning. But the discouraging truth is that, as was the case in 1961 and 1963 and 1965, we have not found the formula, the catalyst, for training and inspiring them into effective actions.

2 **Recommended actions.** In such an unpromising state of affairs, what should we do? We must continue to press the enemy militarily; we must make demonstrable progress in pacification; at the same time, we must add a new ingredient forced on us by the facts. Specifically, we must improve our position by getting ourselves into a military posture that we credibly would maintain indefinitely—a posture that makes trying to "wait us out" less attractive. I recommend a five-pronged course of action to achieve those ends.

a **Stabilize U.S. force-levels in Vietnam.** It is my judgment that, barring a dramatic change in the war, we should limit the increase in U.S. forces in SVN in 1967 to 70,000 men and we should level off at the total of 470,000 which such an increase would provide.* It is my view that this is enough to punish the enemy at the large-unit operations level and to keep the enemy's main forces from interrupting pacification. I believe also that even many more than 470,000 would not kill the enemy off in such numbers as to break their morale so long as they think they can wait us out. It is possible that such a 40 percent increase over our present level of 325,000 will break the enemy's morale in the short term; but if it does not, we must, I believe, be prepared for and have underway a long-term program premised on more than breaking the morale of main force units. A stabilized U.S. force level would be part of such a long-term program. It would put us in a position where negotiations would be more likely to be productive, but if they were not we could pursue the all-important pacification task with proper attention and resources and without the spectre of apparently endless escalation of U.S. deployments.

b **Install a barrier.** A portion of the 470,000 troops—perhaps 10,000 to 20,000—should be devoted to the construction and maintenance of an infiltration barrier. Such a barrier would lie near the 17th parallel—would run from the sea, across the neck of South Vietnam (choking off the new infiltration routes through the DMZ) and across the trails in Laos. This interdiction system (at an approximate cost of $1 billion) would comprise to the east a ground barrier of fences, wire, sensors, artillery, aircraft and mobile troops and to the west—mainly in Laos—an interdiction zone covered by air-laid mines and bombing attacks pinpointed by air-laid acoustic sensors.

The barrier may not be fully effective at first, but I believe that it can be effective in time and that even the threat of its becoming effective can substantially change to our advantage the character of the war. It would hinder enemy efforts, would permit more efficient use of the limited number of friendly troops, and would be persuasive evidence both that our sole aim is to protect the South from the North and that we intend to see the job through.

c **Stabilize the ROLLING THUNDER program against the North.** Attack sorties in North Vietnam have risen from about 4,000 per month at the end of last year to 6,000 per month in

---

* Admiral Sharp has recommended a 12/31/67 strength of 570,000. However, I believe both he and General Westmoreland recognize that the danger of inflation will probably force an end 1967 deployment limit of about 470,000.

the first quarter of this year and 12,000 per month at present. Most of our 50 percent increase of deployed attack-capable aircraft has been absorbed in the attacks on North Vietnam. In North Vietnam, almost 84,000 attack sorties have been flown (about 25 percent against fixed targets), 45 percent during the past seven months.

Despite these efforts, it now appears that the North Vietnamese–Laotian road network will remain adequate to meet the requirements of the Communist forces in South Vietnam—this is so even if its capacity could be reduced by one-third and if combat activities were to be doubled. North Vietnam's serious need for trucks, spare parts and petroleum probably can, despite air attacks, be met by imports. The petroleum requirement for trucks involved in the infiltration movement, for example, has not been enough to present significant supply problems, and the effects of the attacks on the petroleum distribution system, while they have not yet been fully assessed, are not expected to cripple the flow of essential supplies. Furthermore, it is clear that, to bomb the North sufficiently to make a radical impact upon Hanoi's political, economic and social structure, would require an effort which we could make but which would not be stomached either by our own people or by world opinion; and it would involve a serious risk of drawing us into open war with China.

The North Vietnamese are paying a price. They have been forced to assign some 300,000 personnel to the lines of communication in order to maintain the critical flow of personnel and material to the South. Now that the lines of communication have been manned, however, it is doubtful that either a large increase or decrease in our interdiction sorties would substantially change the cost to the enemy of maintaining the roads, railroads, and waterways or affect whether they are operational. It follows that the marginal sorties—probably the marginal 1,000 or even 5,000 sorties—per month against the lines of communication no longer have a significant impact on the war. (See the attached excerpts from intelligence estimates.)

When this marginal inutility of added sorties against North Vietnam and Laos is compared with the crew and aircraft losses implicit in the activity (four men and aircraft and $20 million per 1,000 sorties), I recommend, as a minimum, against increasing the level of bombing of North Vietnam and against increasing the intensity of operations by changing the areas or kinds of targets struck.

Under these conditions, the bombing program would continue the pressure and would remain available as a bargaining counter to get talks started (or to trade off in talks). But, as in the case of a stabilized level of U.S. ground forces, the stabilization of ROLLING THUNDER would remove the prospect of ever escalating bombing as a factor complicating our political posture and distracting from the main job of pacification in South Vietnam.

At the proper time, as discussed on pages 6–7 below, I believe we should consider terminating bombing in all of North Vietnam, or at least in the Northeast zones, for an indefinite period in connection with covert moves toward peace.

d Pursue a vigorous pacification program. As mentioned above, the pacification (Revolutionary Development) program has been and is thoroughly stalled. The large-unit operations war, which we know best how to fight and where we have had our successes, is largely irrelevant to pacification as long as we do not lose it. By and large, the people in rural areas believe that the GVN when it comes will not stay but that the VC will; that cooperation with the GVN will be punished by the VC; that the GVN is really indifferent to the people's welfare; that the low-level GVN are tools of the local rich; and that the GVN is ridden with corruption.

Success in pacification depends on the interrelated functions of providing physical security, destroying the VC apparatus, motivating the people to cooperate and establishing responsive local government. An obviously necessary but not sufficient requirement for success of the Revolutionary Development cadre and police is vigorously conducted and adequately prolonged clearing operations by military troops, who will "stay" in the area, who behave themselves decently and who show some respect for the people.

This elemental requirement of pacification has been missing.

In almost no contested area designed for pacification in recent years have ARVN forces actually "cleared and stayed" to a point where cadre teams, if available, could have stayed overnight in hamlets and survived, let alone accomplish their mission. VC units of company and even battalion size remain in operation, and they are more than large enough to overrun anything the local security forces can put up.

Now that the threat of a Communist main-force military victory has been thwarted by our emergency efforts, we must allocate far more attention and a portion of the regular military forces (at least half of the ARVN and perhaps a portion of the U.S. forces) to the task of providing an active and permanent security screen behind which the Revolutionary Development teams and police can operate and behind which the political struggle with the VC infrastructure can take place.

The U.S. cannot do this pacification security job for the Vietnamese. All we can do is "Massage the heart." For one reason, it is known that we do not intend to stay; if our efforts worked at all, it would merely postpone the eventual confrontation of the VC and GVN infrastructures. The GVN must do the job; and I am convinced that drastic reform is needed if the GVN is going to be able to do it.

The first essential reform is in the attitude of GVN officials. They are generally apathetic, and there is corruption high and low. Often appointments, promotions, and draft deferments must be bought; and kickbacks on salaries are common. Cadre at the bottom can be no better than the system above them.

The second needed reform is in the attitude and conduct of the ARVN. The image of the government cannot improve unless and until the ARVN improves markedly. They do not understand the importance (or respectability) of pacification nor the importance to pacification of proper, disciplined conduct. Promotions, assignments and awards are often not made on merit, but rather on the basis of having a diploma, friends or relatives, or because of bribery. The ARVN is weak in dedication, direction and discipline.

Not enough ARVN are devoted to area and population security, and when the ARVN does attempt to support pacification, their actions do not last long enough; their tactics are bad despite U.S. prodding (no aggressive small-unit saturation patrolling, hamlet searches, quick-reaction contact, or offensive night ambushes); they do not make good use of intelligence; and their leadership and discipline are bad.

Furthermore, it is my conviction that a part of the problem undoubtedly lies in bad management on the American as well as the GVN side. Here split responsibility—or "no responsibility"—has resulted in too little hard pressure on the GVN to do its job and no really solid or realistic planning with respect to the whole effort. We must deal with this management problem and deal with it effectively.

One solution would be to consolidate all U.S. activities which are primarily part of the civilian pacification program and all persons engaged in such activities, providing a clear assignment of responsibility and a unified command under a civilian relieved of all other duties.* Under this approach, there would be a carefully delineated division of responsibility between the civilian-in-charge and an element of COMUSMACV under a senior officer, who would give the subject of planning for and providing hamlet security the highest priority in attention and resources. Success will depend on the men selected for the jobs on both sides (they must be among the highest rank and most competent administrators in the U.S. Government), on complete cooperation among the U.S. elements, and on the extent to which the South Vietnamese can be shocked out of their present pattern of behavior. The first work of this reorganized U.S. pacification organization should be to produce within 60 days a realistic and detailed plan for the coming year.

From the political and public-relations viewpoint, this solution is preferable—if it works. But we cannot tolerate continued failure. If it fails after a fair trial, the only alternative in my view is to place the entire pacification program—civilian and military—under General Westmoreland. This alternative would result in the establishment of a Deputy COMUSMACV for Pacification who would be in command of all pacification staffs in Saigon and of all pacification staffs and activities in the field; one person in each corps, province and district would be responsible for the U.S. effort.

(It should be noted that progress in pacification, more than anything else, will persuade the enemy to negotiate or withdraw.)

e **Press for negotiations.** I am not optimistic that Hanoi or the VC will respond to peace overtures now (explaining my recommendations above that we get into a level-off posture for the long pull). The ends sought by the two sides appear to be irreconcilable and the relative power balance is not in their view unfavorable to them. But three things can be done, I believe, to increase the prospects:

(1) Take steps to increase the credibility of our peace gestures in the minds of the enemy. There is considerable evidence both in private statements by the Communists and in the reports of competent Western officials who have talked with them that charges of U.S. bad faith are not solely propagandistic, but reflect deeply held beliefs. Analyses of Communists' statements and actions indicate that they firmly believe that American leadership really does not

---

* If this task is assigned to Ambassador [William] Porter, another individual must be sent immediately to Saigon to serve as Ambassador Lodge's deputy.

want the fighting to stop, and, that we are intent on winning a military victory in Vietnam and on maintaining our presence there through a puppet regime supported by U.S. military bases.

As a way of projective U.S. bona fides, I believe that we should consider two possibilities with respect to our bombing program against the North, to be undertaken, if at all, at a time very carefully selected with a view to maximizing the chances of influencing the enemy and world opinion and to minimizing the chances that failure would strengthen the hand of the "hawks" at home: First, without fanfare, conditions, or avowal, whether the stand-down was permanent or temporary, stop bombing all of North Vietnam. It is generally thought that Hanoi will not agree to negotiations until they can claim that the bombing has stopped unconditionally. We should see what develops, retaining freedom to resume the bombing if nothing useful was forthcoming.

Alternatively, we could shift the weight-of-effort away from "Zones 6A and 6B"—zones including Hanoi and Haiphong and areas north of those two cities to the Chinese border. This alternative has some attraction in that it provides the North Vietnamese a "face saver" if only problems of "face" are holding up Hanoi peace gestures; it would narrow the bombing down directly to the objectionable infiltration (supporting the logic of a stop-infiltration/full-pause deal); and it would reduce the international heat on the U.S. Here, too, bombing of the Northeast could be resumed at any time, or "spot" attacks could be made there from time to time to keep North Vietnam off balance and to require her to pay almost the full cost by maintaining her repair crews in place. The sorties diverted from Zones 6A and 6B could be concentrated on infiltration routes in Zones 1 and 2 (the southern end of North Vietnam, including the Mu Gia Pass), in Laos and in South Vietnam.*

* Any limitation on the bombing of North Vietnam will cause serious psychological problems among the men who are risking their lives to help achieve our political objectives; among their commanders up to and including the JCS; and among those of our people who cannot understand why we should withhold punishment from the enemy. General Westmoreland, as do the JCS, strongly believes in the military value of the bombing program. Further, Westmoreland reports that the morale of his Air Force personnel may already be showing signs of erosion—an erosion resulting from current operational restrictions.

To the same end of improving our credibility, we should seek ways—through words and deeds—to make believable our intention to withdraw our forces once the North Vietnamese aggression against the South stops. In particular, we should avoid any implication that we will stay in South Vietnam with bases or to guarantee any particular outcome to a solely South Vietnamese struggle.

(2) Try to split the VC off from Hanoi. The intelligence estimate is that evidence is overwhelming that the North Vietnamese dominate and control the National Front and the Viet Cong. Nevertheless, I think we should continue and enlarge efforts to contact the VC/NLF and to probe ways to split members or sections off the VC/NLF organization.

(3) Press contacts with North Vietnam, the Soviet Union and other parties who might contribute toward a settlement.

(4) Develop a realistic plan providing a role for the VC in negotiations, postwar life, and government of the nation. An amnesty offer and proposals for national reconciliation would be steps in the right direction and should be parts of the plan. It is important that this plan be one which will appear reasonable, if not at first to Hanoi and the VC, at least to world opinion.

3 **The prognosis.** The prognosis is bad that the war can be brought to a satisfactory conclusion within the next two years. The large-unit operations probably will not do it; negotiations probably will not do it. *While we should continue to pursue both of these routes in trying for a solution in the short run, we should recognize that success from them is a mere possibility, not a probability.*

The solution lies in girding, openly, for a longer war and in taking actions immediately which will in 12 to 18 months give clear evidence that the continuing costs and risks to the American people are acceptably limited, that the formula for success has been found, and that the end of the war is merely a matter of time. All of my recommendations will contribute to this strategy, but the one most difficult to implement is perhaps the most important one—enlivening the pacification program. The odds are less than even for this task, if only because we have failed consistently since 1961 to make a dent in the problem. But, because the 1967 trend of pacification will, I believe, be the main talisman of ultimate U.S. success or failure in Vietnam, extraordinary imagination and effort should go into changing the stripes of that problem.

President [Nguyen Van] Thieu and Prime Minister Ky are

thinking along similar lines. They told me that they do not expect the Enemy to negotiate or to modify his program in less than two years. Rather, they expect that enemy to continue to expand and to increase his activity. They expressed agreement with us that the key to success is pacification and that so far pacification has failed. They agree that we need clarification of GVN and U.S. roles and that the bulk of the ARVN should be shifted to pacification. Ky will, between January and July 1967, shift all ARVN infantry divisions to that role. And he is giving [General Nguyen Ngoc] Thang, a good Revolutionary Development director, added powers. Thieu and Ky see this as part of a two-year (1967–68) schedule, in which offensive operations against enemy main force units are continued, carried on primarily by the U.S. and other Free-World forces. At the end of the two-year period, they believe the enemy may be willing to negotiate or to retreat from his current course of action.

Note: Neither the Secretary of State nor the JCS have [sic] yet had an opportunity to express their views on this report. Mr. [Nicholas deB.] Katzenbach [undersecretary of state] and I have discussed many of its main conclusions and recommendations—in general, but not in all particulars, it expresses his views as well as my own.

APPENDIX

Extracts from CIA/DIA Report "An Appraisal of the Bombing of North Vietnam through 12 September 1966."

1 There is no evidence yet of any shortage of POL in North Vietnam and stocks on hand, with recent imports, have been adequate to sustain necessary operations.

2 Air strikes against all modes of transportation in North Vietnam increased during the past month, but there is no evidence of serious transport problems in the movement of supplies to or within North Vietnam.

3 There is no evidence yet that the air strikes have significantly weakened popular morale.

4 Air strikes continue to depress economic growth and have been responsible for the abandonment of some plans for economic development, but essential economic activities continue.

Extracts from a March 16, 1966 CIA Report "An Analysis of the ROLLING THUNDER Air Offensive against North Vietnam."

1 Although the movement of men and supplies in North Vietnam has been hampered and made somewhat more costly (by our bombing), the Communists have been able to increase the flow of supplies and manpower to South Vietnam.

2 Hanoi's determination (despite our bombing) to continue its policy of supporting the insurgency in the South appears as firm as ever.

3 Air attacks almost certainly cannot bring about a meaningful reduction in the current level at which essential supplies and men flow into South Vietnam.

Bomb Damage Assessment in the North by the Institute for Defense Analyses' "Summer Study Group."

What surprised us (in our assessment of the effect of bombing North Vietnam) was the extent of agreement among various intelligence agencies on the effects of past operations and probable effects of continued and expanded Rolling Thunder. The conclusions of our group, to which we all subscribe, are therefore merely sharpened conclusions of numerous Intelligence summaries. They are that Rolling Thunder does not limit the present logistic flow into SVN because NVN is neither the source of supplies nor the choke-point on the supply routes from China and USSR. Although an expansion of Rolling Thunder by closing Haiphong harbor, eliminating electric power plants and totally destroying railroads, will at least indirectly impose further privations on the populace of NVN and make the logistic support of VC costlier to maintain, such expansion will not really change the basic assessment. This follows because NVN has demonstrated excellent ability to improvise transportation, and because the primitive nature of their economy is such that Rolling Thunder can affect directly only a small fraction of the population. There is very little hope that the Ho Chi Minh Government will lose control of population because of Rolling Thunder. The lessons of the Korean War are very relevant in these respects. Moreover, foreign economic aid to NVN is large compared to the damage we inflict, and growing. Probably the government of NVN has assurances that the USSR and / or China will assist the rebuilding of its economy after the war, and hence its concern about the damage being inflicted may be moderated by long-range favorable expectations.

Specifically:

1   As of July 1966 the U.S. bombing of North Vietnam had had no measurable direct affect on Hanoi's ability to mount and support military operations in the South at the current level.

2   Since the initiation of the Rolling Thunder program the damage to facilities and equipment in North Vietnam has been more than offset by the increased flow of military and economic aid, largely from the USSR and Communist China.

3   The aspects of the basic situation that have enabled Hanoi to continue its support of military operations in the South and to neutralize the impact of U.S. bombing by passing the economic costs to other Communist countries are not likely to be altered by reducing the present geographic constraints, mining Haiphong and the principal harbors in North Vietnam, increasing the number of armed reconnaissance sorties and otherwise expanding the U.S. air offensive along the lines now contemplated in military recommendations and planning studies.

4   While conceptually it is reasonable to assume that some limit may be imposed on the scale of military activity that Hanoi can maintain in the South by continuing the Rolling Thunder program at the present, or some higher level of effort, there appears to be no basis for defining that limit in concrete terms, or for concluding that the present scale of VC / NVN activities in the field has approached that limit.

5   The indirect effects of the bombing on the will of the North Vietnamese to continue fighting and on their leaders' appraisal of the prospective gains and costs of maintaining the present policy have not shown themselves in any tangible way. Furthermore, we have not discovered any basis for concluding that the indirect punitive effects of bombing will prove decisive in these respects.

JCS Oppose Cutback in Bombing

From the beginning of the air war to its end, military leaders disputed the pessimistic analyses of its effectiveness, arguing

that it could achieve its objectives if it were properly employed. These excerpts from a Joint Chiefs of Staff memorandum, signed by General Earle G. Wheeler, chairman, to Secretary of Defense McNamara, October 14, 1966, as provided in
the body of the Pentagon study, challenged McNamara's proposals to stabilize the bombing and called for escalation of the
air war.

The Joint Chiefs of Staff do not concur in your recommendation that
there should be no increase in level of bombing effort and no modification in areas and targets subject to air attack. They believe our air campaign against NVN to be an integral and indispensable part of over all
war effort. To be effective, the air campaign should be conducted with
only those minimum constraints necessary to avoid indiscriminate
killing of population. . . .

The Joint Chiefs of Staff do not concur with your proposal that, as
a carrot to induce negotiations, we should suspend or reduce our bombing campaign against NVN. Our experiences with pauses in bombing
and resumption have not been happy ones. Additionally, the Joint
Chiefs of Staff believe that the likelihood of the war being settled by
negotiation is small, and that, far from inducing negotiations, another
bombing pause will be regarded by North Vietnamese leaders, and our
Allies, as renewed evidence of lack of U.S. determination to press the
war to a successful conclusion. The bombing campaign is one of the
two trump cards in the hands of the President (the other being the presence of U.S. troops in SVN). It should not be given up without an end
to the NVN aggression in SVN. . . .

The Joint Chiefs of Staff believe that the war has reached a stage
at which decisions taken over the next sixty days can determine the outcome of the war and, consequently, can affect the overall security interests of the United States for years to come. Therefore, they wish to provide to you and to the President their unequivocal views on two salient
aspects of the war situation: the search for peace and military pressures
on NVN.

A The frequent, broadly-based public offers made by the President to
   settle the war by peaceful means on a generous basis, which would
   take from NVN nothing it now has, have been admirable. Certainly,

no one—American or foreigner—except those who are determined
not to be convinced, can doubt the sincerity, the generosity, the al-
truism of U.S. actions and objectives. In the opinion of the Joint
Chiefs of Staff the time has come when further overt actions and offers on our part are not only nonproductive, they are counter-productive. A logical case can be made that the American people, our
Allies, and our enemies alike are increasingly uncertain as to our
resolution to pursue the war to a successful conclusion. The Joint
Chiefs of Staff advocate the following:

(1) A statement by the President during the Manila Conference of
     his unswerving determination to carry on the war until NVN
     aggression against SVN shall cease;

(2) Continued covert exploration of all avenues leading to a
     peaceful settlement of the war; and

(3) Continued alertness to detect and react appropriately to with-
     drawal of North Vietnamese troops from SVN and cessation
     of support to the VC.

B In JCSM-955-64, dated 14 November 1964, and in JCSM-962-64,
dated 23 November 1964, the Joint Chiefs of Staff provided their
views as to the military pressures which should be brought to bear
on NVN. In summary, they recommended a "sharp knock" on NVN
military assets and war-supporting facilities rather than the campaign of slowly increasing pressure which was adopted. Whatever
the political merits of the latter course, we deprived ourselves of the
military effects of early weight of effort and shock, and gave to the
enemy time to adjust to our slow quantitative and qualitative increase of pressure. This is not to say that it is now too late to derive
military benefits from more effective and extensive use of our air
and naval superiority. The Joint Chiefs of Staff recommend:

(1) Approval of their ROLLING THUNDER 52 program, which
     is a step toward meeting the requirement for improved target
     systems. This program would decrease the Hanoi and
     Haiphong sanctuary areas, authorize attacks against the steel
     plant, the Hanoi rail yards, the thermal power plants, selected
     locks and dams controlling water LOC's, SAM support facili-
     ties within the residual Hanoi and Haiphong sanctuaries, and
     POL at Haiphong, Hai Gia (Phuc Yen) and Can Thon (Kep).

(2) Use of naval surface forces to interdict North Vietnamese
     coastal waterborne traffic and appropriate land LOCs and to
     attack other coastal military targets such as radar and AAA
     sites.
     . . . The Joint Chiefs of Staff request that their views as
     set forth above be provided to the President.

McNamara November 1966 DPM

In a draft presidential memorandum of November 17, 1966, excerpts from which appear below, McNamara admitted that the bombing produced certain military benefits but reiterated the larger arguments against its expansion.

A substantial air interdiction campaign is clearly necessary and worthwhile. In addition to putting a ceiling on the size of the force that can be supported, it yields three significant military effects. First, it effectively harasses and delays truck movements down through the southern panhandles of NVN and Laos, though it has no effect on troops infiltrating on foot over trails that are virtually invisible from the air. Our experience shows that daytime armed reconnaissance above some minimum sortie rate makes it prohibitively expensive to the enemy to attempt daylight movement of vehicles, and so forces him to night movement. Second, destruction of bridges and cratering of roads forces the enemy to deploy repair crews, equipment, and porters to repair or bypass the damage. Third, attacks on vehicles, parks, and rest camps destroy some vehicles with their cargoes and inflict casualties. Moreover, our bombing campaign may produce a beneficial effect on U.S. and SVN morale by making NVN pay a price for its enemy [sic]. But at the scale we are now operating, I believe our bombing is yielding very small marginal returns, not worth the cost in pilot lives and aircraft.

The first effect, that of forcing the enemy into a system of night movement, occurs at a lower frequency of armed reconnaissance sorties than the level of the past several months. The enemy was already moving at night in 1965, before the sorties rate had reached half the current level; further sorties have no further effect on the enemy's overall operating system. The second effect, that of forcing the enemy to deploy repair crews, equipment, and porters, is also largely brought about by a comparatively low interdiction effort. Our interdiction campaign in 1965 and early this year forced NVN to assign roughly 300,000 additional personnel to LOCs; there is no indication that recent sortie increases have caused further increases in the number of these personnel. Once the enemy system can repair road cuts and damaged bridges in a few hours, as it has demonstrated it can, additional sorties may work this system harder but are unlikely to cause a significant increase in its costs. Only the third effect, the destruction of vehicles and their cargoes, continues to increase in about the same proportion as the number of armed reconnaissance sorties, but without noticeable impact on VC/NVA operations. The overall capability of the NVN transport system to move supplies within NVN apparently improved in September in spite of 12,200 attack sorties.

In a summary paragraph, the draft memo made the entire case against the bombings:

The increased damage to targets is not producing noticeable results. No serious shortage of POL in North Vietnam is evident, and stocks on hand, with recent imports, have been adequate to sustain necessary operations. No serious transport problem in the movement of supplies to or within North Vietnam is evident; most transportation routes appear to be open, and there has recently been a major logistical build-up in the area of the DMZ. The raids have disrupted the civil populace and caused isolated food shortages, but have not significantly weakened popular morale. Air strikes continue to depress economic growth and have been responsible for abandonment of some plans for economic development, but essential economic activities continue. The increasing amounts of physical damage sustained by North Vietnamese are in large measure compensated by aid received from other Communist countries. Thus, in spite of an interdiction campaign costing at least $250 million per month at current levels, no significant impact on the war in South Vietnam is evident. The monetary value of damage to NVN since the start of bombing in February 1965 is estimated at about $140 million through October 10, 1966.

Westmoreland Requests Additional Troops

In a cablegram to the Pacific command (excerpted below), March 18, 1967, General Westmoreland requested a major increase in U.S. ground forces, thus setting off a heated debate on U.S. strategy in Vietnam. Paragraphs in italics are the Pentagon study's paraphrase or explanation.

On 18 March, General Westmoreland submitted his analysis of current MACV force requirements projected through FY 68. This request was to furnish the base line for all further force deployment calculations during the Program 5 period. In preface to his specific request, CO-MUSMACV reviewed his earlier CY 67 requirement which asked for 124 maneuver battalions with their necessary combat and combat service support, a total strength of 555,741. This figure was the maximum figure requested during the Program 4 deliberations. The approved Program 4 package included only 470,336 and was considerably below the MACV request, a fact which led to the series of reclamas described in Section II. Westmoreland related that MACVCINCPAC had not strongly objected earlier to 470,000 man ceiling because of adverse piaster impact and the realities of service capabilities, but, subsequent reassessment of the situation had indicated clearly to him that the Program 4 force, although enabling U.S. force to gain the initiative did not "permit sustained operations of the scope and intensity required to avoid an unreasonably protracted war."

As the cable continued, the American commander in Vietnam briefly restated his earlier assessment of enemy trends: That the enemy had increased his force structure appreciably and was now confronting Free World Military Forces with large bodies of troops in and above the DMZ, in the Laotian and Cambodian sanctuaries and certain areas within SVN. In light of this new appraisal, he had established an early requirement for an additional 2⅓ divisions which he proposed be accommodated by restructuring the original 555,741-man force package proposed during Program 4. This force was required "as soon as possible but not later than 1 July 1968." Part of the reasoning was that this in effect constituted no more than a 6-month "extension" of the CY 67 program and as such would permit shifting force programming from a Calendar Year to a Fiscal Year basis, a shift long needed in COMUS-MACV's estimation to make force programming for Vietnam compatible with other programs and to provide essential lead time in the procurement of hardware. Westmoreland then looked further ahead, noting:

. . . It is entirely possible that additional forces, over and above the immediate requirement for 2⅓ Divisions, will materialize. Present planning, which will undergo continued refinement, suggests an additional 2⅓ division equivalents whose availability is seen as extending beyond FY 68.

Then as if to take the edge off his request, COMUSMACV turned attention to two programs which were becoming increasingly attractive to American decision-makers. These were development of an improved

RVNAF and an increase in the other Free World Military Forces committed to the war in Vietnam. He commented that despite the force ceiling on RVNAF currently in effect some selective increase in Vietnamese capabilities was required, such as creation of a suitable base for establishing a constabulary, an organization vital to the success of the Revolutionary Development program. Westmoreland stated that it was the position of his headquarters that provision for any and all Free World Military Forces was welcomed as "additive reinforcements," but they would be treated as additions only, thereby having no effect upon U.S. force computations.

The concept of operations under which the new forces he requested were to be employed varied little in its essential aspects from that outlined in MACV's February "Assessment of the Military Situation and Concept of Operations," which had reached Washington but a week earlier. However, the new cable integrated the new forces as part of the MACV operational forces. Westmoreland reviewed the period just past then turned to the future:

. . . our operations were primarily holding actions characterized by border surveillance, reconnaissance to locate enemy forces, and spoiling attacks to disrupt the enemy offensive. As a result of our buildup and successes, we were able to plan and initiate a general offensive. We now have gained the tactical initiative, and are conducting continuous small and occasional large-scale offensive operations to decimate the enemy forces; to destroy enemy base areas and disrupt his infrastructure; to interdict his land and water LOC's and to convince him, through the vigor of our offensive and accompanying psychological operations, that he faces inevitable defeat.

Military success alone will not achieve the U.S. objectives in Vietnam. Political, economic and psychological victory is equally important, and support of Revolutionary Development program is mandatory. The basic precept for the role of the military in support of Revolutionary Development is to provide a secure environment for the population so that the civil aspects of RD can progress.

He then detailed corps by corps the two troop request requirements labeling them the "optimum force" [4⅔ Divs] and the "minimum essential force" [2⅓ Divs]:

B. FORCE REQUIREMENTS FY 68

(1) The MACV objectives for 1967 were based on the assumption that the CY 67 force requirements would be approved and pro-

vided expeditiously within the capabilities of the services. However, with the implementation of Program Four, it was recognized that our accomplishments might fall short of our objectives. With the additional forces cited above, we would have had the capability to extend offensive operations into an exploitation phase designed to take advantage of our successes.

(2)   With requisite forces, we shall be able to complete more quickly the destruction or neutralization of the enemy main forces and bases and, by continued presence, deny to him those areas in RVN long considered safe havens. As the enemy main forces are destroyed or broken up, increasingly greater efforts can be devoted to rooting out and destroying the VC guerrilla and communist infrastructure. Moreover, increased assistance can be provided the RVNAF in support of its effort to provide the required level of security for the expanding areas undergoing Revolutionary Development.

(3)   Optimum Force. The optimum force required [to] implement the concept of operations and to exploit success is considered 4⅔ divisions or the equivalent; 10 tactical fighter squadrons with one additional base; and the full mobile riverine force. The order of magnitude estimate is 201,250 spaces in addition to the 1967 ceiling of 470,366 for a total of 671,616.

    (a)   In I Corps, the situation is the most critical with respect to existing and potential force ratios. As a minimum, a division plus a regiment is required for Quang Tri Province as a containment force. The latter has been justified previously in another plan. Employment of this force in the containment role would release the units now engaged there for expansion of the DaNang, Hue-Phu Bai and Chu Lai TAOR's as well as increase security and control along the corps northern coastal areas. One of the most critical areas in RVN today is Quang Ngai Province even if a major operation were conducted in this area during 1967, the relief would be no more than temporary. A force is needed in the province to maintain continuous pressure on the enemy to eliminate his forces and numerous base areas, and to remove his control over the large population and food reserves. The sustained employment of a division of 10 battalions is mandatory in Quang Ngai Province if desired results are to be realized. Employment of this force would provide security for the vital coastal areas, facilitate opening and securing Route 1 and the railroad and, perhaps equally important, relieve pressure on northern Binh Dinh Province.

    (b)   In II Corps, the task is two fold: destroy the enemy main and guerrilla forces in the coastal areas; and contain the infiltration of NVA forces from Cambodia and Laos. Continual expansion both north and south of the present capital coastal TAOR's opening and securing Route 1 and the railroad, securing Route 20 from Dalat south to the III Corps boundary, destruction of enemy forces in Pleiku and Kontum Provinces, and containment of enemy forces in the Cambodian and Laotian sanctuaries are all tasks to be accomplished given the large area in II Corps and the continuous enemy threat, an optimum force augmentation of four separate brigades is required to execute effectively an exploitation of our successes. An infantry brigade is needed in northern Binh Dinh Province to expand security along the coastal area and to facilitate operations in Quang Ngai Province to the north. A mechanized brigade in the western highlands will assist in offensive and containment operations in the Pleiku-Kontum area. An infantry brigade in the region of Nam Me Thout is needed to conduct operations against enemy forces and bases there and to add security to this portion of II Corps now manned with limited ARVN forces, and finally, a mechanized brigade is needed in Binh Thuan Province to neutralize the enemy forces and bases in the southern coastal area, and to open and secure highway 1 and the national railroad to the III Corps boundary.

(c) In III Corps, operations to destroy VC/NVA forces and bases in the northwestern & central parts of the corps area and to intensify the campaign against the enemy's infrastructure are being conducted. These operations are to be completed by intensive efforts to open and secure the principal land and water LOC's throughout the Corps Zone. However, deployment of the U.S. 9th Div to IV Corps will create a gap in the forces available in III Corps to operate against seen significant base areas in Phuoc Tuy, Bin Tuy, and Long Lhanh Provinces. These areas constitute the home base of the still formidable 5th VC Division. This unit must be destroyed, its bases neutralized and Route 1 and the national railroad opened and secured. Other critical locales that will require considerable effort are War Zone D and Phuoc Long area in which the VC 7th Division is believed to be located. With the forces operating currently in III Corps, substantial progress can be made, but to exploit effectively our successes an addition of one division, preferably air mobile is required. By basing this division in Bien Hoa province just

north of the RSSZ, it would be in position to conduct operations against the 5th Div, and War Zone D, as well as to reinforce the U.S. 9th Div in Delta operations as required.

(d) In IV Corps, with deployment of the U.S. 9th Div to the
Corps area and with increasing success of ARVN operations
there, the situation will be greatly improved. Primary emphasis will be given to destroying VC main and guerrilla
units and their bases, to intensifying operations to extend
GVN control, to stopping the flow of food stuffs and materials to the enemy through Cambodia, and to assisting in the
flow of goods to GVN outlets in Saigon. In addition emphasis will be accorded the opening and securing of principal
water and land LOC's which are the key to all operations in
the Delta. It is noteworthy on this score, that effectiveness of
forces available is hampered severely by an inadequate mobile riverine force. In IV Corps, the essential requirement is
to flesh out the mobile riverine force with three APB's (Barracks Ships) one ARL (repair ship), and two RAS (river assault squadrons).

(4) The Minimum Essential Force necessary to exploit success of the
current offensive and to retain effective control of expanding areas
being cleaned of enemy influence is 2⅓ divisions with a total of 21
maneuver battalions. One division, with nine infantry battalions—
each with 4 rifle companies—and an ACR of three squadrons are
required. The other division of nine maneuver battalions, each battalion organized with four rifle companies is required in Quang
Ngai Province. Four tactical fighter squadrons, each generating
113 sorties per month per identified maneuver battalion, are required. Two squadrons will be stationed at Phu Cat and two at
Tuy Hoa. One C130 or equivalent type squadron can provide adequate airlift and is justified on the basis of current planning factors: This SQD would be based at Cam Ranh Bay. A minimum essential logistic base can be provided by selective augmentation of
NSA Danang, and by provision for lift capability equivalent to
eight LST's in addition to two LST's identified previously for the
containment force in Quang Tri Province. Two nondivisional
Army combat engineer battalions and four Army construction battalions will be required to support divisional engineering effort to
augment two navy construction battalions that previously have
been identified with the containment force in Quang Tri Province. . . .

(b) Effectiveness of the U.S. 9th Division's operations in IV
Corps will be degraded unacceptably without adequate mo-

bility on the waterways. For this reason, addition of two
river assault squadrons with their associated support is
deemed essential. The Mekong Delta Mobile Riverine Force
originally was tailored and justified as a four RAS level.
This requirement still is valid. The primary media of transport in the Delta are air and water. Air mobility is recognized as critical to success of operations in the area, but the
size of offensive operations that can be mounted is limited
by the inherent physical limitations of airborne vehicles. Accordingly, any sizeable offensive operation such as those vi-
sualized for the U.S. 9th Division must utilize the 300km of
waterways in the Delta to exploit tactical mobility. Maintenance of LOC's and population control in the areas secured
by the division's operations, along with extension of the interdiction effort, necessitates expansion of the game warden
operation. Fifty PBR's can provide this capability based on
experience factors accrued thus far. . . .

JCS Support Westmoreland Request

Joint Chiefs of Staff Memorandum 218–67 to Secretary of Defense McNamara, April 20, 1967, as provided in the body of
the Pentagon study and excerpted below, supported Westmoreland's call for additional troops and itself pressed for expansion of the war. Paragraphs in italics are the study's paraphrase or explanation.

*On 20 April, the JCS, in JCSM–218–67, formally reported to the Secre-
tary of Defense that MACV required additional forces to achieve the
objectives they considered the U.S. was pursuing in Vietnam. The JCS
announcement came as little surprise to the Secretary of Defense since
as early as 23 March he had seen the original message in which
COMUSMACV had outlined the minimum essential and optimum force
requirements.*

*JCSM 218–67 reaffirmed the basic objectives and strategic con-
cepts contained in JCSM 702–66 dated 4 November 1966. Briefly,
these entailed a national objective of attaining a stable and indepen-*

dent non-communist government in South Vietnam and a fourfold military contribution toward achieving the objectives of:

(a)   Making it as difficult and costly as possible for the NVA to continue effective support of the VC and to cause North Vietnam to cease direction of the VC insurgency.

(b)   To defeat the VC/NVA and force the withdrawal of NVA forces.

(c)   Extend government dominion, direction and control.

(d)   To deter Chinese Communists from direct intervention in SEA.

The JCS listed three general areas of military effort that they felt should be pursued in the war:

(1)   Operations against the Viet Cong / North Vietnamese Army (VC/NVA) forces in SVN while concurrently assisting the South Vietnamese Government in their nation-building effort.

(2)   Operations to obstruct and reduce the flow of men and materials from North Vietnam (NV) to SVN.

(3)   Operations to obstruct and reduce imports of war-sustaining materials into NVN.

They continued by assessing the achievements of the U.S. and allies in these three areas:

In the first area, the United States and its allies have achieved considerable success in operations against VC/NVA forces. However, sufficient friendly forces have not been made available to bring that degree of pressure to bear on the enemy throughout SVN which would be beyond his ability to accommodate and which would provide the secure environment essential to sustained progress in Revolutionary Development. The current reinforcement of I CTZ by diversion of forces from II to III CTZs reduces the existing pressure in those areas and inevitably will cause a loss of momentum that must be restored at the earliest practicable date.

In the second area, U.S. efforts have achieved appreciable success. Greater success could be realized if an expanded system of targets were made available.

In the third area, relatively little effort has been permitted. This failure to obstruct and reduce imports of war-sustaining materials into NVN has affected unfavorably the desired degree of success of operations in the other areas.

The Joint Chiefs strongly recommended not only the approval of additional forces to provide an increased level of effort in SVN but that action be taken to reduce and obstruct the enemy capability to import the material support required to sustain the war effort. They argued that the cumulative effect of all these operations, in South Vietnam, in North Vietnam and against the enemy's strategic lines of communication would hasten the successful conclusion of the war and would most likely reduce the overall ultimate force requirements. Their rationale for the 1968 forces was summarized as follows:

The FY 1968 force for SVN is primarily needed to offset the enemy's increased posture in the vicinity of the DMZ and to improve the environment for Revolutionary Development in I and IV CTZs. To achieve the secure environment for lasting progress in SVN, additional military forces must be provided in order to (1) destroy the enemy main force, (2) locate and destroy district and provincial guerrilla forces, and (3) provide security for the population. The increased effort required to offset VC/NVA main forces' pressure is diminishing the military capability to provide a secure environment to villages and hamlets. Diversion of forces from within SVN and the employment of elements of CINCPAC's reserve are temporary measures at the expense of high-priority programs in other parts of SVN. Thus, if sufficient units are to be available to provide both direct and indirect support to Revolutionary Development throughout SVN, added forces must be deployed.

The three-TFS force for Thailand and the additional Navy forces in the South China Sea and the Gulf of Tonkin are required to bring increased pressures to bear on NVN.

Johnson, Wheeler, and Westmoreland Discuss Force Needs

The following excerpts from the Pentagon study describe a conversation on April 27, 1967, between President Johnson and Generals Wheeler and Westmoreland. The narrative says the conversation was reported in notes by John T. Mc-

Naughton, assistant secretary of defense for international security affairs. Italicized emphasis and words in parentheticals
are those of the Pentagon study. Johnson's concern with
Westmoreland's proposals is palpable.

Westmoreland was quoted as saying that without the 2⅓ additional divisions which he had requested "we will not be in danger of being defeated but it will be nip and tuck to oppose the reinforcements the enemy is capable of providing. In the final analysis we are fighting a war
of attrition in Southeast Asia."

Westmoreland predicted that the next step if we were to pursue
our present strategy to fruition would probably be the second addition
of 2⅓ divisions or approximately another 100,000 men. Throughout the
conversations he repeated his assessment that the war would not be lost
but that progress would certainly be slowed down. To him this was "not
an encouraging outlook but a realistic one." When asked about the influence of increased infiltration upon his operations the general replied
that as he saw it "this war is action and counteraction. Anytime we take
an action we expect a reaction." The President replied: "When we add
divisions can't the enemy add divisions? If so, where does it all end?"
Westmoreland answered: "The VC and DRV strength in SVN now totals 285,000 men. It appears that last month we reached the crossover
point in areas *excluding the two northern provinces.*" (Emphasis
added.) "Attritions will be greater than additions to the force. . . . The
enemy has 8 divisions although he would have difficulty supporting all
of these. He would be hard pressed to support more than 12 divisions.
If we add 2⅓ divisions, it is likely the enemy will react by adding
troops." The President then asked "At what point does the enemy ask
for volunteers?" Westmoreland's only reply was, "That is a good question."

COMUSMACV briefly analyzed the strategy under the present
program of 470,000 men for the President. He explained his concept of
a "meatgrinder" where we would kill large numbers of the enemy but
in the end do little better than hold our own, with the shortage of troops
still restricting MACV to a fire brigade technique—chasing after enemy main force units when and where it could find them. He then predicted that "unless the will of the enemy is broken or unless there was
an unraveling of the VC infrastructure the war could go on for five
years. If our forces were increased, that period could be reduced, al-

though not necessarily in proportion to increases in strength," since factors other than increase in strength had to be considered. For instance, a non-professional force, such as that which would result from fulfilling the requirement for 100,000 additional men by calling reserves, would cause some degradation of normal leadership and effectiveness. Westmoreland concluded by estimating that with a *force level of 565,000 men, the war could well go on for three years. With a second increment of 2⅓ divisions leading to a total of 665,000 men, it could go on for two years.*

General Wheeler . . . listed three matters . . . which were bothering the JCS. These were:

(a)   DRV troop activity in Cambodia. U.S. troops may be forced to move against these units in Cambodia.

(b)   DRV troop activity in Laos. U.S. troops may be forced to move against these units.

(c)   Possible invasion of North Vietnam. We may wish to take offensive action against the DRV with ground troops.

The bombing which had always attracted considerable JCS attention was in Wheeler's estimation about to reach the point of target saturation—when all worthwhile fixed targets except the ports had been struck. Once this saturation level was reached the decision-makers would be impelled to address the requirement to deny to the North Vietnamese use of the ports. He summarized the JCS position saying that the JCS firmly believed that the President must review the contingencies which they faced, the troops required to meet them and additional punitive action against DRV. Westmoreland parenthetically added that he was "frankly dismayed at even the thought of stopping the bombing program.". . .

The President closed the meeting by asking: "What if we do not add the 2⅓ divisions?" General Wheeler replied first, observing that the momentum would die; in some areas the enemy would recapture the initiative, an important but hardly disastrous development, meaning that we wouldn't lose the war but it would be a longer one. He added that:

"Of the 2⅓ divisions, I would add one division on the DMZ to relieve the Marines to work with ARVN on pacification; and I would put one division east of Saigon to relieve the 9th Division to deploy to the Delta to increase the effectiveness of the three good ARVN divisions now there; the brigade I would send to Quang Ngai to make there the progress in the next year that we have made in Binh Dinh in the past year."

The President reacted by saying:

"We should make certain we are getting value received from the South Vietnamese troops. Check the dischargees to determine whether we could make use of them by forming additional units, by mating them with US troops, as is done in Korea, or in other ways."

There is no record of General Westmoreland's reply, if any. . . .

McGeorge Bundy Opposes Escalation

McGeorge Bundy resurfaced in 1967 as an informal adviser to Johnson on Vietnam and other issues. In these excerpts from a document entitled "Memorandum on Vietnam Policy," as provided in the body of the Pentagon study, Bundy came out strongly against the military's recommendations to escalate the war and alluded to the increasingly important war at home. According to the study, the document bore no date but a copy was marked in pencil "rec'd 5–4–67 12n." Paragraphs in italics are the study's paraphrase or explanation.

Since the Communist turndown of our latest offers [to negotiate] in February, there has been an intensification of bombing in the North, and press reports suggest that there will be further pressure for more attacks on targets heretofore immune. There is also obvious pressure from the military for further reinforcements in the South, although General Westmoreland has been a model of discipline in his public pronouncements. One may guess, therefore, that the President will soon be confronted with requests for 100,000–200,000 more troops and for authority to close the harbor in Haiphong. Such recommendations are inevitable, in the framework of strictly military analysis. It is the thesis of this paper that in the main they should be rejected, and that as a matter of high national policy there should be a publicly stated ceiling to the level of American participation in Vietnam, as long as there is no further marked escalation on the enemy side.

There are two major reasons for this recommendation: the situation in Vietnam and the situation in the United States. As to Vietnam, it seems very doubtful that further intensifications of bombing in the North or major increases in U.S. troops in the South are really a good way of bringing the war to a satisfactory conclusion. As to the United States, it seems clear that uncertainty about the future size of the war is now having destructive effects on the national will.

Unlike the vocal critics of the Administrations, Mac Bundy was not opposed to the bombing per se, merely to any further extension of it since he felt such action would be counter-productive. Because his views carry such weight, his arguments against extending the bombing are reproduced below in full:

On the ineffectiveness of the bombing as a means to end the war, I think the evidence is plain—though I would defer to expert estimators. Ho Chi Minh and his colleagues simply are not going to change their policy on the basis of losses from the air in North Vietnam. No intelligence estimate that I have seen in the last two years has ever claimed that the bombing would have this effect. The President never claimed that it would. The notion that this was its purpose has been limited to one school of thought and has never been the official Government position, whatever critics may assert.

I am very far indeed from suggesting that it would make sense now to stop the bombing of the North altogether. The argument for that course seems to me wholly unpersuasive at the present. To stop the bombing today would be to give the Communists something for nothing, and in a very short time all the doves in this country and around the world would be asking for some further unilateral concessions. (Doves and hawks are alike in their insatiable appetites; we can't really keep the hawks happy by small increases in effort—they come right back for more.)

The real justification for the bombing, from the start, has been double—its value for Southern morale at a moment of great danger, and its relation to Northern infiltration. The first reason has disappeared but the second remains entirely legitimate. Tactical bombing of communications and of troop concentrations—and of airfields as necessary—seems to me sensible and practical. It is strategic bombing that seems both unproductive and unwise. It is true, of course, that all careful bombing does some damage to the enemy. But the net effect of this damage upon the military capability of a primitive country is almost sure to be slight. (The lights have not stayed off in Haiphong, and even if they had, electric lights are in no sense essential to the Communist war effort.) And against this distinctly marginal impact we have to weigh the fact that strategic bombing does tend to divide the U.S., to distract us all from the real struggle in the South, and to accentuate the unease and distemper which surround the war in Vietnam, both at home and abroad. It is true that careful polls show majority support for the bombing, but I believe this support rests upon an erroneous belief in its effectiveness as a means to end the war. Moreover, I think those against extension of the bombing are more passionate on balance than those who favor it. Finally, there is certainly a point at which such bombing does increase the risk of conflict with China or the Soviet Union, and I am sure there is no majority for that. In particular, I think it clear that the case against going after Haiphong Harbor is so strong that a majority would back the Government in rejecting that course.

So I think that with careful explanation there would be more approval than disapproval of an announced policy restricting the bombing closely to activities that support the war in the South. General Westmoreland's speech to the Congress made this tie-in, but attacks on power plants really do not fit the picture very well. We are attacking them, I fear, mainly because we have "run out" of other targets. Is it a very good reason? Can anyone demonstrate that such targets have been rewarding? Remembering the claims made for attacks on [rest illegible].

In a similar fashion Bundy developed his arguments against a major increase in U.S. troop strength in the South and urged the President not to take any new initiatives for the present. But the appeal of Bundy's analysis for the President must surely have been its finale in which Bundy, acutely aware of the President's political sensitivities, cast his arguments in the context of the forthcoming 1968 Presidential elections. Here is how he presented the case:

There is one further argument against major escalation in 1967 and 1968 which is worth stating separately, because of the surface it seems cynically political. It is that Hanoi is going to do everything it possibly can to keep its position intact until after our 1968 elections. Given their history, they are bound to hold out for a possible U.S. shift in 1969—that's what they did against the French, and they got most of what they wanted when [Pierre] Mendes[-France] took power [during the 1954 Geneva Conference]. Having held on so long this time, and having nothing much left to lose—compared to the chance of victory— they are bound to keep on fighting. Since only atomic bombs could really knock them out (an invasion of North Vietnam would not do it in two years, and is of course ruled out on other grounds), they have it in their power to "prove" that military escalation does not bring peace—at least over the next two years. They will surely do just that. However much they may be hurting, they are not going to do us any favors before November 1968. (And since this was drafted, they have been publicly advised by [U.S. newspaper columnist] Walter Lippmann to wait for the Republicans—as if they needed the advice and as if it was his place to give it!)

It follows that escalation will not bring visible victory over Hanoi before the election. Therefore the election will have to be fought by the Administration on other grounds. I think those other grounds are clear and important, and that they will be obscured if our policy is thought to be one of increasing—and ineffective—military pressure.

If we assume that the war will still be going on in November 1968, and that Hanoi will not give us the pleasure of consenting to negotiations sometime before then what we must plan to offer as a defense of Administration policy is not victory over Hanoi, but growing success— and self reliance—in the South. This we can do, with luck, and on this side of the parallel, the Vietnamese authorities should be prepared to help us out (though of course the VC will do their damndest against us). Large parts of Westy's speech (if not quite all of it) were wholly consistent with this line of argument. . . .

If we can avoid escalation-that-does-not-seem-to-work, we can focus attention on the great and central achievement of these last two years: on the defeat we have prevented. The fact that South Vietnam has not been lost and is not going to be lost is a fact of truly massive importance in the history of Asia, the Pacific, and the U.S. An articulate minority of "Eastern intellectuals" (like Bill [Senator J. William] Fulbright [D-Ark.]) may not believe in what they call the domino theory, but most Americans (along with nearly all Asians) know better. Under this administration the United States has already saved the hope of freedom for hundreds of millions—in this sense, the largest part of the job is done. This critically important achievement is obscured by seeming to act as if we have to do much more lest we fail.

Enthoven Opposes Increase in Ground Forces

This May 4, 1967, memorandum for McNamara from his systems-analysis chief, Alain C. Enthoven, used statistics to

question whether further escalation of U.S. ground forces
would significantly affect the course of the war.

Although MACV has admitted to you that the VC/NVA forces can
refuse to fight when they want to, this fact has played no role in
MACV's analysis of strategy and force requirements. (For example, in
his October 1965 briefing, General [William] DePuy said, "The more
often we succeed at (search and destroy operations) the less often will
the VC stand and fight.") Because enemy attrition plays such a central
role in MACV's thinking, and because the enemy's degree of control
over the pace of the action determines how well he can control his attrition, we have taken a hard look at the facts on the enemy's tactical initiative. From reliable, detailed accounts of 56 platoon-sized and larger
fire-fights in 1966 we have classified these fights according to how
they developed. The first four categories in the table all represent cases
in which the enemy willingly and knowingly stood and fought in a
pitched battle; these categories include 47 (84%) of the 56 battles. The
first three categories, enemy ambushes and assaults on our forces, have
66% of the cases; these three plus category 4a, comprising the cases
where the enemy has the advantage of surprise, have 78% of the cases.

The results are independently confirmed from two sources. First,
the ARCOV study, which analyzed a different set of battles in late 1965
and early 1966, found that 46% of the fights begin as enemy ambushes
and that the enemy starts the fight in 88% of the cases; moreover, it
found that 63% of the infantry targets encountered were personnel in
trenches or bunkers. Second, we have analyzed the After-Action Reports submitted to MACV by the line commanders in the field; although generally vague and incomplete in their descriptions of what
happened, they broadly confirm the drift of the above numbers.

These results imply that the size of the force we deploy has little
effect on the rate of attrition of enemy forces. This conclusion should
scarcely surprise you in view of the trend of enemy losses in 1966 and
in view of the obvious sensitivity of month-to-month enemy losses to
his known strategic initiatives. What is surprising to me is that MACV
has ignored this type of information in discussing force levels. I recommend that you inject this factor into the discussion.

Rostow Analysis of Air War

Walt W. Rostow, presidential assistant for national security and long a forceful advocate of the bombing of North Vietnam, joined the debate on May 6, 1967, with this memorandum addressed to several top officials. Arguing with McNamara and McGeorge Bundy, he developed a position that also differed in some particulars from that of the Joint Chiefs of Staff. Paragraphs in italics are the study's paraphrase or explanation.

Rostow's paper began by reviewing what the U.S. was attempting to do in the war: frustrate a Communist take-over "by defeating their main force units; attacking the guerrilla infrastructure; and building a South Vietnamese governmental and security structure. . . ." The purpose of the air war in the North was defined as "To hasten the decision in Hanoi to abandon the aggression . . . ," for which we specifically sought:

(i)   to limit and harass infiltration; and
(ii) to impose on the North sufficient military and civil cost to make them decide to get out of the war earlier rather than later.

Sensitive to the criticisms of the bombing, Rostow tried to dispose of certain of their arguments:

We have never held the view that bombing could stop infiltration. We have never held the view that bombing of the Hanoi-Haiphong area alone would lead them to abandon the effort in the South. We have never held the view that bombing Hanoi-Haiphong would directly cut back infiltration. We have held the view that the degree of military and civilian cost felt in the North and the diversion of resources to deal with our bombing could contribute marginally—and perhaps significantly—to the timing of a decision to end the war. But it was no substitute for making progress in the South.

Rostow argued that while there were policy decisions to be made about the war in the South, particularly with respect to new force levels, there existed no real disagreement with the Administration as to our general strategy on the ground. Where contention did exist was in the matter of the air war. Here there were three broad strategies that could be pursued. Rostow offered a lengthy analysis of the three options. . . .

A. CLOSING THE TOP OF THE FUNNEL

Under this strategy we would mine the major harbors and, perhaps, bomb port facilities and even consider blockade. In addition, we would attack systematically the rail lines between Hanoi and mainland China. At the moment the total import capacity into North Viet Nam is about 17,200 tons per day. Even with expanded import requirement due to the food shortage, imports are, in fact, coming in at about 5700 tons per day. It is possible with a concerted and determined effort that we could cut back import capacity somewhat below the level of requirements; but this is not sure. On the other hand, it would require a difficult and sustained effort by North Viet Nam and its allies to prevent a reduction in total imports below requirements if we did all these things.

The costs would be these:

•   The Soviet Union would have to permit a radical increase in Hanoi's dependence upon Communist China, or introduce minesweepers, etc., to keep its supplies coming into Hanoi by sea;

•   The Chinese Communists would probably introduce many more engineering and anti-aircraft forces along the roads and rail lines between Hanoi and China in order to keep the supplies moving;

•   To maintain its prestige, in case it could not or would not open up Hanoi-Haiphong in the face of mines, the Soviet Union might contemplate creating a Berlin crisis. With respect to a Berlin crisis, they would have to weigh the possible split between the U.S. and its Western European allies under this pressure against damage to the atmosphere of détente in Europe which is working in favor of the French communist Party and providing the Soviet Union with generally enlarged influence in Western Europe.

I myself do not believe that the Soviet Union would go to war with us over Viet Nam unless we sought to occupy North Viet Nam; and, even then, a military response from Moscow would not be certain.

With respect to Communist China, it always has the option of invading Laos and Thailand; but this would not be a rational response to naval and air operations designed to strangle Hanoi. A war throughout Southeast Asia would not help Hanoi; although I do believe Communist China would fight us if we invaded the northern part of North Viet Nam.

One can always take the view that, given the turmoil inside Communist China, an irrational act by Peiping is possible. And such irrationality cannot be ruled out.

I conclude that if we try to close the top of the funnel, tension between ourselves and the Soviet Union and Communist China would increase; if we were very determined, we could impose additional burdens on Hanoi and its allies; we might cut capacity below requirements; and the outcome is less likely to be a general war than more likely.

B. ATTACKING WHAT IS INSIDE THE FUNNEL

This is what we have been doing in the Hanoi-Haiphong area for some weeks. I do not agree with the view that the attacks on Hanoi-Haiphong have no bearing on the war in the South. They divert massive amounts of resources, energies, and attention to keeping the civil and military establishment going. They impose general economic, political, and psychological difficulties on the North which have been complicated this year by a bad harvest and food shortages. I do not believe that they "harden the will of the North." In my judgment, up to this point, our bombing of the North has been a painful additional cost they have thus far been willing to bear to pursue their efforts in the South.

On the other hand:

• There is no direct, immediate connection between bombing the Hanoi-Haiphong area and the battle in the South;
• If we complete the attack on electric power by taking out the Hanoi station—which constitutes about 80% of the electric power supply of the country now operating—we will have hit most of the targets whose destruction imposes serious military-civil costs on the North.
• With respect to risk, it is unclear whether Soviet warnings about our bombing Hanoi-Haiphong represent decisions already taken or decisions which might be taken if we persist in banging away in that area.

It is my judgment that the Soviet reaction will continue to be addressed to the problem imposed on Hanoi by us; that is, they might introduce Soviet pilots as they did in the Korean War; they might bring ground-to-ground missiles into North Viet Nam with the object of attacking our vessels at sea and our airfields in the Danang area.

I do not believe that the continuation of attacks at about the level we have been conducting them in the Hanoi-Haiphong area will lead to pressure on Berlin or a general war with the Soviet Union. In fact, carefully read, what the Soviets have been trying to signal is: Keep away from our ships, we may counter-escalate to some degree; but we do not want a nuclear confrontation over Viet Nam.

C.   CONCENTRATION IN ROUTE PACKAGES 1 AND 2

The advantage of concentrating virtually all our attacks in this area are three:

- We would cut our loss rate in pilots and planes;
- We would somewhat improve our harassment of infiltration of South Viet Nam;
- We would diminish the risks of counter-escalatory action by the Soviet Union and Communist China, as compared with courses A and B.

He rejected course A as incurring too many risks with too little return. . . . Here is how he formulated his conclusions:
With respect to Course B I believe we have achieved greater results in increasing the pressure on Hanoi and raising the cost of their continuing to conduct the aggression in the South than some of my most respected colleagues would agree. I do not believe we should lightly abandon what we have accomplished; and specifically, I believe we should mount the most economical and careful attack on the Hanoi power station our air tacticians can devise. Moreover, I believe we should keep open the option of coming back to the Hanoi-Haiphong area, depending upon what we learn of their repair operations; and what Moscow's and Peiping's reactions are; especially when we understand better what effects we have and have not achieved thus far.

I believe the Soviet Union may well have taken certain counter-steps addressed to the more effective protection of the Hanoi-Haiphong area and may have decided—or could shortly decide—to introduce into North Viet Nam some surface-to-surface missiles.

With respect to option C, I believe we should, while keeping open the B option, concentrate our attacks to the maximum in Route Packages 1 and 2; and, in conducting Hanoi-Haiphong attacks, we should do so only when the targets make sense. I do not expect dramatic results

from increasing the weight of attack in Route Packages 1 and 2; but I
believe we are wasting a good many pilots in the Hanoi-Haiphong area
without commensurate results. The major objective of maintaining the
B option can be achieved at lower cost.

McNamara Turns Dove

With this May 19, 1967, draft presidential memorandum, a by-
now deeply troubled McNamara stamped himself as a full-
fledged critic of the prevailing strategy. He called not only for
stabilizing the ground war and cutting back the bombing or
stopping it altogether but also for accepting a compromise
settlement. The text, as provided in the body of the Pentagon
study, is labeled "first rough draft—data and estimates have
not been checked." Paragraphs in italics are the study's paraphrase or explanation.

*By the 19th of May the opinions of McNamara and his key aides with
respect to the bombing and Westy's troop requests had crystalized sufficiently that another Draft Presidential Memorandum was written. It
was entitled, "Future Actions in Vietnam," and was a comprehensive
treatment of all aspects of the war—military, political, and diplomatic.
It opened with an appraisal of the situation covering both North and
South Vietnam, the U.S. domestic scene and international opinion. The
estimate of the situation in North Vietnam hewed very close to the opinions of the intelligence community already referred to. Here is how the
analysis proceeded:*

C. NORTH VIETNAM

Hanoi's attitude towards negotiations has never been soft nor open-
minded. Any concession on their part would involve an enormous loss
of face. Whether or not the Polish and [Wilfred] Burchett- [Alexei]
Kosygin initiatives had much substance to them, it is clear that Hanoi's
attitude currently is hard and rigid. They seem uninterested in a political settlement and determined to match U.S. military expansion of the

conflict. This change probably reflects these factors: (1) increased assurances of help from the Soviets received during [North Vietnamese
premier] Pham Van Dong's April trip to Moscow; (2) arrangements
providing for the unhindered passage of materiel from the Soviet Union
through China; and (3) a decision to wait for the results of the U.S.
elections in 1968. Hanoi appears to have concluded that she cannot secure her objectives at the conference table and has reaffirmed her strategy of seeking to erode our ability to remain in the South. The Hanoi
leadership has apparently decided that it has no choice but to submit to
the increased bombing. There continues to be no sign that the bombing
has reduced Hanoi's will to resist or her ability to ship the necessary
supplies south. Hanoi shows no signs of ending the large war and advising the VC to melt into the jungles. The North Vietnamese believe
they are right; they consider the Ky regime to be puppets; they believe
the world is with them and that the American public will not have staying power against them. Thus, although they may have factions in the
regime favoring different approaches, they believe that, in the long run,
they are stronger than we are for the purpose. They probably do not
want to make significant concessions, and could not do so without serious loss of face.

*When added to the continuing difficulties in bringing the war in
the south under control, the unchecked erosion of U.S. public support
for the war, and the smoldering international disquiet about the need
and purpose of such U.S. intervention, it is not hard to understand the
DPM's statement that, "This memorandum is written at a time when
there appears to be no attractive course of action." Nevertheless, "alternatives" was precisely what the DPM had been written to suggest.
These were introduced with a recapitulation of where we stood militarily and what the Chiefs were recommending. With respect to the war in
the North, the DPM states:*

Against North Vietnam, an expansion of the bombing program
(ROLLING THUNDER 56) was approved mid-April. Before it was approved, General Wheeler said, "The bombing campaign is reaching the
point where we will have struck all worthwhile fixed targets except the
ports. At this time we will have to address the requirement to deny the
DRV the use of the ports." With its approval, excluding the port areas,
no major military targets remain to be struck in the North. All that remains are minor targets, restrikes of certain major targets, and armed
reconnaissance of the lines of communication (LOCs)—and, under new
principles, mining the harbors, bombing dikes and locks, and invading

North Vietnam with land armies. These new military moves against North Vietnam, together with land movements into Laos and Cambodia, are now under consideration by the Joint Chiefs of Staff.

The broad alternative courses of action it considered were two:

Course A. Grant the request and intensify military actions outside the South—especially against the North. Add a minimum of 200,000 men—100,000 (2⅓ divisions plus 5 tactical air squadrons) would be deployed in FY 1968, another 100,000 (2⅓ divisions and 8 tactical air squadrons) in FY 1969, and possibly more later to fulfill the JCS ultimate requirement for Vietnam and associated world-wide contingencies. Accompanying these force increases (as spelled out below) would be greatly intensified military actions outside South Vietnam—including in Laos and Cambodia but especially against the North.

Course B. Limit force increases to no more than 30,000; avoid extending the ground conflict beyond the borders of South Vietnam; and concentrate the bombing on the infiltration routes south of 20%. Unless the military situation worsens dramatically, add no more than 9 battalions of the approved program of 87 battalions. This course would result in a level of no more than 500,000 men (instead of the currently planned 470,000) on December 31, 1968. (See Attachment IV for details.) A part of this course would be a termination of bombing in the Red River basin unless military necessity required it, and a concentration of all sorties in North Vietnam on the infiltration routes in the neck of North Vietnam, between 17° and 20°.

BOMBING PURPOSES AND PAYOFFS

Our bombing of North Vietnam was designed to serve three purposes:

(1) To retaliate and to lift the morals [sic] of the people in the South who were being attacked by agents of the North.

(2) To add to the pressure on Hanoi to end the war.

(3) To reduce the flow and / or to increase the cost of infiltrating men and material from North to South.

We cannot ignore that a limitation on bombing will cause serious psychological problems among the men, officers and commanders, who will not be able to understand why we should withhold punishment from the enemy. General Westmoreland said that he is "frankly dismayed at even the thought of stopping the bombing program." But this reason for attacking North Vietnam must be scrutinized carefully. We should not bomb for punitive reasons if it serves no other purpose—especially if analysis shows that the actions may be counterproductive. It costs American lives; it creates a backfire of revulsion and opposition by killing civilians; it creates serious risks; it may harden the enemy.

With respect to added pressure on the North, it is becoming apparent that Hanoi may already have "written off" all assets and lives that might be destroyed by U.S. military actions short of occupation of annihilation [sic]. They can and will hold out at least so long as a prospect of winning the "war of attrition" in the South exists. And our best judgment is that a Hanoi prerequisite to negotiations is significant retrenchment (if not complete stoppage) of U.S. military actions against them—at the least, a cessation of bombing. In this connection, Consul-General Rice (Hong Kong 7581, 5/1/67) said that, in his opinion, we cannot by bombing reach the critical level of pain in North Vietnam and that, "below that level, pain only increases the will to fight." [British counterinsurgency expert] Sir Robert Thompson said to Mr. [Cyrus] Vance [deputy secretary of defense] on April 28 that our bombing, particularly in the Red River Delta, "is unifying North Vietnam."

With respect to interdiction of men and materiel, it now appears that no combination of actions against the North short of destruction of the regime or occupation of North Vietnamese territory will physically reduce the flow of men and materiel below the relatively small amount needed by enemy forces to continue the war in the South. Our effort can and does have severe disruptive effects, which Hanoi can and does plan on and prestock against. Our efforts physically to cut the flow meaningfully by actions in North Vietnam therefore largely fail and, in failing, transmute attempted interdiction into pain, or pressure on the North (the factor discussed in the paragraph next above). The lowest "ceiling" on infiltration can probably be achieved by concentration on the North Vietnamese "funnel" south of 20° and on the Trail in Laos.

But what if the above analyses are wrong? Why not escalate the bombing and mine the harbors (and perhaps occupy southern North Vietnam)—on the gamble that it would constrict the flow, meaningfully limiting enemy action in the South, and that it would bend Hanoi? The answer is that the costs and risks of the actions must be considered.

The primary costs of course are U.S. lives: The air campaign against heavily defended areas costs us one pilot in every 40 sorties. In addition, an important but hard-to-measure cost is domestic and world opinion: There may be a limit beyond which many Americans and much of the world will not permit the United States to go. The picture of the world's greatest superpower killing or seriously injuring 1,000 non-combatants a week, while trying to pound a tiny backward nation into submission on an issue whose merits are hotly disputed, is not a pretty one. It could conceivably produce a costly distortion in the American national consciousness and in the world image of the United States—especially if the damage of North Vietnam is complete enough to be "successful."

The most important risk, however, is the likely Soviet, Chinese and North Vietnamese reaction to intensified US air attacks, harbor-mining, and ground actions against North Vietnam.

LIKELY COMMUNIST REACTIONS

At the present time, no actions—except air strikes and artillery fire necessary to quiet hostile batteries across the border—are allowed against *Cambodian* territory. In Laos, we average 5,000 attack sorties a month against the infiltration routes and base areas, we fire artillery from South Vietnam against targets in Laos, and we will be providing 3-man leadership for each of 20 12-man U.S.-Vietnamese Special Forces teams that operate to a depth of 20 kilometers in Laos. Against North Vietnam, we average 8,000 or more attack sorties a month against all worthwhile fixed and LOC targets; we use artillery against ground targets across the DMZ; we fire from naval vessels at targets ashore and afloat up to 19°; and we mine their inland waterways, estuaries . . . up to 20°.

Intensified air attacks against the same types of targets, we would anticipate, would lead to no great change in the policies and reactions of the Communist powers beyond the furnishing of some new equipment and manpower. China, for example, has not reacted to our striking MIG fields in North Vietnam, and we do not expect them to, although there are some signs of greater Chinese participation in North Vietnamese air defense.

Mining the harbors would be much more serious. It would place Moscow in a particularly galling dilemma as to how to preserve the Soviet position and prestige in such a disadvantageous place. The Soviets might, but probably would not, force a confrontation in Southeast Asia—where even with minesweepers they would be at as great a military disadvantage as we were when they blocked the corridor to Berlin in 1961, but where their vital interest, unlike ours in Berlin (and in Cuba), is not so clearly at stake. Moscow in this case should be expected to send volunteers, including pilots, to North Vietnam; to provide some new and better weapons and equipment; to consider some action in Korea, Turkey, Iran, the Middle East or, most likely, Berlin, where the Soviets can control the degree of crisis better; and to show across-the-board hostility toward the U.S. (interrupting any on-going conversations on ABMs, non-proliferation, etc.). China could be expected to seize upon the harbor-mining as the opportunity to reduce Soviet political influence in Hanoi and to discredit the USSR if the Soviets took no military action to open the ports. Peking might read the harbor-mining as indicating that the U.S. was going to apply military pressure until North Vietnam capitulated, and that this meant an eventual invasion. If so, China might decide to intervene in the war with combat troops and air power, to which we would eventually have to respond by bombing Chinese airfields and perhaps other targets as well. **Hanoi** would tighten belts, refuse to talk, and persevere—as it could without too much difficulty. North Vietnam would of course be fully dependent for supplies on China's will, and Soviet influence in Hanoi would therefore be reduced. (Ambassador [to Laos William] Sullivan feels very strongly that it would be a serious mistake, by our actions against the port, to tip Hanoi away from Moscow and toward Peking.)

To U.S. ground actions in North Vietnam, we would expect China to respond by entering the war with both ground and air forces. The Soviet Union could be expected in these circumstances to take all actions listed above under the lesser provocations and to generate a serious confrontation with the United States at one or more places of her own choosing.

The arguments against Course A were summed up in a final paragraph:

Those are the likely costs and risks of **COURSE A.** They are, we believe, both unacceptable and unnecessary. Ground action in North Vietnam, because of its escalatory potential, is clearly unwise despite the open invitation and temptation posed by enemy troops operating freely back and forth across the DMZ. Yet we believe that, short of threatening and perhaps toppling the Hanoi regime itself, pressure against the North will, if anything, harden Hanoi's unwillingness to talk and her settlement terms if she does. China, we believe, will oppose settlement throughout. We believe that there is a chance that the Soviets, at the brink, will exert efforts to bring about peace; but we believe also that intensified bombing and harbor-mining, even if coupled with political pressure from Moscow, will neither bring Hanoi to negotiate nor affect North Vietnam's terms.

With Course A rejected, the DPM turned to consideration of the levelling-off proposals of Course B. The analysis of the de-escalated bombing program of this option proceeded in this manner:

The bombing program that would be a part of this strategy is, basically, a program of concentration of effort on the infiltration routes near the south of North Vietnam. The major infiltration-related targets in the Red River basin having been destroyed, such interdiction is now best served by concentration of all effort in the southern neck of North Vietnam. All of the sorties would be flown in the area between 17° and 20°. This shift, despite possible increases in anti-aircraft capability in the area, should reduce the pilot and aircraft loss rates by more than 50 per cent. The shift will, if anything, be of positive military value to General Westmoreland while taking some steam out of the popular effort in the North.

The above shift of bombing strategy, now that almost all major targets have been struck in the Red River basin, can to military advantage be made at any time. It should not be done for the sole purpose of getting Hanoi to negotiate, although that might be a bonus effect. To maximize the chances of getting that bonus effect, the optimum scenario would probably be (1) to inform the Soviets quietly that within a few days the shift would take place, stating no time limits but making no promises not to return to the Red River basin to attack targets which later acquire military importance (any deal with Hanoi is likely to be midwifed by Moscow); (2) to make the shift as predicted, without fanfare; and (3) to explain publicly, when the shift had become obvious, that the northern targets had been destroyed, and that that had been militarily important, and that there would be no need to return to the northern areas unless military necessity dictated it. The shift should not be huckstered. Moscow would almost certainly pass its information on to Hanoi, and might urge Hanoi to seize the opportunity to de-escalate the war by talks or otherwise Hanoi, not having been asked a question by us and having no ultimatum-like time limit, would be in a better posture to answer favorably than has been the case in the past. The military side of the shift is sound, however, whether or not the diplomatic spill-over is successful.

In a section dealing with diplomatic and political considerations, the DPM outlined the political view of the significance of the struggle as seen by the U.S. and by Hanoi. It then developed a conception of large U.S. interests in Asia around the necessity of containing China. This larger interest required settling the Vietnam war into perspective as only one of three fronts that required U.S. attention (the other two being Japan-Korea and India-Pakistan). In the overall view, the DPM argued, long-run trends in Asia appeared favorable to our interests:

The fact is that the trends in Asia today are running mostly for, not against, our interests (witness Indonesia and the Chinese confusion); there is no reason to be pessimistic about our ability over the next decade or two to fashion alliances and combinations (involving especially Japan and India) sufficient to keep China from encroaching too far. To the extent that our original intervention and our existing actions in Vietnam were motivated by the perceived need to draw the line against Chinese expansionism in Asia, our objective has already been attained, and **COURSE B** will suffice to consolidate it!

With this perspective in mind the DPM went on to reconsider and restate U.S. objectives in the Vietnam contest under the heading "Commitment and Hopes Distinguished":

The time has come for us to eliminate the ambiguities from our minimum objectives—our commitments—in Vietnam. Specifically, two principles must be articulated, and policies and actions brought in line with them: (1) Our commitment is only to see that the people of South Vietnam are permitted to determine their own future. (2) This commitment ceases if the country ceases to help itself.

It follows that no matter how much we might *hope* for some things, our *commitment* is *not*:

- to expel from South Vietnam regroupees, who are South Vietnamese (though we do not like them),
- to ensure that a particular person or group remains in power, nor that the power runs to every corner of the land (though we prefer certain types and we hope their writ will run throughout South Vietnam),
- to guarantee that the self-chosen government is non-Communist (though we believe and strongly hope it will be), and
- to insist that the independent South Vietnam remain separate from North Vietnam (though in the short-run, we would prefer it that way).

(Nor do we have an obligation to pour in effort out of proportion to the effort contributed by the people of South Vietnam or in the face of coups, corruption, apathy or other indications of Saigon failure to co-operate effectively with us.)

We *are* committed to stopping or off setting the effect of North Vietnam's application of force in the South, which denies the people of the South the ability to determine their own future. Even here, however, the line is hard to draw. Propaganda and political advice by Hanoi (or by Washington) is presumably not barred; nor is economic aid or economic advisors. Less clear is the rule to apply to military advisors and war materiel supplied to the contesting factions.

The importance of nailing down and understanding the implications of our limited objectives cannot be overemphasized. It relates intimately to strategy against the North, to troop requirements and missions in the South, to handling of the Saigon government, to settlement terms, and to US domestic and international opinion as to the justification and the success of our efforts on behalf of Vietnam.

This articulation of American purposes and commitments in Vietnam pointedly rejected the high blown formulations of U.S. objectives in NSAM 288 ["an independent non-communist South Vietnam," "defeat the Viet Cong," etc.], and came forcefully to grips with the old dilemma of the U.S. involvement dating from the Kennedy era: only limited means to achieve excessive ends. Indeed, in the following section of specific recommendations, the DPM urged the President to, "issue a NSAM nailing down U.S. policy as described herein." The emphasis in this scaled down set of goals, clearly reflecting the frustrations of failure, was South Vietnamese self-determination. The DPM even went so far as to suggest that, "the South will be in position, albeit imperfect, to start the business of producing a full-spectrum government in South Vietnam." What this amounted to was a recommendation that we accept a compromise outcome. Let there be no mistake these were radical positions for a senior U.S. policy official within the Johnson Administration to take. They would bring the bitter condemnation of the Chiefs and were scarcely designed to flatter the President on the successes of his efforts to date. That they represented a more realistic mating of U.S. strategic objectives and capabilities is another matter.

The scenario for the unfolding of the recommendations in the DPM went like this:

(4)   **June:** Concentrate the bombing of North Vietnam on physical interdiction of men and materiel. This would mean terminating, ex-

cept where the interdiction objective clearly dictates otherwise, all bombing north of 20° and improving interdiction as much as possible in the infiltration "funnel" south of 20° by concentration of sorties and by an all-out effort to improve detection devices, denial weapons, and interdiction tactics.

(5)   July: Avoid the explosive Congressional debate and U.S. Reserve call-up implicit in the Westmoreland troop request. Decide that, unless the military situation worsens dramatically, U.S. deployments will be limited to Program 4-plus (which according to General Westmoreland, will not put us in danger of being defeated, but will mean slow progress in the South). Associated with this decision are decisions not to use large numbers of U.S. troops in the Delta and not to use large numbers of them in grassroots pacification work.

(6)   September: Move the newly elected Saigon government well beyond its National Reconciliation program to seek a political settlement with the non-Communist members of the NLF—to explore a cease-fire and to reach an accommodation with the non-Communist South Vietnamese who are under the VC banner; to accept them as members of an opposition political party, and, if necessary, to accept their individual participation in the national government—in sum, a settlement to transform the members of the VC from military opponents to political opponents.

(7)   October: Explain the situation to the Canadians, Indians, British, UN and others, as well as nations now contributing forces, requesting them to contribute border forces to help make the inside–South Vietnam accommodation possible, and—consistent with our desire neither to occupy nor to have bases in Vietnam—offering to remove later an equivalent number of U.S. forces. (This initiative is worth taking despite its slim chance of success.)

Having made the case for de-escalation and compromise, the DPM ended on a note of candor with a clear statement of its disadvantages and problems:

The difficulties with this approach are neither few nor small: There will be those who disagree with the circumscription of the U.S. commitment (indeed, at one time or another, one U.S. voice or another has told the Vietnamese, third countries, the U.S. Congress, and the public of "goals" or "objectives" that go beyond the above bare-bones statement of our "commitment"); some will insist that pressure, enough pressure, on the North can pay off or that we will have yielded a blue chip without exacting a price in exchange for our concentrating on interdiction; many will argue that denial of the larger number of troops will prolong the war, risk losing it and increase the casualties of the Americans who are there; some will insist that this course reveals weakness to which Moscow will react with relief, contempt and reduced willingness to help, and to which Hanoi will react by increased demands and truculence; others will point to the difficulty of carrying the Koreans, Filipinos, Australians and New Zealanders with us; and there will be those who point out the possibility that the changed U.S. tone may cause a "rush for the exits" in Thailand, in Laos and especially inside South Vietnam, perhaps threatening cohesion of the government, morale of the army, and loss of support among the people. Not least will be the alleged impact on the reputation of the United States and of its President. Nevertheless, the difficulties of this strategy are fewer and smaller than the difficulties of any other approach.

William Bundy Response to McNamara

In what the authors of the Pentagon study called a "rambling and sometimes contradictory memo," Assistant Secretary of State William Bundy responded to McNamara's draft presidential memorandum on May 30, 1967. Bundy's response suggests, if nothing else, the extent to which McNamara had gone beyond most of his civilian colleagues in his "dovishness." Paragraphs in italics are the study's paraphrase or explanation.

William Bundy at State drafted comments on the DPM on May 30 and circulated them at State and Defense. In his rambling and sometimes contradictory memo, Bundy dealt mainly with the nature and scope of the U.S. commitment—as expressed in the DPM and as he saw it. He avoided any detailed analysis of the two military options and focused his attention on the strategic reasons for American involvement; the objectives we were after; and the terms under which we could consider closing down the operation. His memo began with his contention that:

The gut point can almost be summed up in a pair of sentences. If we can get a reasonably solid GVN political structure and GVN performance at all levels, favorable trends could become really marked over the next 18 months, the war will be won for practical purposes at some point, and the resulting peace will be secured. On the other hand, if we do not get these results from the GVN and the South Vietnamese people, no amount of U.S. effort will achieve our basic objective in South Viet-Nam—a return to the essential provisions of the Geneva Accords of 1954 and a reasonably stable peace for many years based on these Accords.

It is the view of the central importance of the South that dominates the remainder of Bundy's memo. But his own thinking was far from clear about how the U.S. should react to a South Vietnamese failure for at the end of it he wrote:

None of the above decides one other question clearly implicit in the DOD draft. What happens if "the country ceases to help itself." If this happens in the literal sense, if South Viet-Nam performs so badly that it simply is not going to be able to govern itself or to resist the slightest internal pressure, then we would agree that we can do nothing to prevent this. But the real underlying question is to what extent we tolerate imperfection, even gross imperfection, by the South Vietnamese while they are still under the present grinding pressure from Hanoi and the NLF.

This is a tough question. What do we do if there is a military coup this summer and the elections are aborted? There would then be tremendous pressure at home and in Europe to the effect that this negated what we were fighting for, and that we should pull out.

But against such pressure we must reckon that the stakes in Asia will remain. After all, the military rule, even in peacetime, in Thailand, Indonesia, and Burma. Are we to walk away from the South Vietnamese, at least as a matter of principle, simply because they failed in what was always conceded to be a courageous and extremely difficult effort to become a true democracy during a guerrilla war?

Bundy took pointed issue with DPM's reformulation of U.S. objectives. Starting with the DPM's discussion of U.S. larger interests in Asia, Bundy argued that:

In Asian eyes, the struggle is a test case, and indeed much more black-and-white than even we ourselves see it. The Asian view bears little resemblance to the breast-beating in Europe or at home. Asians would quite literally be appalled—and this includes India—if we were to pull out from Viet-Nam or if we were to settle for an illusory peace that produced Hanoi control over all Viet-Nam in short order.

In short, our effort in Viet-Nam in the past two years has not only

prevented the catastrophe that would otherwise have unfolded but has
laid a foundation for a progress that now appears truly possible and of
the greatest historical significance.

*Having disposed of what he saw as a misinterpretation of Asian
sentiment and U.S. interests there, Bundy now turned to the DPM's attempt to minimize the U.S. commitment in Vietnam. He opposed the
DPM language because in his view it dealt too heavily with our military commitment to get NVA off the South Vietnamese back, and not
enough with the equally important commitment to assure that "the political board in South Vietnam is not tilted to the advantage of the
NLF." Bundy's conception of the U.S. commitment was twofold:*

- To prevent any imposed political role for the NLF in South
Vietnamese political life, and specifically the coalition demanded by
point 3 of Hanoi's Four Points, or indeed any NLF part in government
or political life that is not safe and acceptable voluntarily to the South
Vietnamese Government and people.
- To insist in our negotiating position that "regroupees," that is,
people originally native to South Viet-Nam who went North in 1954
and returned from 1959 onward, should be expelled as a matter of principle in the settlement. Alternatively, such people could remain in
South Viet-Nam if, but only if, the South Vietnamese Government itself was prepared to receive them back under a reconciliation concept,
which would provide in essence that they must be prepared to accept
peaceful political activity under the Constitution (as the reconciliation
appeal now does). This latter appears to be the position of the South
Vietnamese Government, which—as Tran Van Do has just stated in
Geneva—argues that those sympathetic to the Northern system of government should go North, while those prepared to accept the Southern
system of government may stay in the South. Legally, the first alternative is sound, in that Southerners who went North in 1954 became for
all legal and practical purposes Northern citizens and demonstrated
their allegiance. But if the South Vietnamese prefer the second alternative, it is in fact exactly comparable to the regroupment provisions of
the 1954 Accords, and can legally be sustained. But in either case the
point is that the South Vietnamese are not obliged to accept as citizens
people whose total pattern of conduct shows that they would seek to
overthrow the structure of government by force and violence.

*The remainder of Bundy's comments were addressed to impor-
tance of this last point. The U.S. could not consider withdrawing its
forces until not only the North Vietnamese troops but also the re-*

groupees had returned to the North. Nowhere in his comments does he specifically touch on the merits of the two military options, but his arguments all seem to support the tougher of the two choices (his earlier support of restricting the bombing thus seems paradoxical). He was, it is clear, less concerned with immediate specific decisions on a military phase of the war than with the long term consequences of this major readjustment of American sights in Southeast Asia.

Chapter 7

The Tet Offensive and the End of Escalation

The North Vietnamese/Vietcong Tet Offensive of 1968 marked a major turning point in the Vietnam War. The enemy attacks were directed against the cities and towns of South Vietnam, presumably the most secure areas in the country, and this, along with the element of surprise and their sheer magnitude, had a stunning impact. Thus although U.S. and South Vietnamese forces in time repulsed the offensive and inflicted crippling losses on the enemy, Tet had a profound psychological effect, especially in the United States. Johnson eventually responded by ending U.S. escalation of the war, cutting back the bombing, and making a new proposal for peace negotiations. Most important, perhaps, he withdrew himself from the 1968 presidential campaign.

The Tet Offensive exceeded in scope and ferocity anything in the war to this point. On January 30, 1968, during the Vietnamese lunar New Year (Tet) holidays, the North Vietnamese and Vietcong launched simultaneous attacks on all the major towns and cities of South Vietnam. Catching the United States and South Vietnam by surprise, they scored stunning successes at the outset, even for a brief period pene-

trating the U.S. Embassy compound in Saigon, the very symbol of U.S. power. The United States and South Vietnam
quickly recovered and drove back the enemy attackers, in all
areas inflicting huge losses, but the offensive had a profoundly
disruptive effect throughout South Vietnam, setting back pacification still further and causing at least a momentary loss of
confidence.

As a result of Tet, the great debate on U.S. strategy that
began in early 1967 came to a crisis point in early 1968. After
a brief period of uncertainty, Westmoreland concluded that
the U.S. position was secure. General Wheeler, on the other
hand, saw Tet as an opportunity to achieve what the JCS had
sought from the beginning, mobilization of the reserves and
expansion of the war, and after a trip to Vietnam in late February he proposed to add 206,000 new U.S. troops and he re-
vived Westmoreland's earlier proposals to expand the war into
Laos, Cambodia, and if necessary North Vietnam.

Those who had opposed expansion of the war in 1967
mobilized a year later to head it off once again. Tet had an
enormous political and psychological impact in the United
States. It appeared to put the lie to the administration's 1967
claims of progress, and many influential Americans concluded
in its aftermath that anything that could be won in Vietnam
would not be worth the prospective cost. Civilians in the Pentagon, supported by McNamara's successor as secretary of
defense, Clark Clifford, and by presidential speechwriter Harry
McPherson, argued that from a domestic political standpoint
further escalation of the war would be suicidal. They eventually persuaded a reluctant Johnson, and in a dramatic speech
on March 31, 1968, the President approved only a modest increase in U.S. ground forces. More important, he cut back the
bombing of North Vietnam to the area below the 20th parallel,
set forth new peace proposals, and, most dramatically, indicated that he would not run for President in 1968.

Tet stands as one of the most important turning points of
America's longest war. After weeks of hesitation, Johnson with
obvious reluctance terminated the open-ended U.S. commitment to maintain an independent, non-Communist South Vietnam and put an end to the policy of gradual escalation
launched in 1965, changes not easily reversed by his successor. To the surprise of some administration officials, the North
Vietnamese responded positively to the U.S. offer to negotiate, and after numerous delays formal peace talks began in
May 1968. It would take four more years, many thousands of

lives, and much destruction before these talks produced results. As a result of Tet, however, the U.S. role changed significantly, and the war after 1968 would be very different from
before.

The Pentagon study documentation for this period is
quite sparse. In fact, the authors were completing their work at
the very time the offensive was taking place. Their study, for
all practical purposes, ended in late 1967, and they did not
deal with this period except as a kind of postscript. The several documents included below do, however, give some sense
of the dramatic developments of February–March 1968 and of
their even more dramatic outcome.

CINCPAC Late 1967 Report on War

In his year-end report for 1967, excerpted below, Admiral U. S. Grant Sharp, commander in chief of Pacific forces, continued to insist that the air war was producing important results. Paragraphs in italics are the study's paraphrase or explanation.

Admiral Sharp outlined three objectives which the air campaign was seeking to achieve: disruption of the flow of external assistance into North Vietnam, curtailment of the flow of supplies from North Vietnam into Laos and South Vietnam, and destruction "in depth" of North Vietnamese resources that contributed to the support of the war. Acknowledging that the flow of fraternal communist aid into the North had grown every year of the war, CINCPAC noted the stepped up effort in 1967 to neutralize this assistance by logistically isolating its primary port of entry—Haiphong. The net results, he felt, had been encouraging:

The overall effect of our effort to reduce external assistance has resulted not only in destruction and damage of the transportation systems and goods being transported thereon but has created additional management, distribution and manpower problems. In addition, the attacks have created a bottleneck at Haiphong where inability effectively to move goods inland from the port has resulted in congestion on the docks and a slowdown in offloading ships as they arrive. By October, road and rail interdictions had reduced the transportation clearance capacity at Haiphong to about 2700 short tons per day. An average of 4400 short tons per day had arrived in Haiphong during the year.

The assault against the continuing traffic of men and material through North Vietnam toward Laos and South Vietnam, however, had produced only marginal results. Success here was measured in the totals of destroyed transport, not the constriction of the flow of personnel and goods.

Although men and material needed for the level of combat now prevailing in South Vietnam continue to flow despite our attacks on LOCs, we have made it very costly to the enemy in terms of material, manpower, management, and distribution. From 1 January through 15 December 1967, 122,960 attack sorties were flown in Rolling Thunder route packages I through V and in Laos, SEA DRAGON offensive operations involved 1,384 ship-days on station and contributed materially in reducing enemy seaborne infiltration in southern NVN and in the vicinity of the DMZ. Attacks against the NVN transport system during the past 12 months resulted in destruction of carriers, cargo carried, and personnel casualties. Air attacks throughout North Vietnam and Laos destroyed or damaged 5,261 motor vehicles, 2,475 railroad rolling stock, and 11,425 watercraft from 1 January through 20 December 1967. SEA DRAGON accounted for another 1,473 WBLC destroyed or damaged from 1 January–30 November. There were destroyed raillines, bridges, ferries, railroad yards and ships, storage areas, and truck parks. Some 3,685 land targets were struck by SEA DRAGON forces, including the destruction or damage of 303 coastal defense and radar sites. Through external assistance, the enemy has been able to replace or rehabilitate many of the items damaged or destroyed, and transport inventories are roughly at the same level they were at the beginning of the year. Nevertheless, construction problems have caused interruptions in the flow of men and supplies, caused a great loss of work-hours, and restricted movement particularly during daylight hours.

The admission that transport inventories were the same at year's end as when it began must have been a painful one indeed for CINCPAC in view of the enormous cost of the air campaign against the transport system in money, aircraft, and lives. As a consolation for this signal failure, CINCPAC pointed to the extensive diversion of civilian manpower to war related activities as a result of the bombing.

A primary effect of our efforts to impede movement of the enemy has been to force Hanoi to engage from 500,000 to 600,000 civilians in full-time and part-time war-related activities, in particular for air defense and repair of the LOCs. This diversion of manpower from other pursuits, particularly from the agricultural sector, has caused a drawdown on manpower. The estimated lower food production yields, coupled with an increase in food imports in 1967 (some six times that of 1966), indicate that agriculture is having great difficulty in adjusting to this changed composition of the work force. The cost and difficulties of the war to Hanoi have sharply increased, and only through the willingness of other communist countries to provide maximum replacement of goods and material has NVN managed to sustain its war effort.

To these manpower diversions CINCPAC added the cost to North Vietnam in 1967 of the destruction of vital resources—the third of his air war objectives:

C Destroying vital resources:

Air attacks were authorized and executed by target systems for the first time in 1967, although the attacks were limited to specific targets within each system. A total of 9,740 sorties was flown against targets on the ROLLING THUNDER target list from 1 January–15 December 1967. The campaign against the power system resulted in reduction of power generating capability to approximately 15 percent of original capacity. Successful strikes against the Thai Nguyen iron and steel plant and the Haiphong cement plant resulted in practically total destruction of these two installations. NVN adjustments to these losses have had to be made by relying on additional imports from China, the USSR or the Eastern European countries. The requirement for additional imports reduces available shipping space for war supporting supplies and adds to the congestion at the ports. Interruptions in raw material supplies and the requirement to turn to less efficient means of power and distribution have degraded overall production.

Economic losses to North Vietnam amounted to more than $130 million dollars [sic] in 1967, representing over one-half of the total economic losses since the war began.

Wheeler's Post-Tet Report to President

When the dust had settled after the initial phase of the enemy's Tet Offensive, General Wheeler journeyed to Saigon to survey the situation and make recommendations to the President. While there, he apparently decided to attempt to use the exigencies of Tet to force the President's hand on mobilizing the reserves and expanding the war. The following are excerpts from Wheeler's memorandum to President Johnson, dated February 27, 1968, headed "Report of Chairman, J.C.S., on Situation in Vietnam and MACV Requirements." The request for 206,000 additional troops set off the public firestorm that eventually led to Johnson's March 31, 1968, decision to halt escalation of the war.

1 The Chairman, JCS and party visited SVN on 23, 24 and 25 February. This report summarizes the impressions and facts developed through conversations and briefings at MACV and with senior commanders throughout the country.

2. SUMMARY

• The current situation in Vietnam is still developing and fraught with opportunities as well as dangers.

• There is no question in the mind of MACV that the enemy went all out for a general offensive and general uprising and apparently believed that he would succeed in bringing the war to an early successful conclusion.

• The enemy failed to achieve his initial objective but is continuing his effort. Although many of his units were badly hurt, the judgement is that he has the will and the capability to continue.

• Enemy losses have been heavy; he has failed to achieve his prime objectives of mass uprisings and capture of a large number of the capital cities and towns. Morale in enemy units which were badly mauled or where the men were oversold the idea of a decisive victory at TET probably has suffered severely. However, with replacements, his indoctrination system would seem capable of maintaining morale at a generally adequate level. His determination appears to be unshaken.

• The enemy is operating with relative freedom in the countryside, probably recruiting heavily and no doubt infiltrating NVA units and personnel. His recovery is likely to be rapid; his supplies are adequate; and he is trying to maintain the momentum of his winter-spring offensive.

• The structure of the GVN held up but its effectiveness has suffered.

• The RVNAF held up against the initial assault with gratifying, and in a way, surprising strength and fortitude. However, RVNAF is now in a defensive posture around towns and cities and there is concern about how well they will bear up under sustained pressure.

• The initial attack nearly succeeded in a dozen places, and defeat in those places was only averted by the timely reaction of U.S. forces. In short, it was a very near thing.

• There is no doubt that the RD Program has suffered a severe set back.

• RVNAF was not badly hurt physically—they should recover strength and equipment rather quickly (equipment in 2–3 months—strength in 3–6 months). Their problems are more psychological than physical.

• U.S. forces have lost none of their pre-TET capability.

• MACV has three principal problems. First, logistic support north of Danang is marginal owing to weather, enemy interdiction and harassment and the massive deployment of U.S. forces into the DMZ/Hue area. Opening Route 1 will alleviate this problem but takes a substantial troop commitment. Second, the defensive posture of ARVN is permitting the VC to make rapid inroads in the formerly pacified countryside. ARVN, in its own words, is in a dilemma as it cannot afford another enemy thrust into the cities and towns and yet if it remains in a defensive posture, against this contingency, the countryside goes by default. MACV is forced to devote much of its troop strength to this problem. Third MACV has been forced to deploy 50% of all U.S. maneuver battalions into I Corps, to meet the threat there, while stripping the rest of the country of adequate reserves. If the enemy synchronizes an attack against Khe Sanh/Hue-Quang Tri with an offensive in the Highlands and around Saigon while keeping the pressure on throughout the remainder of the country, MACV will be hard pressed to meet adequately all threats. Under these circumstances, we must be prepared to accept some reverses.

- For these reasons, General Westmoreland has asked for a 3 division–15 tactical fighter squadron force. This force would provide him with a theater reserve and an offensive capability which he does not now have.

3.   THE SITUATION AS IT STANDS TODAY

a   **Enemy Capabilities:**

(1)   The enemy has been hurt badly in the populated lowlands, is practically intact elsewhere. He committed over 67,000 combat maneuver forces plus perhaps 25% or 17,000 more impressed men and boys, for a total of about 84,000. He lost 40,000 killed, at least 3,000 captured, and perhaps 5,000 disabled or died of wounds. He had peaked his force total to about 240,000 just before TET, by hard recruiting, infiltration, civilian impressment, and drawdowns on service and guerrilla personnel. So he has lost about one fifth of his total strength. About two-thirds of his trained, organized unit strength can continue offensive action. He is probably infiltrating and recruiting heavily in the countryside while allied forces are securing the urban areas. (Discussions of strengths and recruiting are in paragraphs 1, 2 and 3 of Enclosure (1)). The enemy has adequate munitions, stockpiled in-country and available through the DMZ, Laos, and Cambodia, to support major attacks and countrywide pressure; food procurement may be a problem. (Discussion is in paragraph 6 Enclosure (1)). Besides strength losses, the enemy now has morale and training problems which currently limit combat effectiveness of VC guerrilla, main and local forces. (Discussions of forces are in paragraphs 2, 5, Enclosure (1)).

(a)   I Corps Tactical Zone: Strong enemy forces in the north-
        ern two provinces threaten Quanq Tri and Hue cities,
        and U.S. positions at the DMZ. Two NVA divisions
        threaten Khe Sanh. Eight enemy battalion equivalents
        are in the Danang–Hoi An area. Enemy losses in I CTZ
        have been heavy, with about 13,000 killed; some NVA
        as well as VC units have been hurt badly. However,
        NVA replacements in the DMZ area can offset these
        losses fairly quickly. The enemy has an increased ar-
        tillery capability at the DMZ, plus some tanks and possi-
        bly even a limited air threat in I CTZ.

(b)   II Corps Tactical Zone: The 1st NVA Division went vir-
        tually unscathed during TET offensive, and represents a
        strong threat in the western highlands. Seven combat
        battalion equivalents threaten Dak To. Elsewhere in the
        highlands, NVA units have been hurt and VC units
        chopped up badly. On the coast, the 3rd NVA Division
        had already taken heavy losses just prior to the offen-
        sive. The 5th NVA Division, also located on the coast, is
        not in good shape. Local force strength is about 13,000
        killed; some NVA as well as coastal II CTZ had dwin-
        dled long before the offensive. The enemy's strength in
        II CTZ is in the highlands where enemy troops are fresh
        and supply lines short.

(c)   III CTZ: Most of the enemy's units were used in the TET
        effort, and suffered substantial losses. Probably the only
        major unit to escape heavy losses was the 7th NVA Di-
        vision. However, present dispositions give the enemy the
        continuing capability of attacking in the Saigon area
        with 10 to 11 combat effective battalion equivalents. His
        increased movement southward of supporting arms and
        infiltration of supplies has further developed his capacity
        for attacks by fire.

(d)   IV Corps Tactical Zone: All enemy forces were commit-
        ted in IV Corps, but losses per total strength were the
        lightest in the country. The enemy continues to be capa-
        ble of investing or attacking cities throughout the area.

(2)   New weapons or tactics:
        We may see heavier rockets and tube artillery, additional
      armor, and the use of aircraft, particularly in the I CTZ. The
      only new tactic in view is infiltration and investment of cities
      to create chaos, to demoralize the people, to discredit the gov-
      ernment, and to tie allied forces to urban security.

b   RVNAF Capabilities:
  (1)   Current Status of RVNAF:
    (a)   Strength
        —As of 31 Dec RVNAF strength was 643,116 (Regular Forces—342,951; RF—151,376; and PF—148,789)

Date	Auth	PFD	% of Strength
31 Dec.	112,435	96,667	86
10 Feb.	112,435	77,000	68.5
15 Feb.	112,435	83,935	74.7

. . .

    (d)   The redeployment of forces has caused major relocations of support forces, logistical activities and supplies.
    (e)   The short range solutions to the four major areas listed above were: (a) Emergency replacement of major equipment items and ammunition from the CONUS and (b) day-to-day emergency actions and relocation of resources within the theater. In summary, the logistics system in Vietnam has provided adequate support throughout the TET offensive. . . . .

d   GVN Strength and Effectiveness:
  (1)   Psychological—the people in South Vietnam were handed a psychological blow, particularly in the urban areas where the feeling of security had been strong. There is a fear of further attacks.
  (2)   The structure of the Government was not shattered and continues to function but at greatly reduced effectiveness.
  (3)   In many places, the RD program has been set back badly. In other places the program was untouched in the initial stage of the offensive. MACV reports that of the 555 RD cadre groups, 278 remain in hamlets, 245 are in district and province towns on security duty, while 32 are unaccounted for. It is not clear as to when, or even whether, it will be possible to return to the RD program in its earlier form. As long as the VC prowl the countryside it will be impossible, in many places, even to tell exactly what has happened to the program.
  (4)   Refugees—An additional 470,000 refugees were generated during the offensive. A breakdown of refugees is at Enclosure (7). The problem of caring for refugees is part of the larger problem of reconstruction in the cities and towns. It is antici-

pated that the care and reestablishment of the 250,000 persons or 50,000 family units who have lost their homes will require from GVN sources the expenditure of 500 million piasters for their temporary care and resettlement plus an estimated 30,000 metric tons of rice. From U.S. sources, there is a requirement to supply aluminum and cement for 40,000 refugee families being reestablished under the Ministry of Social Welfare and Refugee self-help program. Additionally, the GVN/Public Works City Rebuilding Plan will require the provision of 400,000 double sheets of aluminum, plus 20,000 tons [words illegible].

4.   WHAT DOES THE FUTURE HOLD

a   **Probable Enemy Strategy.** (Reference paragraph 7b, Enclosure (1).) We see the enemy pursuing a reinforced offensive to enlarge his control throughout the country and keep pressures on the government and allies. We expect him to maintain strong threats in the DMZ area, at Khe Sanh, in the highlands, and at Saigon, and to attack in force when conditions seem favorable. He is likely to try to gain control of the country's northern provinces. He will continue efforts to encircle cities and province capitals to isolate and disrupt normal activities, and infiltrate them to create chaos. He will seek maximum attrition of RVNAF elements. Against U.S. forces, he will emphasize attacks by fire on airfields and installations, using assaults and ambushes selectively. His central objective continues to be the destruction of the Government of SVN and its armed forces. As a minimum he hopes to seize sufficient territory and gain control of enough people to support establishment of the groups and committees he proposes for participation in an NLF dominated government.

b   **MACV Strategy:**
   (1)   MACV believes that the central thrust of our strategy now must be to defeat the enemy offensive and that if this is done well, the situation overall will be greatly improved over the pre-TET condition.
   (2)   MACV accepts the fact that its first priority must be the security of Government of Vietnam in Saigon and provincial capitals. MACV describes its objectives as:
      •   First, to counter the enemy offensive and to destroy or eject the NVA invasion force in the north.
      •   Second, to restore security in the cities and towns.

- Third, to restore security in the heavily populated areas of the countryside.
- Fourth, to regain the initiative through offensive operations.

c **Tasks:**

(1) Security of Cities and Government. MACV recognizes that U.S. forces will be required to reinforce and support RVNAF in the security of cities, towns and government structure. At this time, 10 U.S. battalions are operating in the environs of Saigon. It is clear that this task will absorb a substantial portion of U.S. forces.

(2) Security in the Countryside. To a large extent the VC now control the countryside. Most of the 54 battalions formerly providing security for pacification are now defending district or province towns. MACV estimates that U.S. forces will be required in a number of places to assist and encourage the Vietnamese Army to leave the cities and towns and reenter the country. This is especially true in the Delta.

(3) Defense of the Borders, the DMZ and Northern Provinces. MACV considers that it must meet the enemy threat in I Corps Tactical Zone and has already deployed there slightly over 50% of all U.S. maneuver battalions. U.S. forces have been thinned out in the highlands, notwithstanding an expected enemy offensive in the early future.

(4) Offensive Operations. Coupling the increased requirement for the defense of the cities and subsequent reentry into the rural areas, and the heavy requirement for defense of the I Corps Zone, MACV does not have adequate forces at this time to resume the offensive in the remainder of the country, nor does it have adequate reserves against the contingency of simultaneous large-scale enemy offensive action throughout the country.

5. FORCE REQUIREMENTS

a Forces currently assigned to MACV, plus the residual Program Five forces yet to be delivered, are inadequate in numbers to carry out the strategy and to accomplish the tasks described above in the proper priority. To contend with, and defeat, the new enemy threat, MACV has stated requirements for forces over the 525,000 ceiling imposed by Program Five. The add-on requested totals 206,756 spaces for a new proposed ceiling of 731,756, with all forces being deployed into country by the end of CY 68. Principal forces included in the add-on are three division equivalents, 15 tactical fighter squadrons and augmentation for current Navy programs. MACV desires that these additional forces be delivered in three packages as follows:

(1) Immediate Increment, Priority One: To be deployed by 1 May 68. Major elements include one brigade of the 5th Mechanized Division with a mix of one infantry, one armored and one mechanized battalion; the Fifth Marine Division (less RLT-26); one armored cavalry regiment; eight tactical fighter squadrons; and a groupment of Navy units to augment on going programs.

(2) Immediate Increment, Priority Two: To be deployed as soon as possible but prior to 1 Sept 68. Major elements include the remainder of the 5th Mechanized Division, and four tactical fighter squadrons. It is desirable that the ROK Light Division be deployed within this time frame.

(3) Follow-on Increment: To be deployed by the end of CY 68. Major elements include one infantry division, three tactical fighter squadrons, and units to further augment Navy Programs.

b Enclosure (9) treats MACV's force requirements for CY 68 to include troop lists, and service strengths for each of the three packages which comprise the total MACV request.

c Those aspects of MACV's CY 68 force requirements recommendations meriting particular consideration are:

(1) Civilianization. Approximately 150,000 Vietnamese and troop contributing nations' civilians are currently employed by MACV components. Program Five contains provisions to replace 12,545 military spaces by civilians during CY 68. MACV is experiencing difficulties with the civilian program because of curfew impositions, disrupted transportation, fear, movement of military units which include civilians, strikes, and prospective mobilization [rest illegible].

LBJ's March 31, 1968, Decisions

These excerpts from a State Department cablegram to U.S. ambassadors in Australia, New Zealand, Thailand, Laos, the

Philippines, and South Korea, March 31, 1968, as provided in the body of the Pentagon study, announced provisions of the major speech President Johnson was to make hours later. The cable did not include Johnson's new appeal for negotiations, nor did it contain his announcement that he would not run for reelection, something he added to the speech at the last minute without informing even his closest advisers. Paragraphs in italics are the study's paraphrase or explanation.

a Major stress on importance of GVN and ARVN increased effectiveness with our equipment and other support as first priority in our own actions.

b 13,500 support forces to be called up at once in order to round out the 10,500 combat units sent in February.

c Replenishment of strategic reserve by calling up 48,500 additional reserves, stating that these would be designed to strategic reserve.

d Related tax increases and budget cuts already largely needed for non-Vietnam reasons.

In addition, after similar consultation and concurrence, President proposes to announce that bombing will be restricted to targets most directly engaged in battlefield area and that this meant that there would be no bombing north of the 20th parallel. Announcement would leave open how Hanoi might respond, and would be open-ended as to time. However, it would indicate that Hanoi's response could be helpful in determining whether we were justified in assumption that Hanoi would not take advantage if we stopped bombing altogether. Thus, it would to this extent foreshadow possibility of full bombing stoppage at a later point.

This cable offered the Ambassadors some additional rationale for this new policy for their discretionary use in conversations with their respective heads of government. This rationale represents the only available statement by the Administration of some of its underlying reasons and purposes for and expectations from this policy decision.

a You should call attention to force increases that would be announced at the same time and would make clear our continued resolve. Also our top priority to re-equipping ARVN forces.

b You should make clear that Hanoi is most likely to denounce the project and thus free our hand after a short period. Nonetheless, we might wish to continue the limitation even after a formal denunciation, in order to reinforce its sincerity and put the monkey firmly on Hanoi's back for whatever follows. Of course, any major military change could compel full-scale resumption at any time.

    c   With or without denunciation, Hanoi might well feel limited in conducting any major offensives at least in the northern areas. If they did so, this could ease the pressure where it is most potentially serious. If they did not, then this would give us a clear field for whatever actions were then required.

    d   In view of weather limitations, bombing north of the 20th parallel will in any event be limited at least for the next four weeks or so— which we tentatively envisage as a maximum testing period in any event. Hence, we are not giving up anything really serious in this time frame. Moreover, air power now used north of 20th can probably be used in Laos (where no policy change planned) and in SVN.

    e   Insofar as our announcement foreshadows any possibility of a complete bombing stoppage, in the event Hanoi really exercises reciprocal restraints, we regard this as unlikely. But in any case, the period of demonstrated restraint would probably have to continue for a period of several weeks, and we would have time to appraise the situation and to consult carefully with them before we undertook any such action.

Glossary of Acronyms and Abbreviations

AA   antiaircraft
AAA   antiaircraft artillery
ABM   antiballistic missile
ACR   Armored Cavalry Regiment
AFB   air force base
AID   Agency for International Development (U.S.)
ARCOV   Army Combat Operations in Vietnam
ARVN   Army of the Republic of (South) Vietnam
ASA   Army Security Agency
ASW   antisubmarine warfare
CAP   White House message sent through CIA
CAS   code name for CIA
CAT   Civil Air Transport, airline based on Taiwan
CHICOM   Chinese Communist
CHMAAG   Chief Military Assistance Advisory Group
CIA   Central Intelligence Agency
CINCPAC   commander in chief, Pacific
CJCS   chairman, Joint Chiefs of Staff
COMINT   communications intelligence
COMUSMACV   commander, U.S. Military Assistance Command, Vietnam

CONUS   Continental United States
CTZ   corps tactical zone
CY   calendar year
DEPTEL   Department of State telegram
DIA   Defense Intelligence Agency
DMZ   demilitarized zone
DOD   Department of Defense
DPM   draft presidential memo
DRV   Democratic Republic of (North) Vietnam
ECM   electronic countermeasures
FEC   French Expeditionary Corps
FOA   Foreign Operations Administration
FY   fiscal year
FYI   for your information
GCI   ground clearance intercept
GVN   Governemnt of (South) Vietnam
HNC   High National Council
ICA   International Cooperation Administration
JCS   Joint Chiefs of Staff
JCSM   Joint Chiefs of Staff memorandum
KIA   killed in action
LOC   lines of communication
LST   tank landing ship
MAAG   Military Assistance Advisory Group
MACV   Military Assistance Command, Vietnam
MAP   Military Assistance Program
MDAP   Mutual Defense Assistance Program
MEF   Marine Expeditionary Force
MIG   Mikoyan and Gorevich, designation for Soviet aircraft formed from
names of designers
NATO   North Atlantic Treaty Organization
NSA   National Security Agency
NSC   National Security Council
NVA   North Vietnamese Army
NVN   North Vietnam
OSS   Office of Strategic Services
PACOM   Pacific Command
PAVN   People's Army of (North) Vietnam
PBR   river patrol boat
PF   popular forces
PL   Pathet Lao
POL   petroleum, oil, and lubricants
RD   Revolutionary Development
REFTEL   reference to telegram

RF   Regional Forces
RLT   regimental landing team
ROK   Republic of (South) Korea
rpt   repeat
RSSZ   Rungsat Special Zone
RVNAF   Republic of (South) Vietnam Armed Forces
SAM   surface-to-air missile
SEA   Southeast Asia
SEATO   Southeast Asia Treaty Organization
SecDef   secretary of defense
SQD   squadron
SVN   South Vietnam
TAOR   tactical area of operations
TF   task force
TFS   tactical fighter squadron
UK   United Kingdom
UN   United Nations
USAF   United States Air Force
USG   United States Government
USIA   United States Information Agency
USIB   United States Intelligence Board
USIS   United States Information Service
USOM   United States Operations Mission
USSR   Union of Soviet Socialist Republics
VC   Vietcong
VM   Vietminh
VN   Vietnam
VNAF   (South) Vietnam Armed Forces
VOA   Voice of America
WBLC   water-borne logistics craft

The Pentagon Papers:
A Bibliographical Essay

There are three published editions of the original collection of Pentagon Papers given to *The New York Times* by Daniel Ellsberg in 1971. Neil Sheehan et al., *The Pentagon Papers as Published by The New York Times* (New York, 1971), abridged here, is the best introduction to the papers, containing readable and generally reliable (although now dated) analyses by *The New York Times* writers of the original Defense Department chapters as well as many of the most important documents. The so-called Gravel edition, U.S. Congress, Senate Subcommittee on Public Buildings and Grounds, *The Pentagon Papers* (*The Senator Gravel Edition*) (4 vols., Boston, 1971) is the most orderly and usable of the larger editions, containing much of the original text and a large collection of documents. A fifth volume includes an index and commentaries on the papers by a number of scholars. U.S. Congress, House Committee on Armed Services, *United States–Vietnam Relations 1945–1967: A Study Prepared by the Department of Defense* (12 vols., Washington, 1971), usually known as the "GPO edition," has the largest collection of documents, but it is awkwardly arranged and poorly printed and contains numerous deletions. Ellsberg withheld from

The New York Times the so-called Negotiating Volumes of the papers, four volumes that dealt with peace initiatives and secret contacts. George C. Herring, ed., *The Secret Diplomacy of the Vietnam War: The Negotiating Volumes of the Pentagon Papers* (Austin, Tex., 1983) provides an annotated edition of these volumes, substantial sections of which are still "sanitized."

Whichever the volume or edition, the papers must be used with caution. The Department of Defense (DOD) essays are uneven in quality and reflect the "dovish" bias of McNamara's civilian advisers and their preference for a population security strategy. They rely primarily on DOD records and do not always adequately reflect the role of the State Department and White House. They emphasize military matters and devote only slight attention to such important things as the operation of the aid program and American involvement in South Vietnamese politics. In terms of documents, at least, they should be supplemented by the State Department publication *Foreign Relations of the United States,* volumes of which for Vietnam are now available to 1964, are much more inclusive and comprehensive in terms of coverage, and are superbly edited. For critical assessments of the Pentagon Papers by an eminent scholar of the Vietnam War, see George McT. Kahin, "The Pentagon Papers: A Critical Evaluation," *American Political Science Review* (June 1975), pp. 675–684. H. Bradford Westerfield, "What Use Are Three Versions of the Pentagon Papers?" ibid., pp. 685–696, assesses the strengths and weaknesses of the three editions as historical sources.

There is no up-to-date study of the compilation of the Pentagon Papers and their subsequent, controversial disposition. These events are best covered in contemporary accounts such as Sanford J. Ungar, *The Papers and the Papers* (New York, 1972), Harrison E. Salisbury, *Without Fear or Favor: The New York Times and Our Times* (New York, 1980), Kenneth W. Salter, *The Pentagon Papers Trial* (Berkeley, Calif., 1975), and Peter Schrag, *Test of Loyalty: Daniel Ellsberg and the Rituals of Secret Government* (New York, 1974).

Two of the authors of the Pentagon Papers subsequently wrote analyses of the Vietnam War based largely on findings derived from the papers. Leslie Gelb with Richard Betts, *The Irony of Vietnam: The System Worked* (Washington, 1978), although curiously titled, develops the argument that American presidents from Truman to Nixon did just enough to keep South Vietnam afloat until the next election. Daniel Ellsberg, *Papers on the War* (New York, 1972), develops a more bitter and more critical variant of the same theme. Because of the author's personal involvement in the affair, Neil Sheehan's monumental *A Bright Shining Lie: John Paul Vann and America in Vietnam* (New York, 1988), contains some valuable insights into the issues and personalities involved in the stormy history of the Pentagon Papers. Floyd Abrams, "The Pentagon Papers: A Decade Later," *New York Times Magazine* (June 7, 1981), pp. 22–26, 76–95, provides a measured assessment of the impact of the Pentagon Papers from the vantage point of 1981.